FOR ORGANS, PIANOS & ELECTRONIC KEYBOARDS

E-Z PLAY TODAY

188

64 STANDARD HITS

P9-DCA-286

E-Z Play TODAY chord notation is designed for playing **standard chord positions** or **single key chords** on all **major brand organs** and **portable keyboards**.

Contents

HAL LEONARD PUBLISHING CORPORATION

Home Office: National Sales Office:
960 East Mark Street   8112 West Bluemound Road
Winona MN 55987   Milwaukee WI 53213

The Breeze And I

Registration 8
Rhythm: Fox Trot or Swing

Words by Al Stillman
Music by Ernesto Lecuona

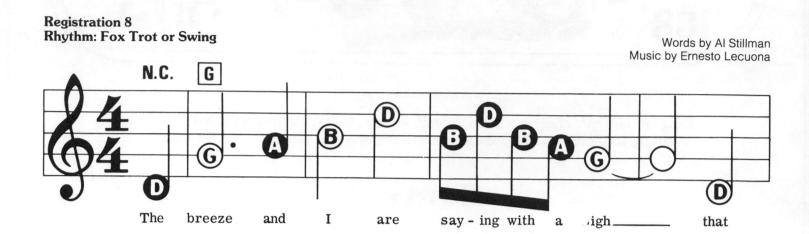

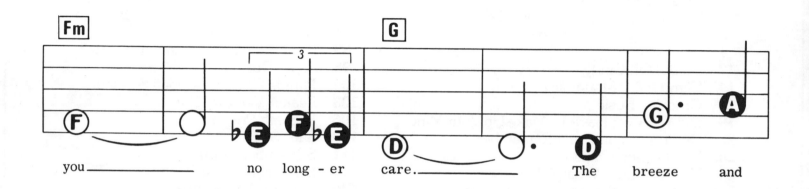

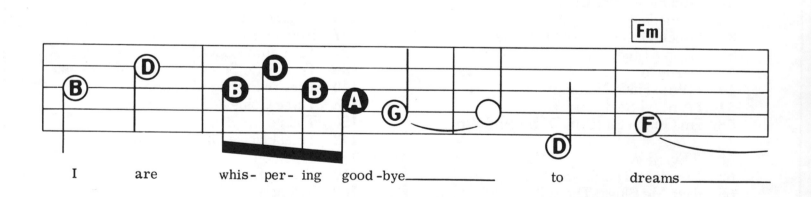

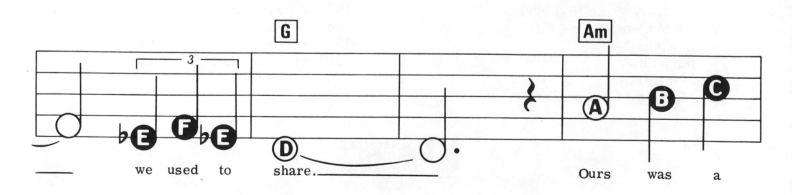

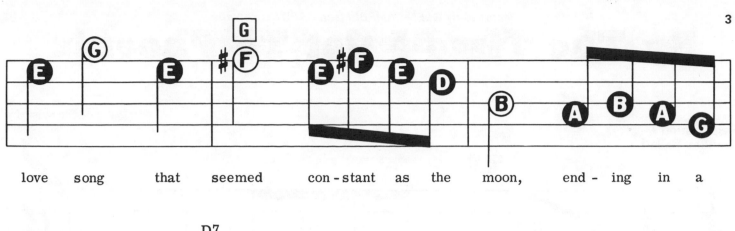

love song that seemed con-stant as the moon, end-ing in a

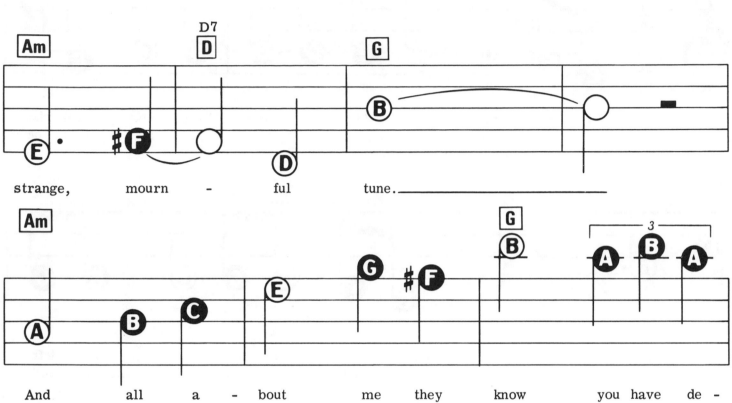

strange, mourn - ful tune._____

And all a - bout me they know you have de -

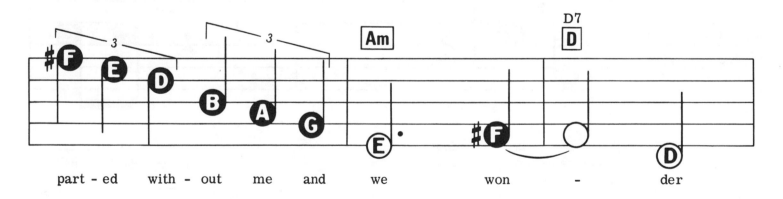

part-ed with-out me and we won - der

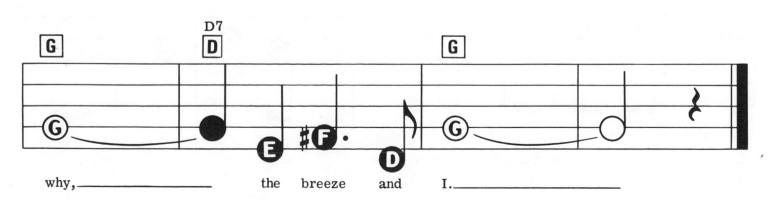

why,_____ the breeze and I._____

Recorded by GLEN CAMPBELL on CAPITOL Records

By The Time I Get To Phoenix

Words and Music by
Jimmy Webb

Registration 1
Rhythm: Ballad

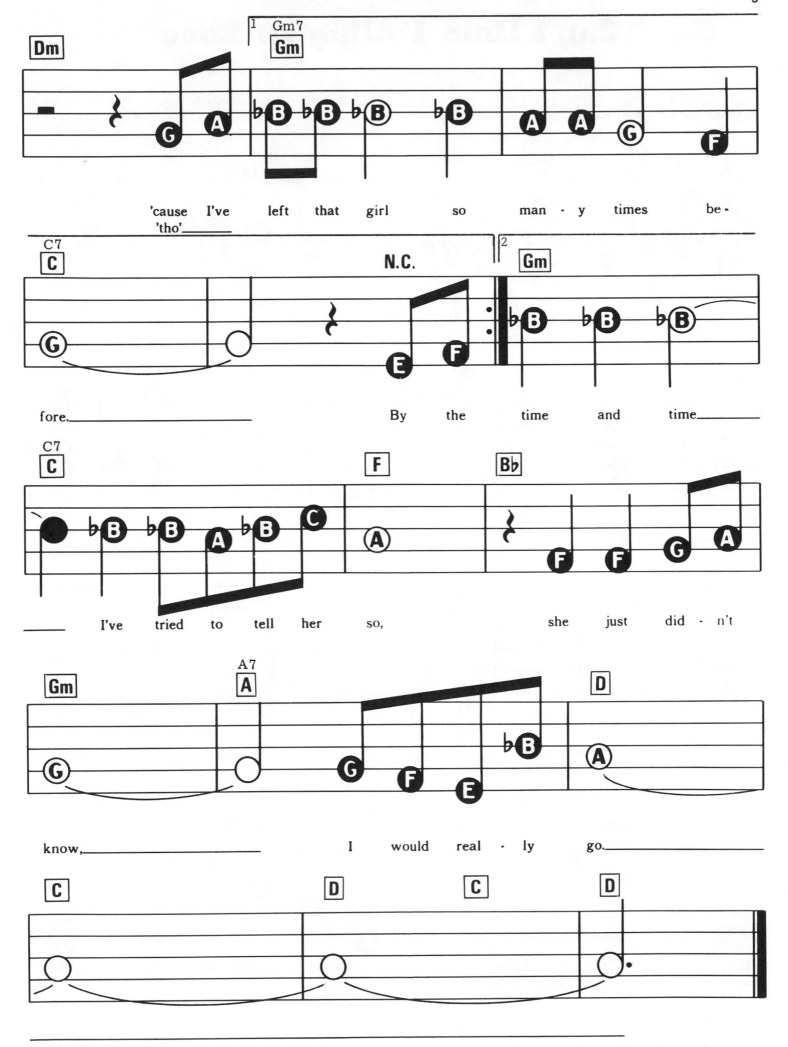

'cause I've left that girl so man-y times be-
'tho'_____

fore._____ By the time and time_____

_____ I've tried to tell her so, she just did-n't

know,_____ I would real-ly go._____

Can't Help Falling In Love

Registration 3
Rhythm: Slow Rock or Ballad

Words and Music by George Weiss,
Hugo Peretti, and Luigi Creatore

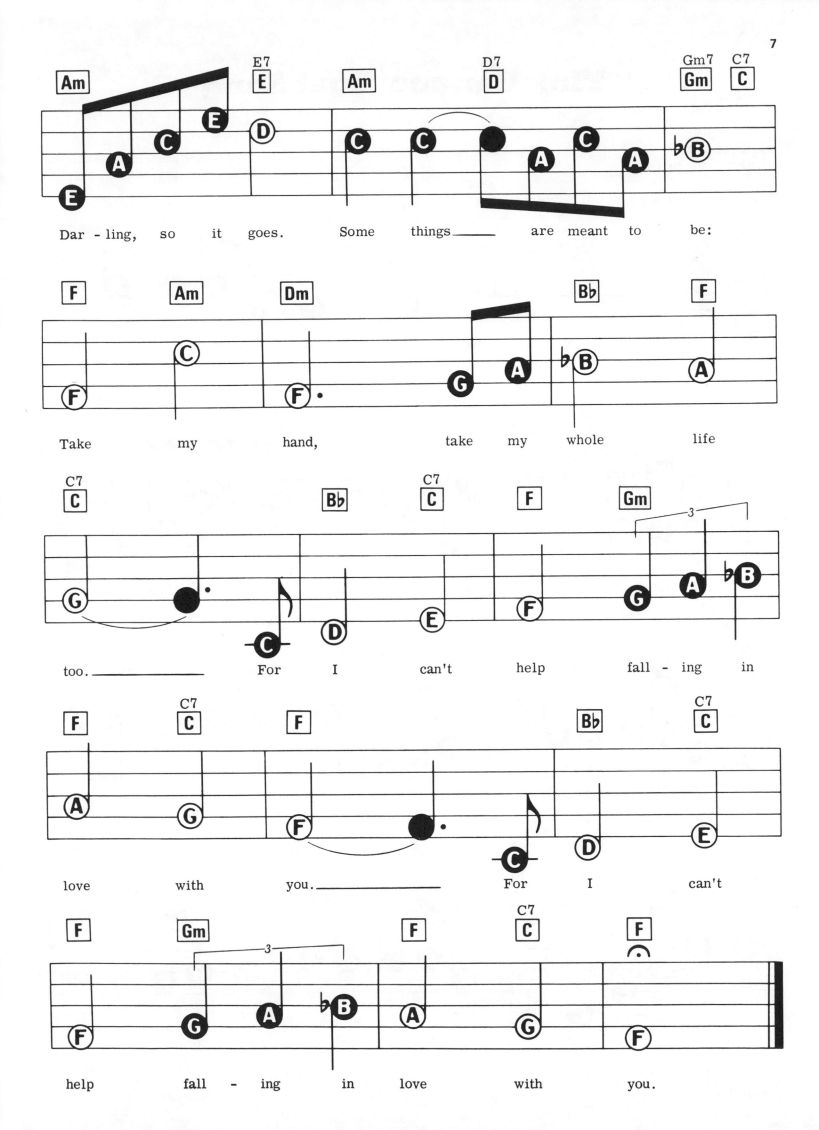

The Banana Boat Song

Registration 4
Rhythm: Latin or Tango

Lyric and Music by Erik Darling,
Bob Carey and Alan Arkin

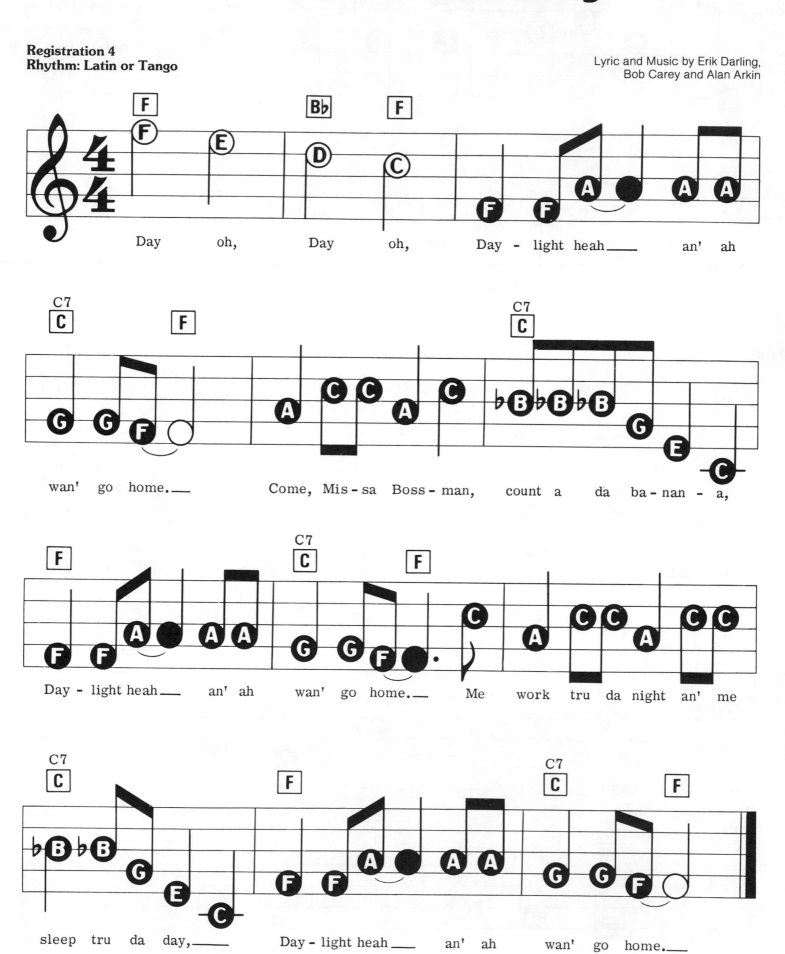

Celebrate

Words and Music by
Alan Gordon and Garry Bonner

Registration 4
Rhythm: Rock or Jazz Rock

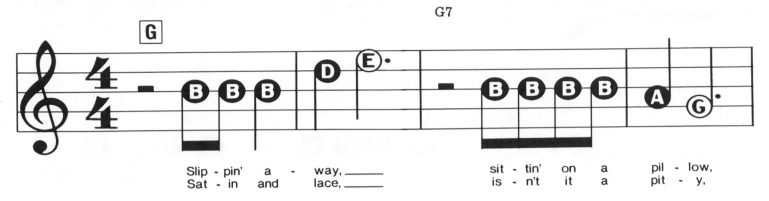

Slip - pin' a - way, _____ sit - tin' on a pil - low,
Sat - in and lace, _____ is - n't it a pit - y,

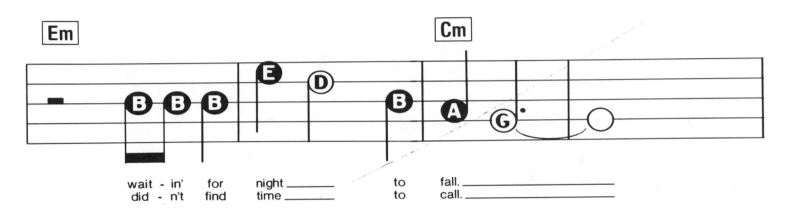

wait - in' for night _____ to fall. _____
did - n't find time _____ to call. _____

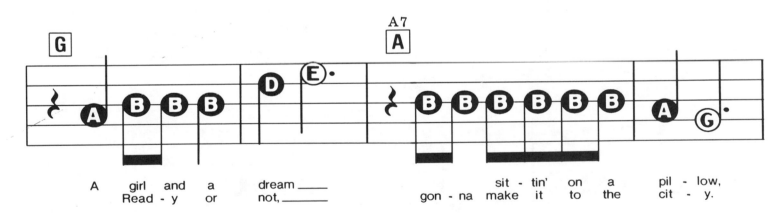

A girl and a dream _____ sit - tin' on a pil - low,
Read - y or not, _____ gon - na make it to the cit - y.

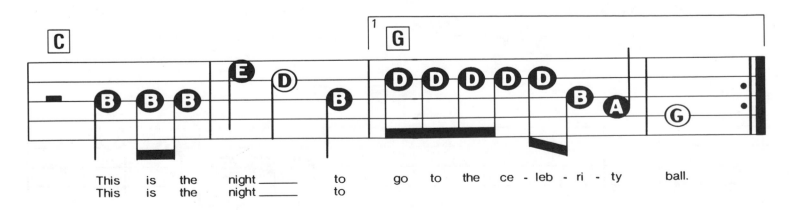

This is the night _____ to go to the ce - leb - ri - ty ball.
This is the night _____ to

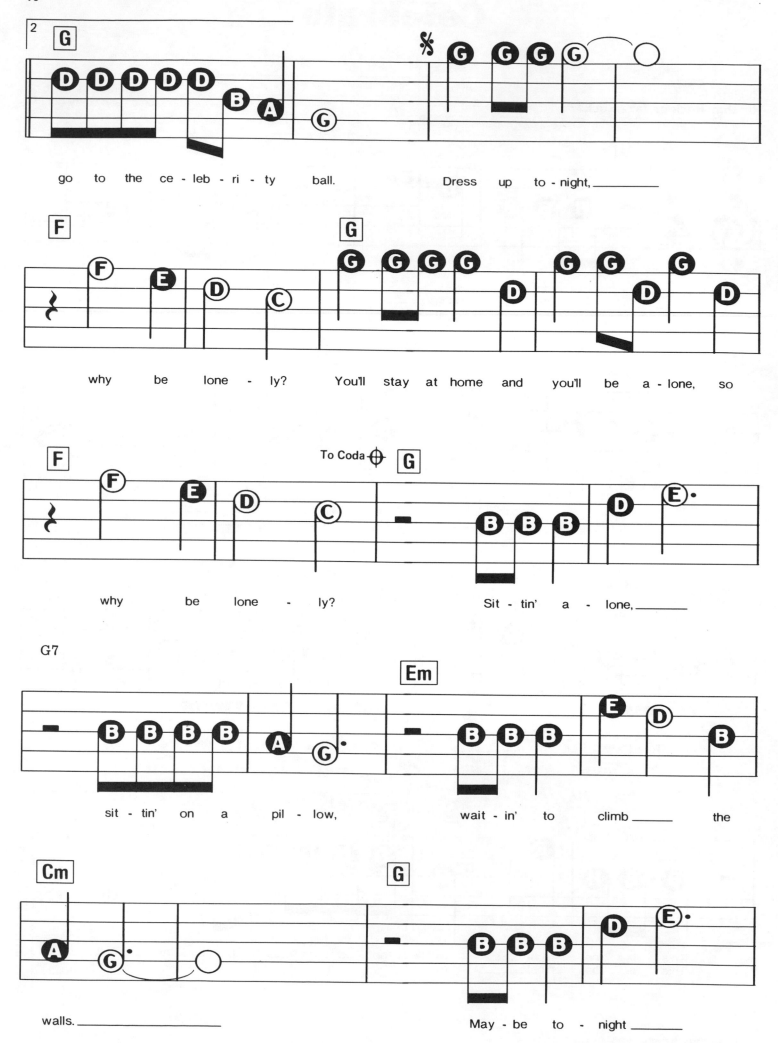

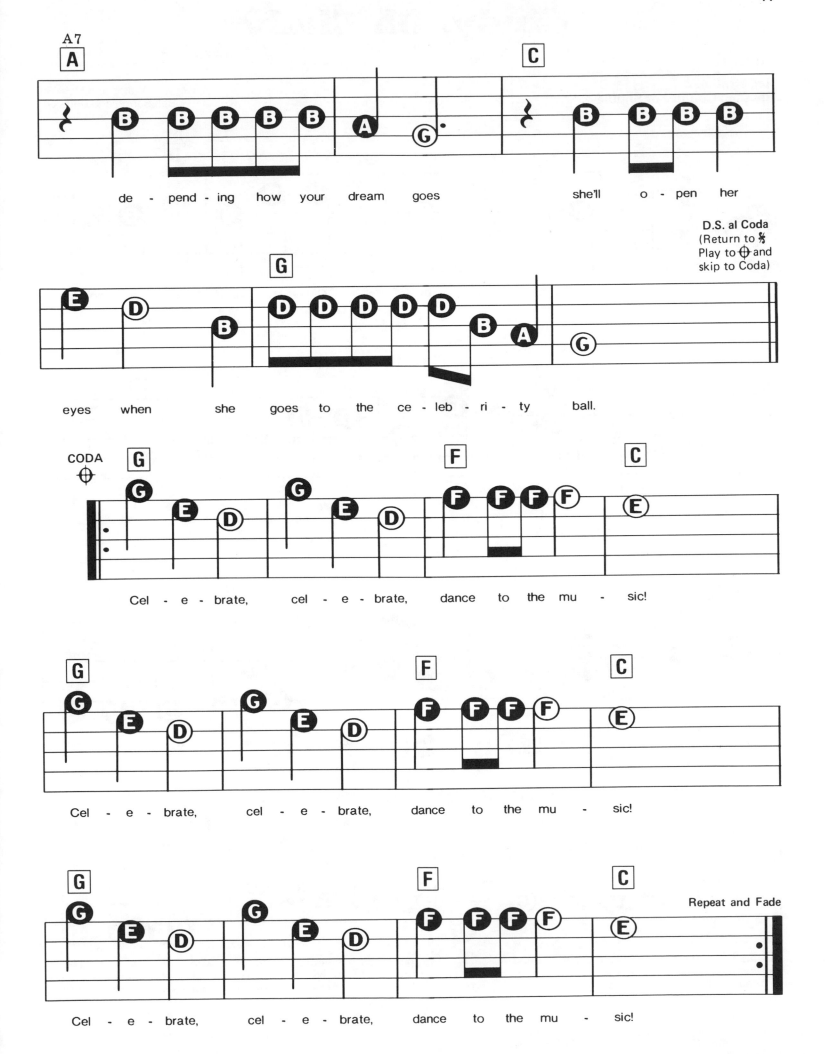

Cindy, Oh Cindy

Registration 2
Rhythm: Country or Shuffle

Words and Music by
Bob Barron and Burt Long

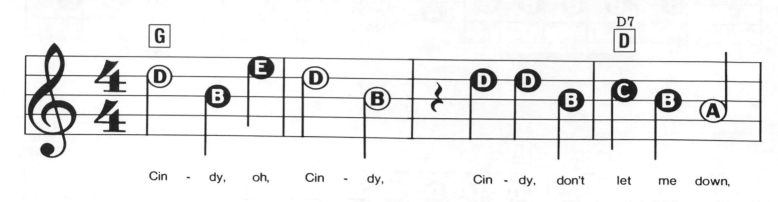

Cin - dy, oh, Cin - dy, Cin - dy, don't let me down,

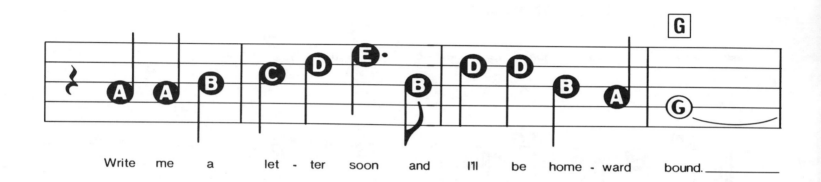

Write me a let - ter soon and I'll be home - ward bound. _____

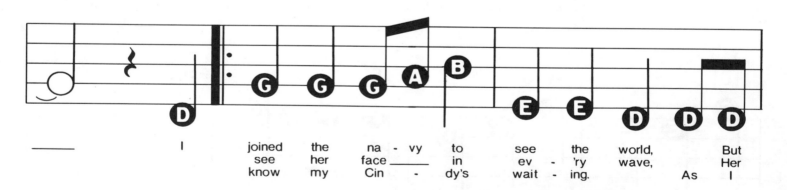

_____	I	joined	the	na-vy	to	see	the	world,	But
	see	her	face___	in	ev-	'ry	wave,	As	I
	know	my	Cin -	dy's	wait -	ing.			

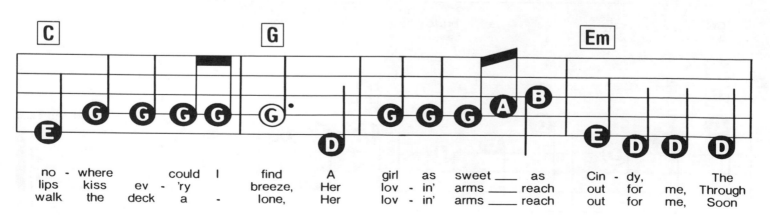

no - where	could	I	find	A	girl	as	sweet___	as	Cin - dy,	The
lips	kiss	ev - 'ry	breeze,	Her	lov - in'	arms___	reach	out	for	me, The
walk	the	deck a -	lone,	Her	lov - in'	arms___	reach	out	for	me, Soon

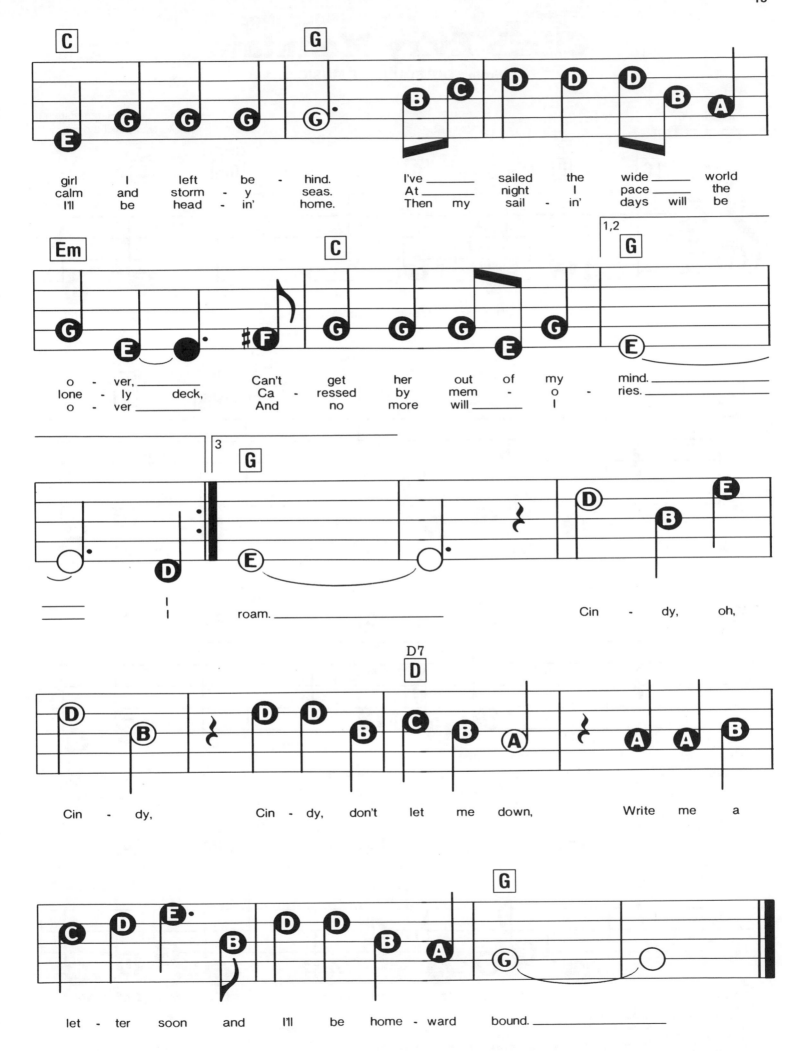

Climb Ev'ry Mountain

(From "THE SOUND OF MUSIC")

Registration 5
Rhythm: Fox Trot

Words by Oscar Hammerstein II
Music by Richard Rodgers

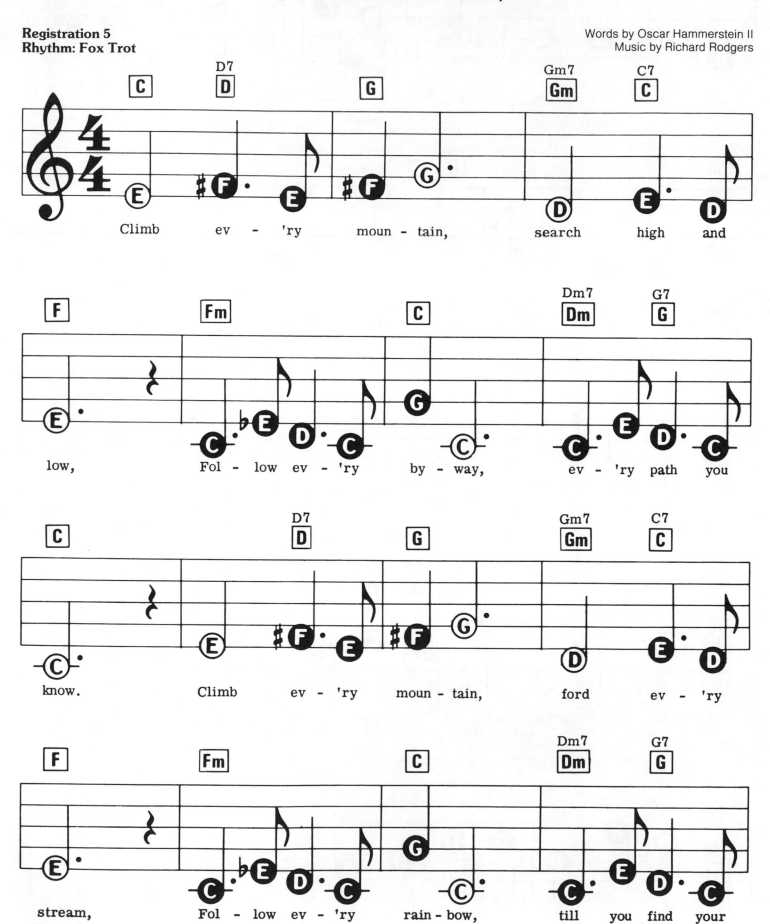

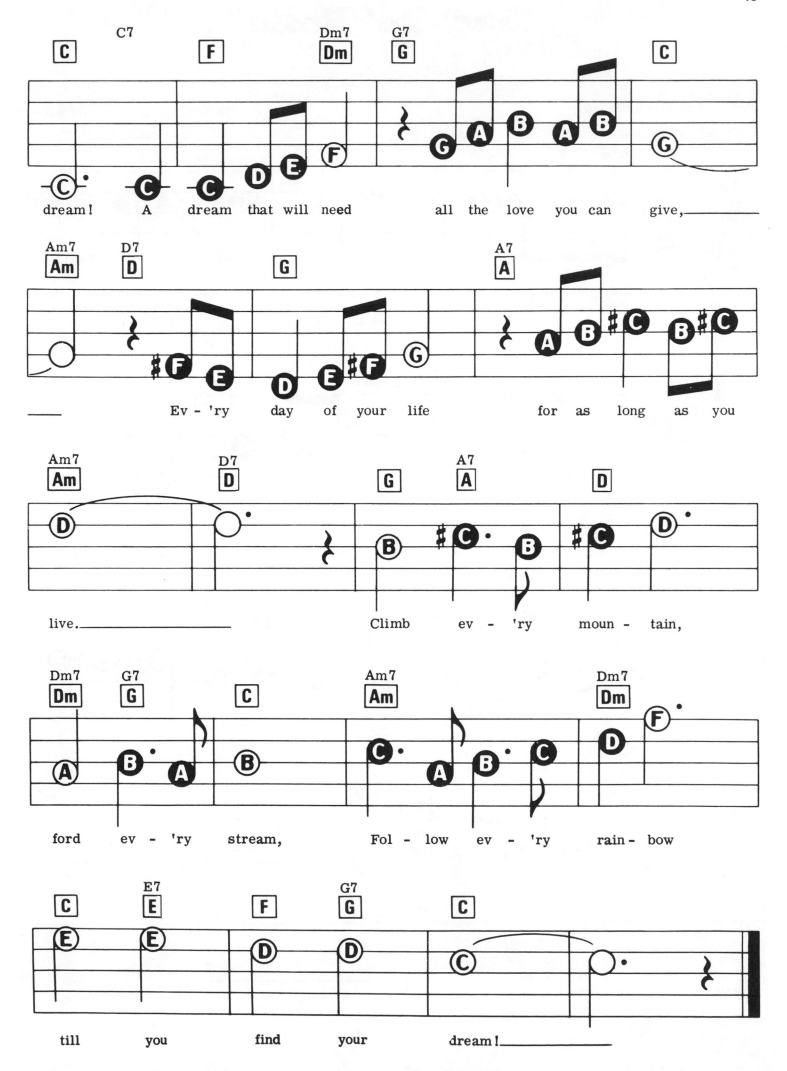

Cracklin' Rosie

Registration 5
Rhythm: Fox Trot or Ballad

Words and Music by
Neil Diamond

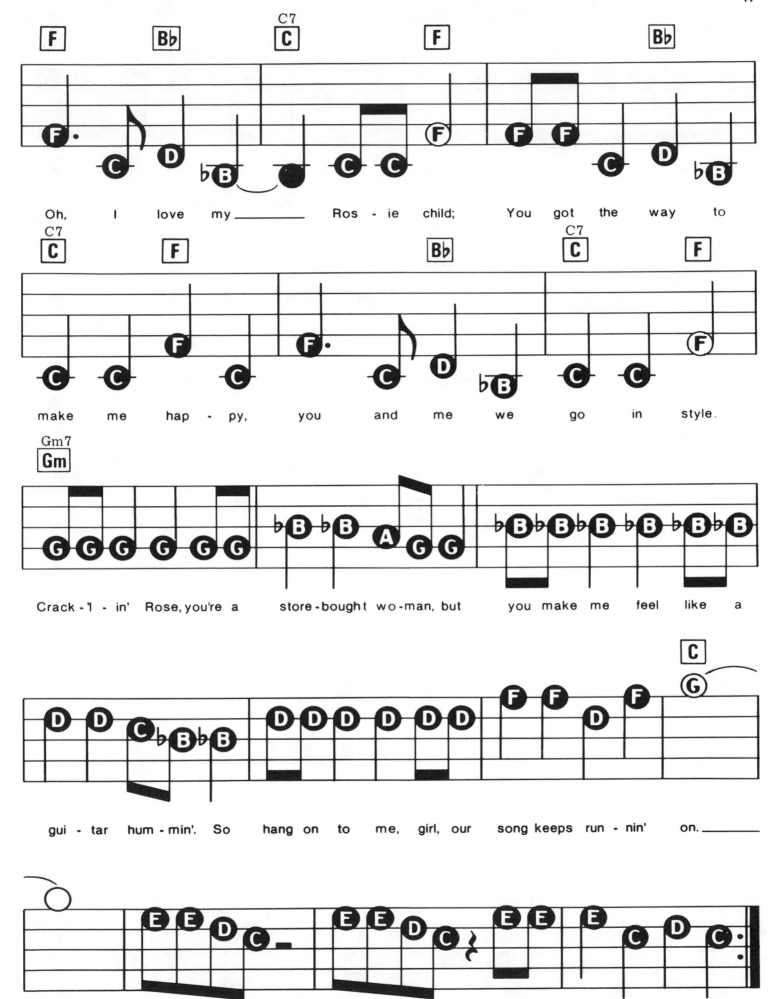

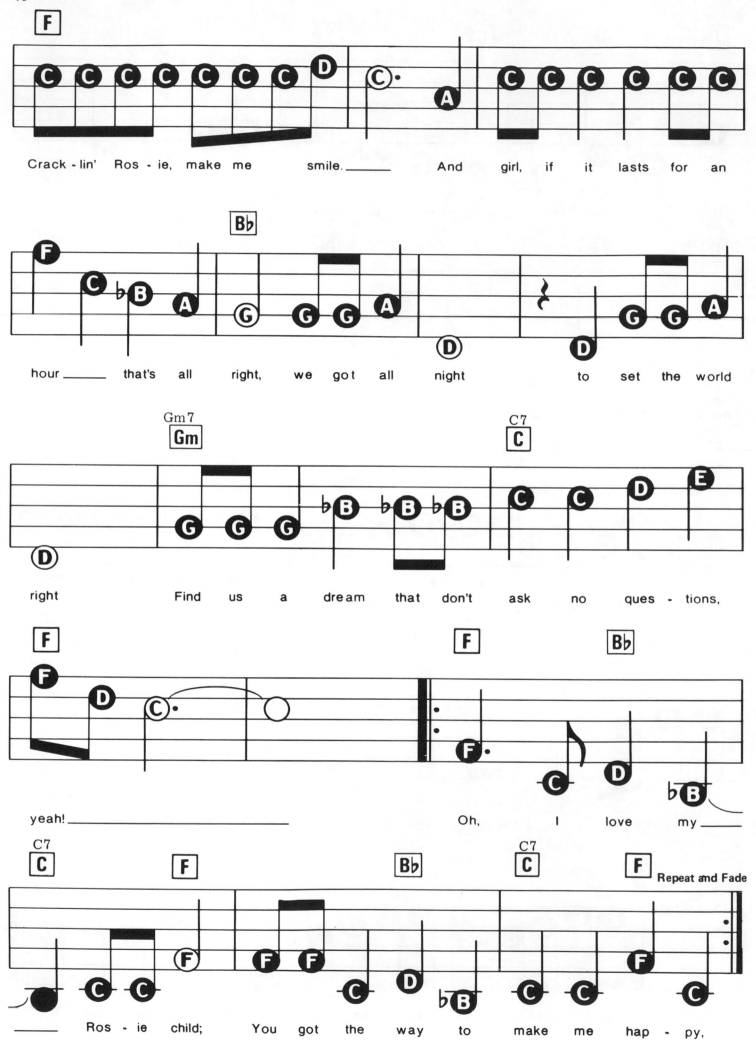

Did You Ever Have To Make Up Your Mind

Registration 4
Rhythm: Country or Shuffle

by John Sebastian

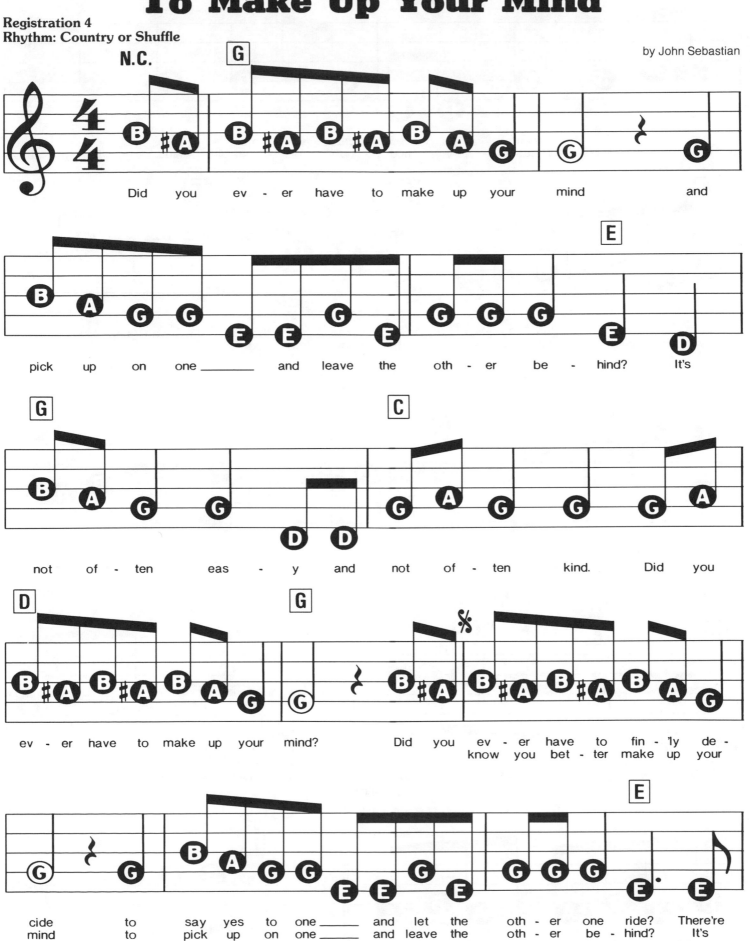

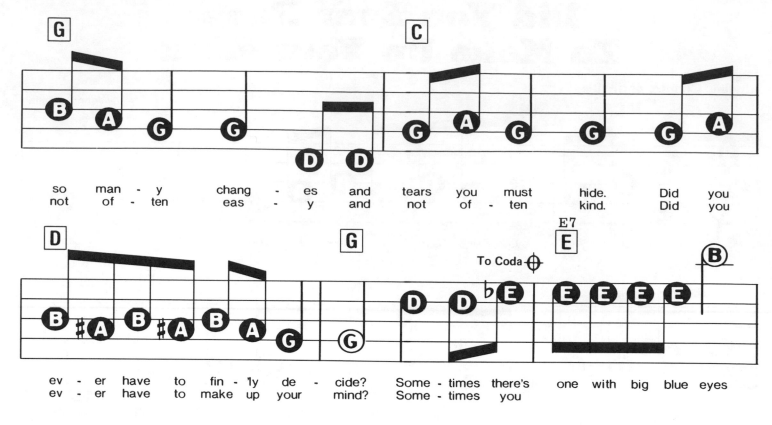

so man - y chang - es and tears you must hide. Did you
not of - ten eas - y and not of - ten kind. Did you

ev - er have to fin - 'ly de - cide? Some - times there's one with big blue eyes
ev - er have to make up your mind? Some - times you

cute as a bun - ny with hair down to here and plen - ty of mon - ey and

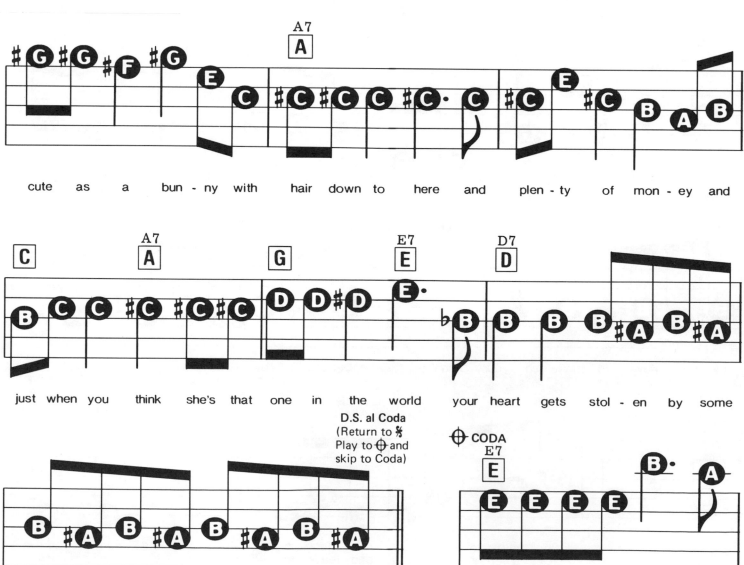

just when you think she's that one in the world your heart gets stol - en by some

mous - ey look - in' girl and then you

real - ly dig a girl the

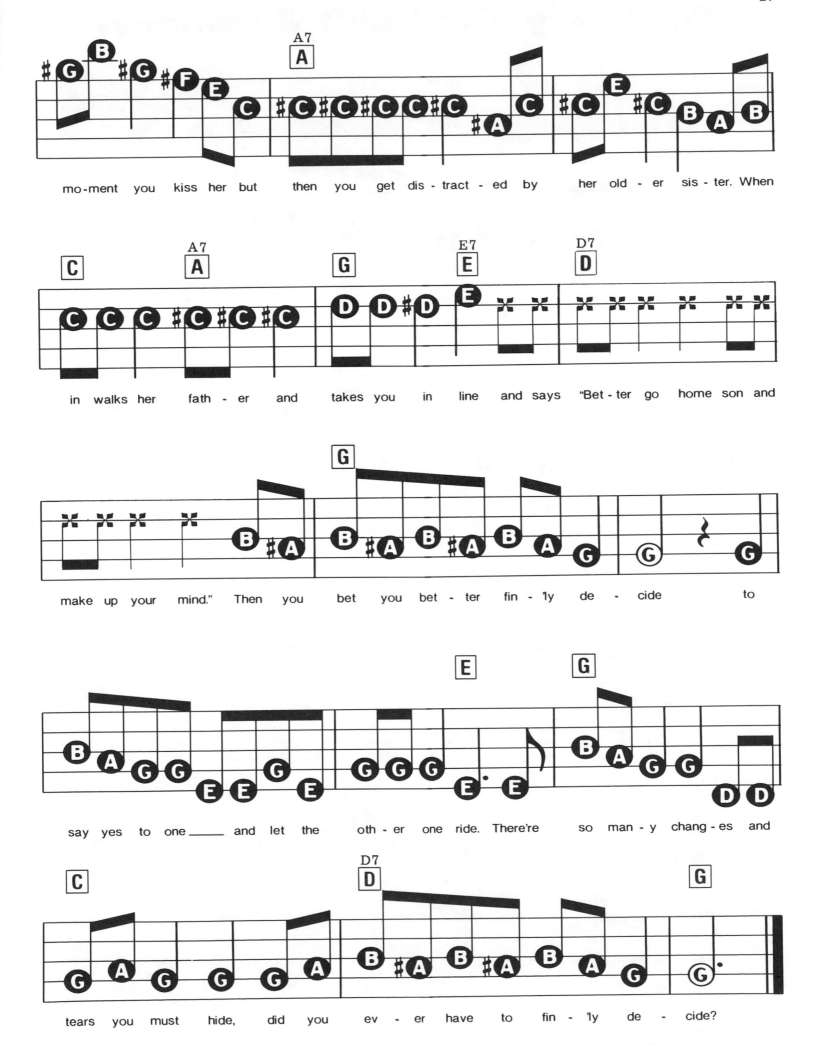

Don't Say You Don't Remember

Registration 7
Rhythm: Swing or Jazz

Words and Music by
Helen Miller and Estelle Levitt

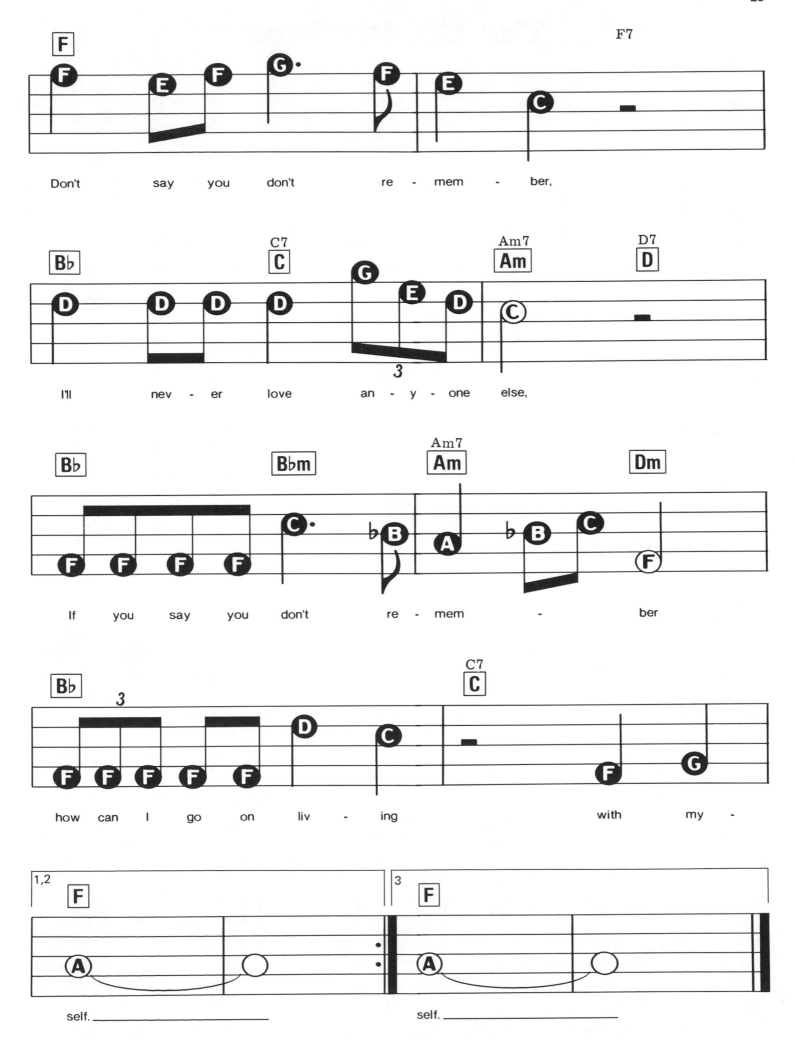

The Exodus Song

Registration 6
Rhythm: Ballad

Words by Pat Boone
Music by Ernest Gold

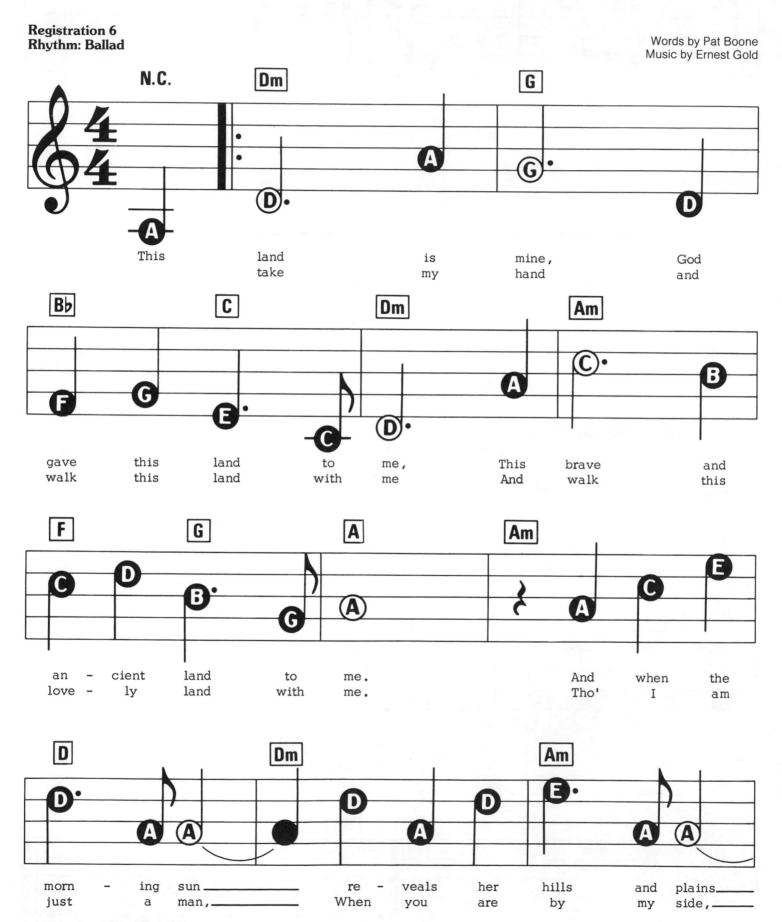

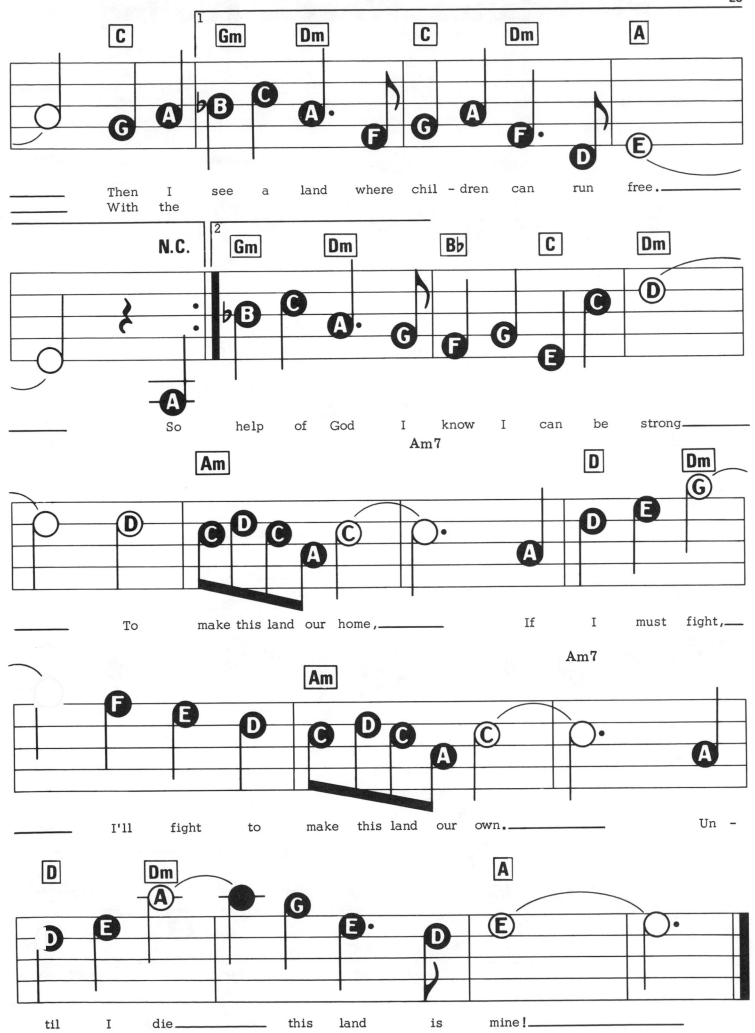

Flashdance...What A Feeling

Registration 5
Rhythm: Rock or Jazz Rock

Lyrics by Keith Forsey and Irene Cara
Music by Giorgio Moroder

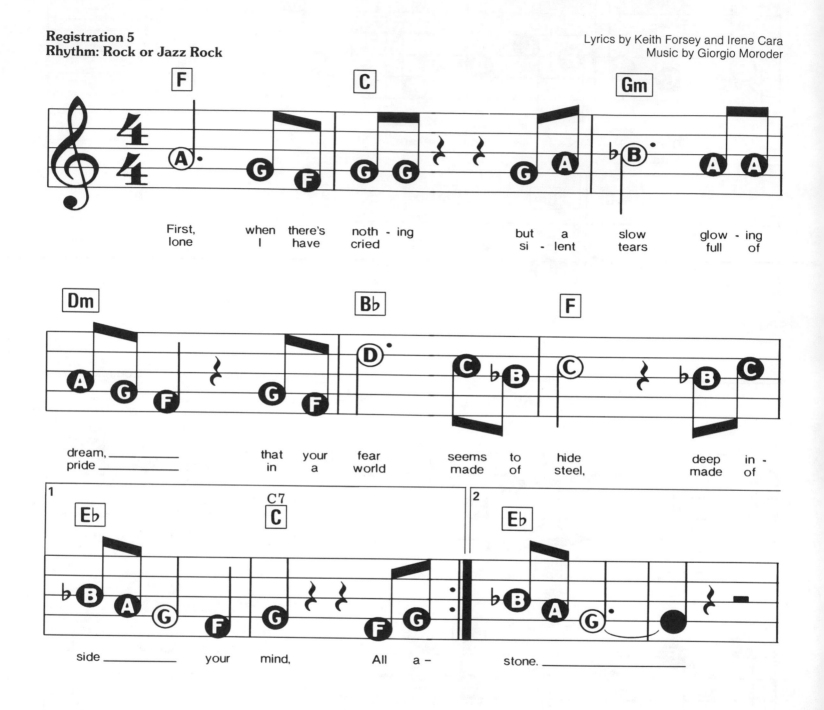

First, when there's noth - ing but a slow glow - ing
lone when I have cried si - lent tears full of

dream, _____ that your fear seems to hide deep in -
pride _____ in a world made of steel, made of

side _____ your mind, All a - stone. _____

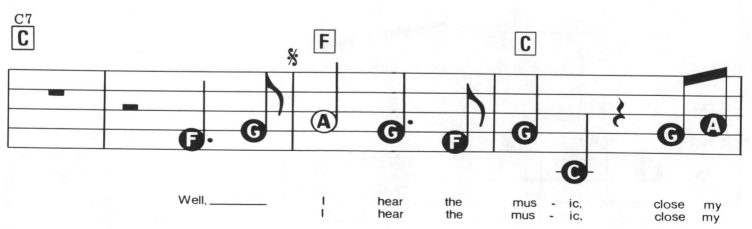

Well, _____ I hear the mus - ic, close my
I hear the mus - ic, close my

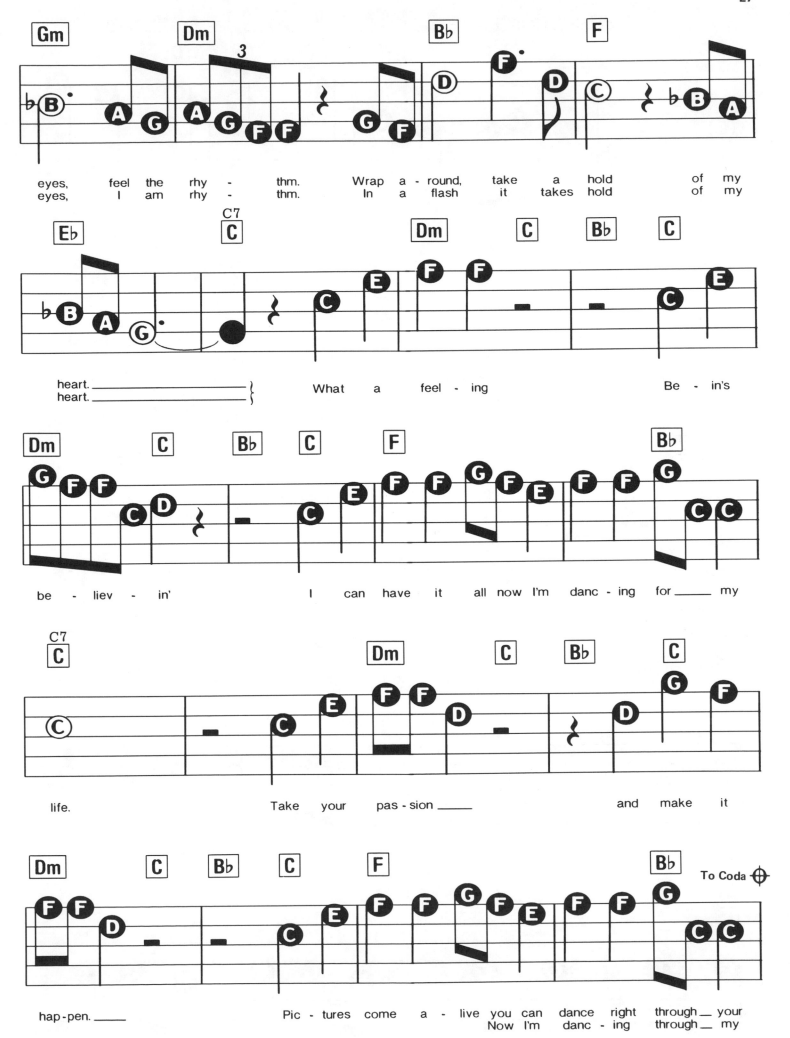

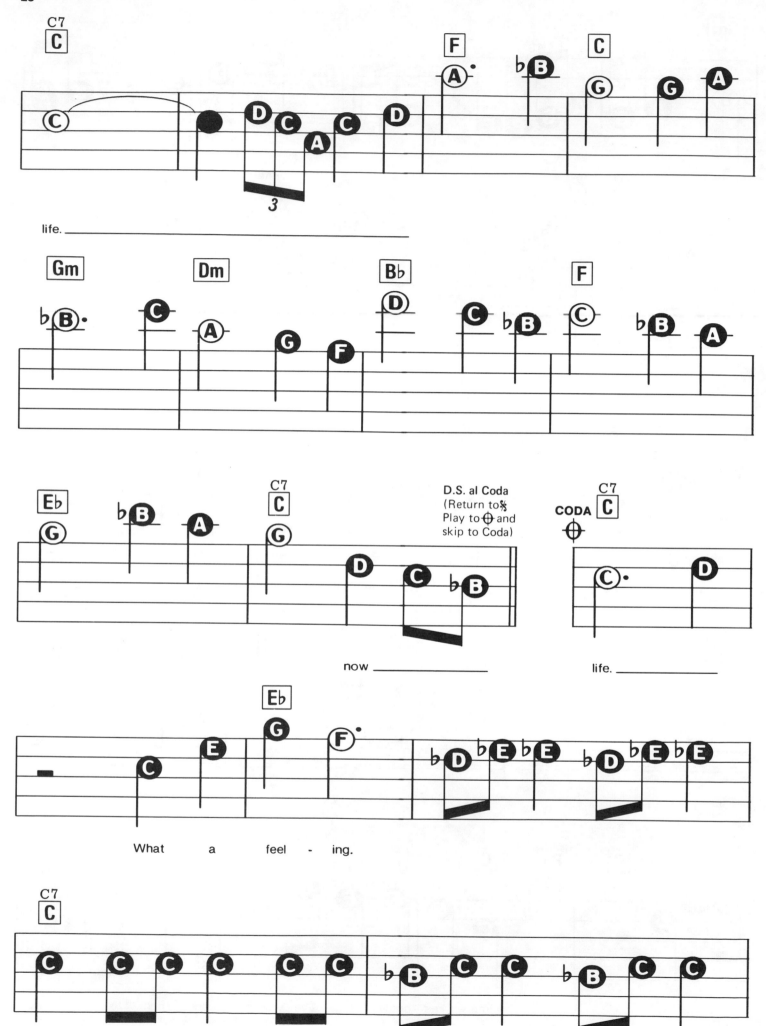

Forty-Five Minutes From Broadway

Registration 10
Rhythm: Waltz or Jazz Waltz

Words and Music by George M. Cohan
Revisions by Mary Cohan

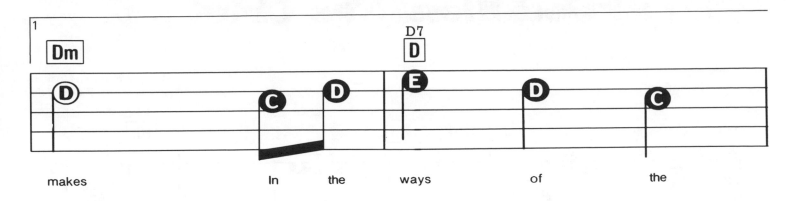

makes   In   the   ways   of   the

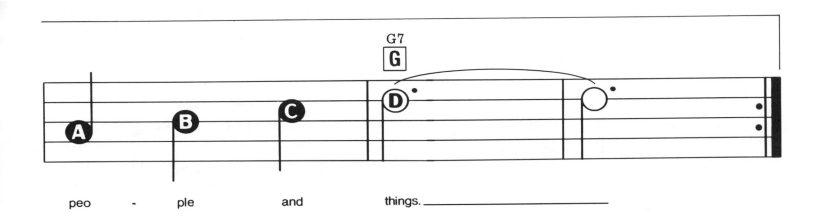

peo - ple   and   things. _____

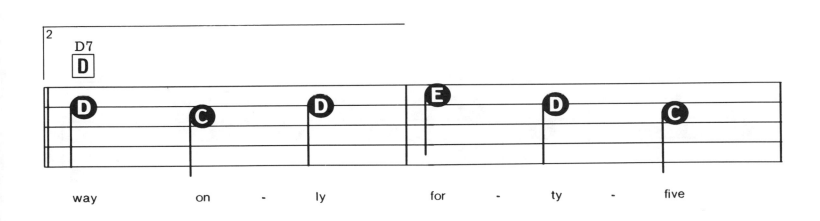

way   on - ly   for - ty - five

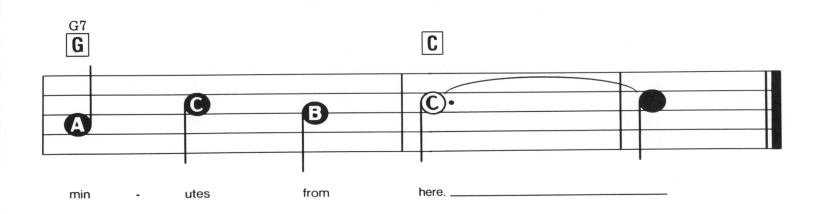

min - utes   from   here. _____

God Bless' The Child

Registration 4
Rhythm: Ballad

Words and Music by
Arthur Herzog Jr. and Billie Holiday

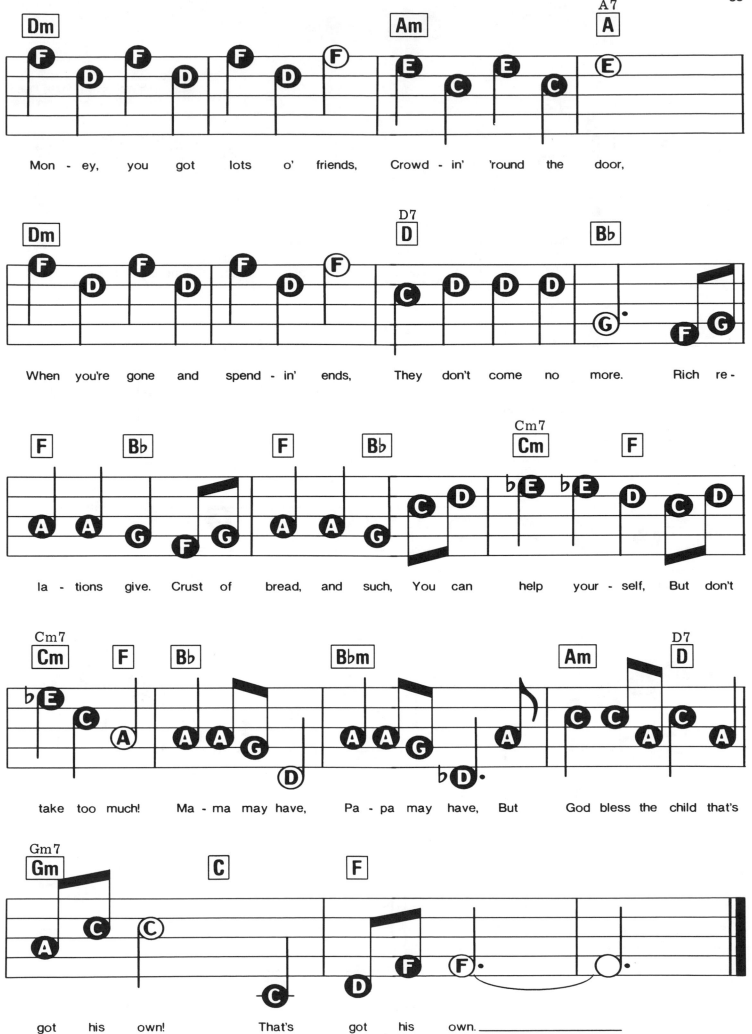

Granada

Registration 5
Rhythm: Waltz

Spanish Words and Music by Agustin Lara
English Words by Dorothy Dodd
Music by Agustin Lara

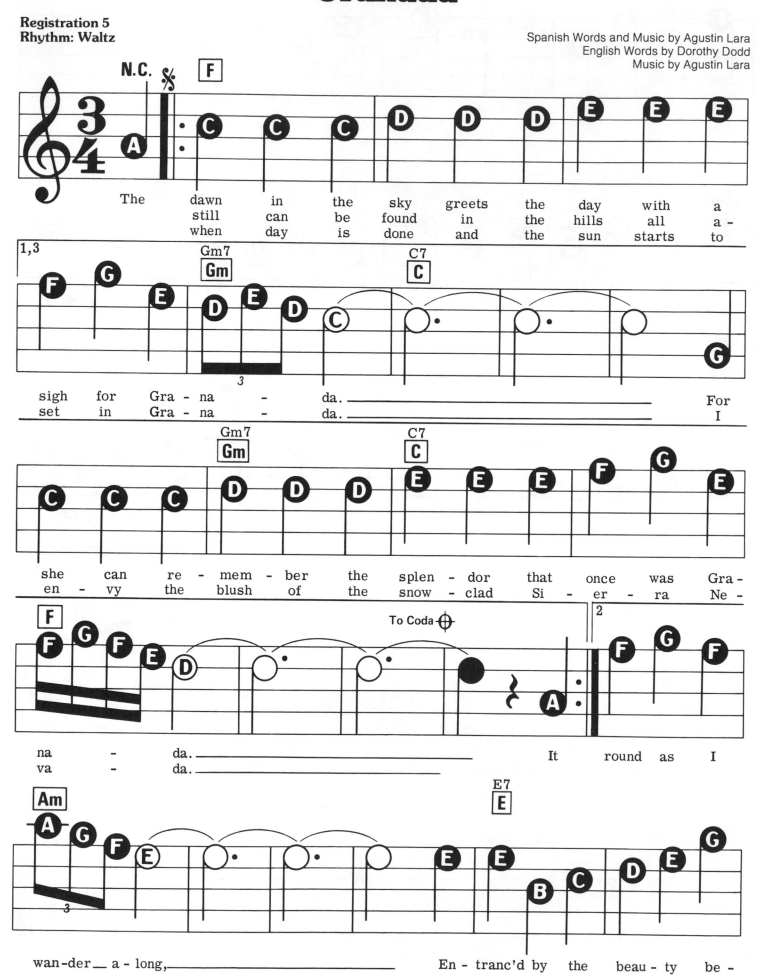

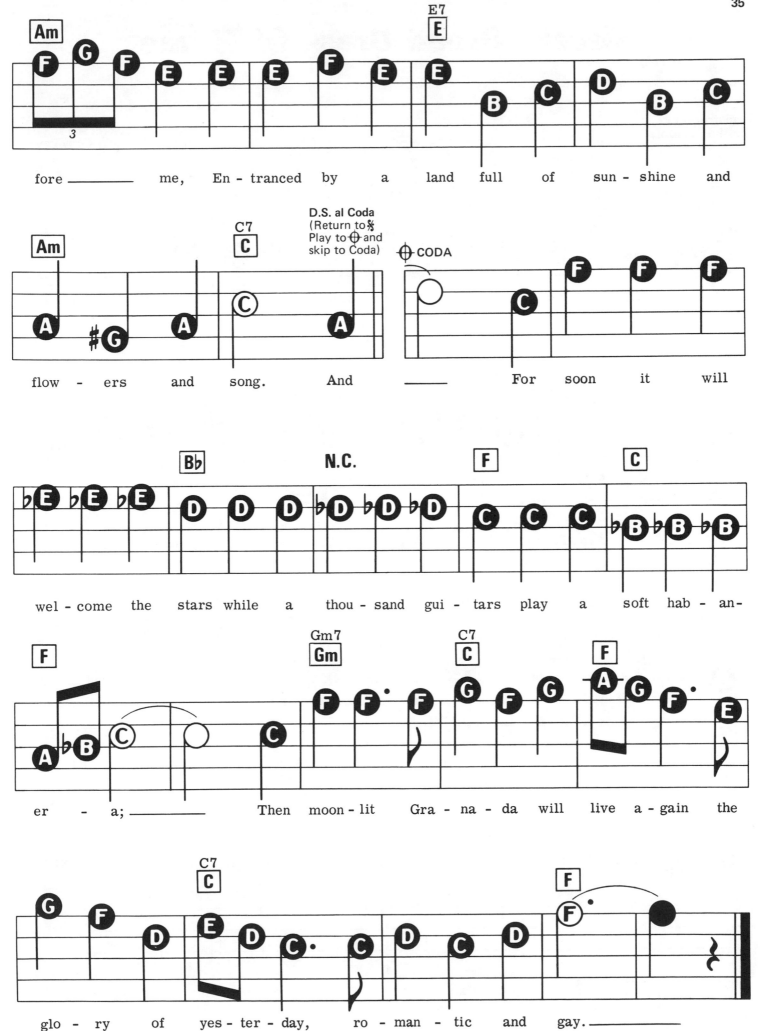

Green, Green Grass Of Home

Registration 2
Rhythm: Country

Words and Music by
Curly Putman

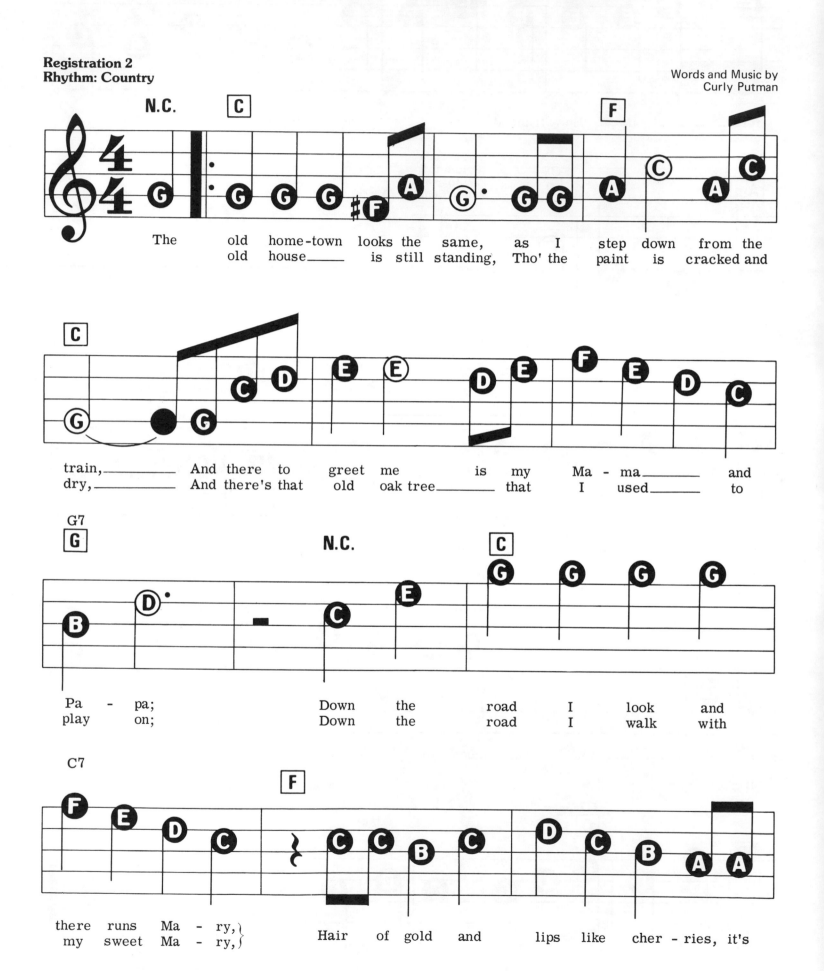

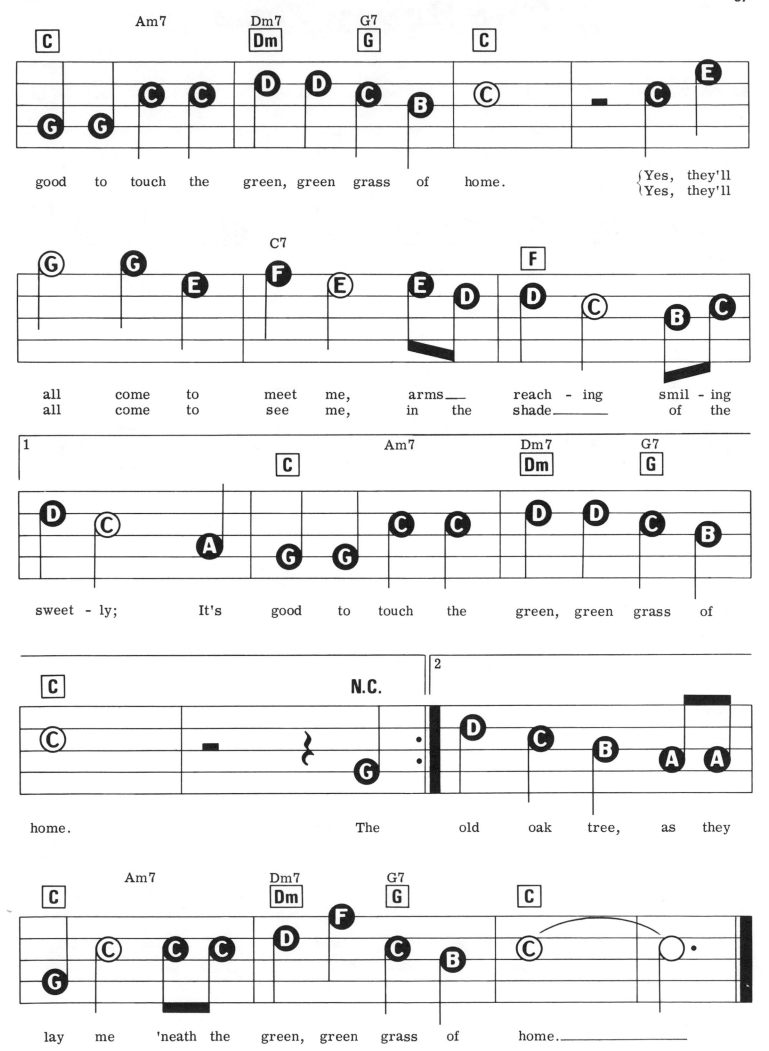

The Happy Time

Registration 1
Rhythm: Waltz

Music by John Kander
Words by Fred Ebb

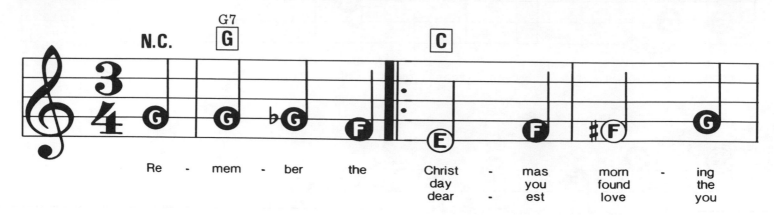

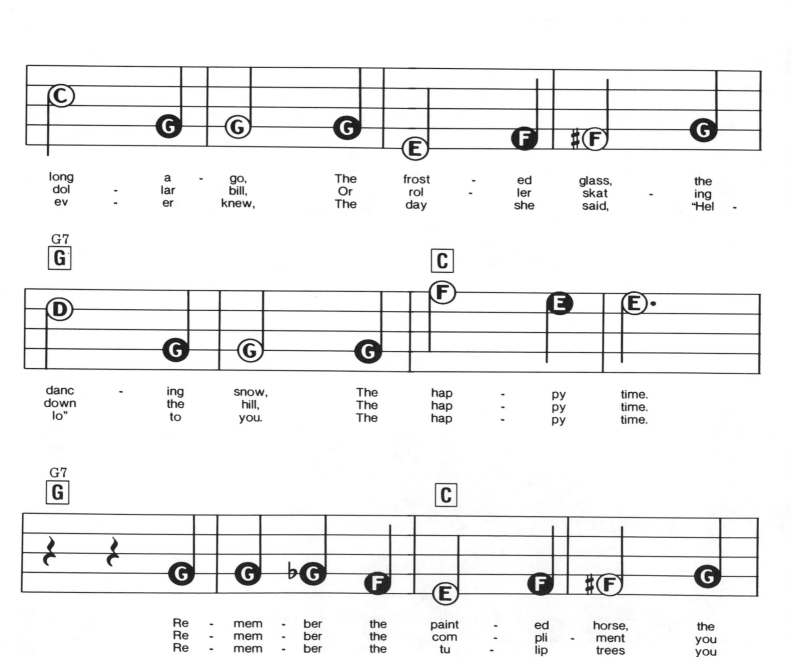

Re - mem - ber the Christ - mas morn - ing
day you found the
dear - est love you

long a - go, The frost - ed glass, the
dol - lar bill, Or rol - ler skat - ing
ev - er knew, The day she said, "Hel -

danc - ing snow, The hap - py time.
down the hill, The hap - py time.
lo" to you. The hap - py time.

Re - mem - ber the paint - ed horse, the
Re - mem - ber the com - pli - ment you
Re - mem - ber the tu - lip trees you

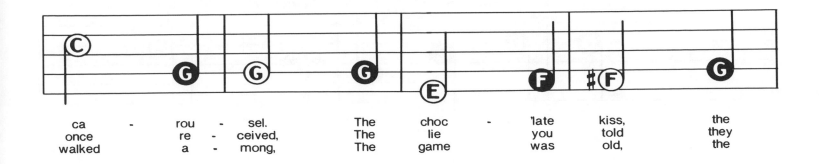

ca - rou - sel. The choc - 'late kiss, the
once re - ceived, The lie you told, they
walked a - mong, The game was old, the

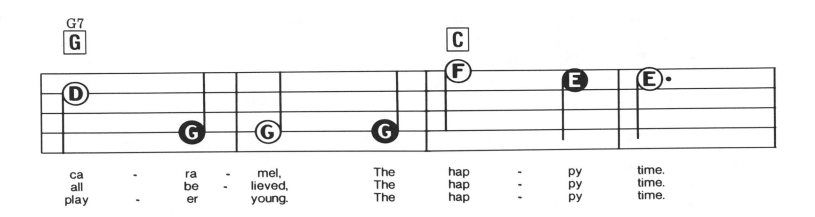

ca - ra - mel, The hap - py time.
all be - lieved, The hap - py time.
play - er young. The hap - py time.

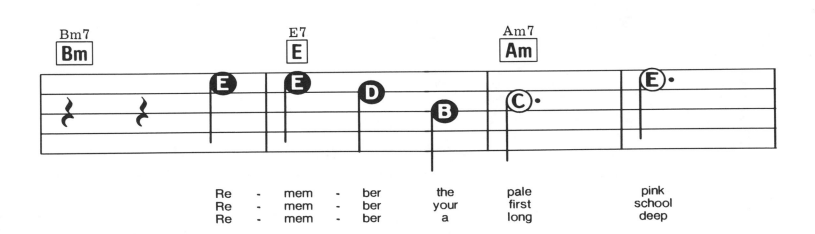

Re - mem - ber the pale pink
Re - mem - ber your first school
Re - mem - ber a long deep

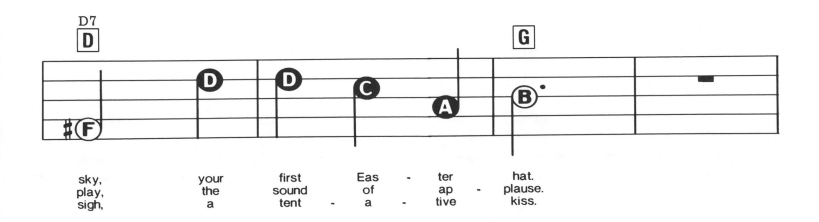

sky, your first Eas - ter hat.
play, the first sound of ap - plause.
sigh, a tent - a - tive kiss.

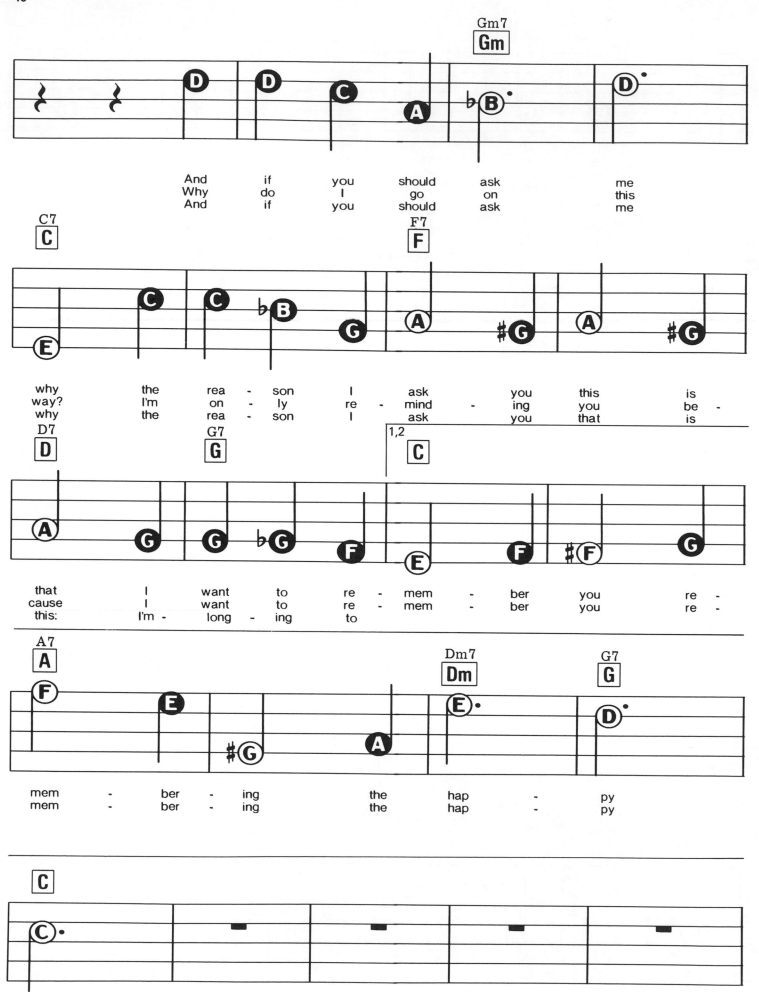

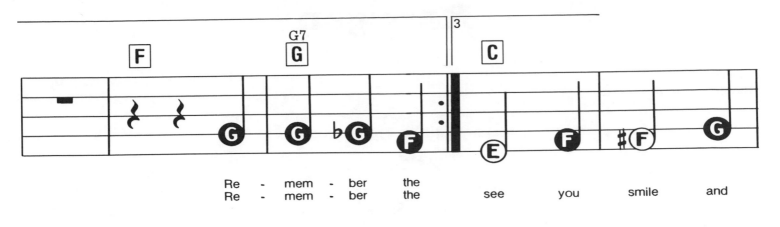

Re - mem - ber the
Re - mem - ber the see you smile and

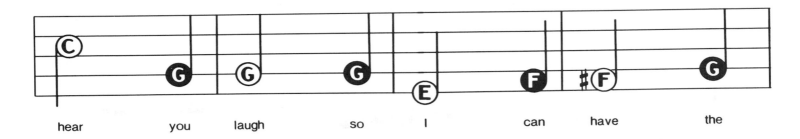

hear you laugh so I can have the

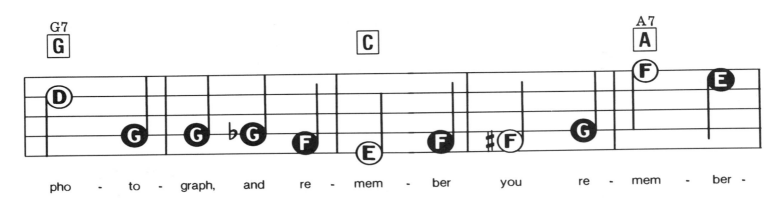

pho - to - graph, and re - mem - ber you re - mem - ber -

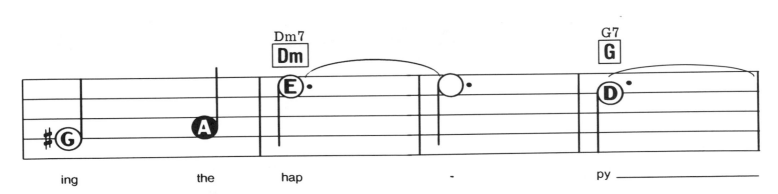

ing the hap - py _____

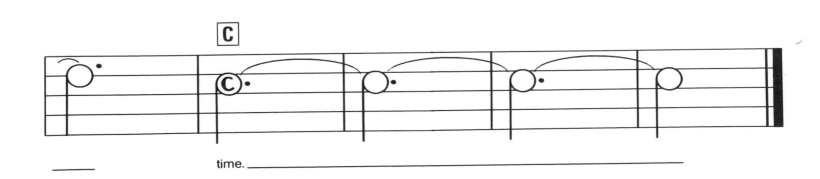

_____ time. _____

Harrigan

Registration 5
Rhythm: March

Words and Music by
George M. Cohan

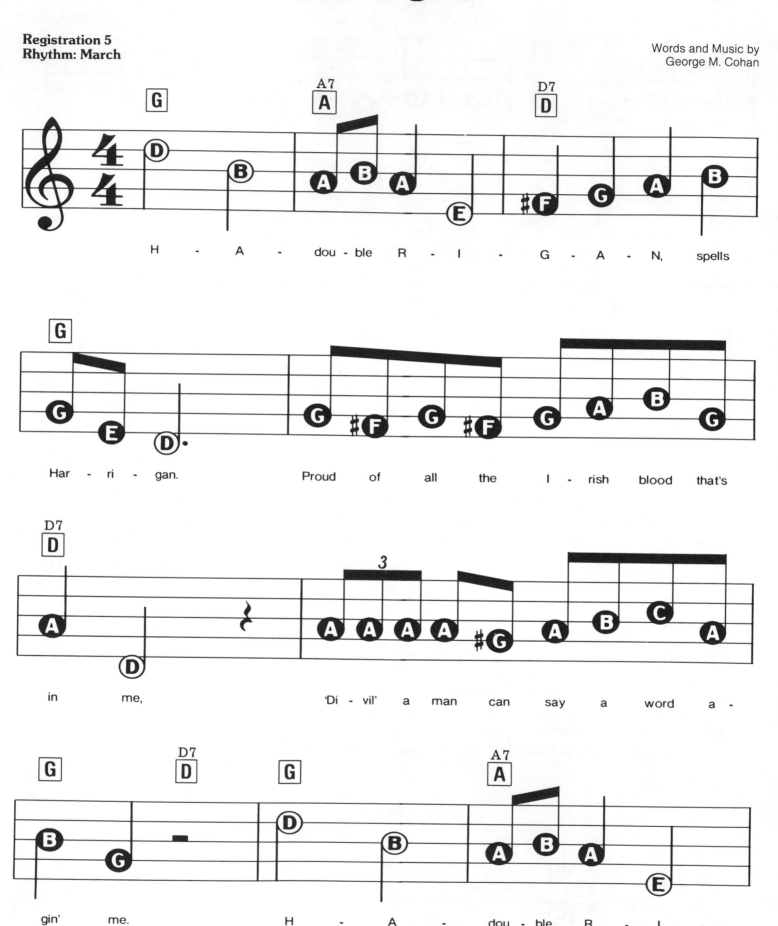

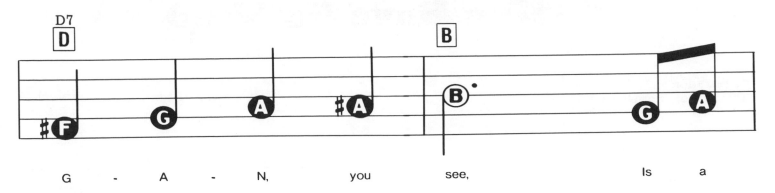

G - A - N, you see, Is a

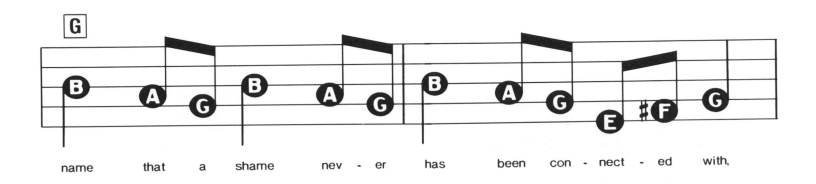

name that a shame nev - er has been con - nect - ed with,

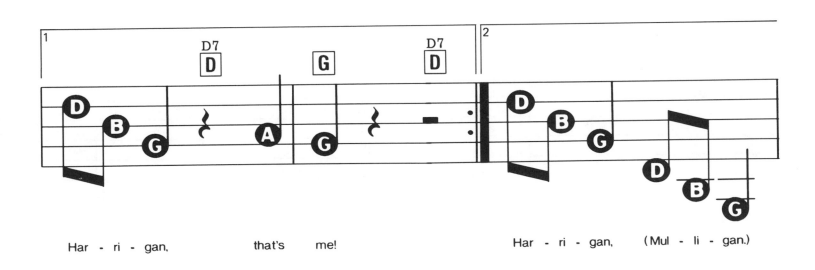

Har - ri - gan, that's me! Har - ri - gan, (Mul - li - gan.)

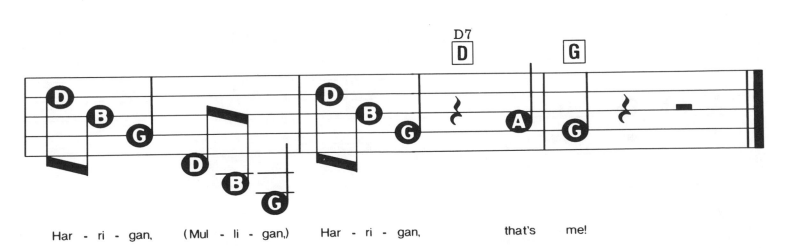

Har - ri - gan, (Mul - li - gan,) Har - ri - gan, that's me!

I (Who Have Nothing)

Registration 9
Rhythm: Rock or Disco

English Lyric by Jerry Lieber and Mike Stoller
Music by C. Donida

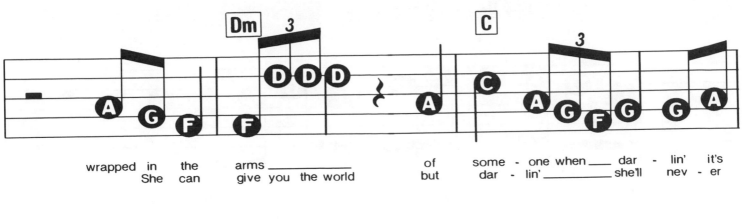

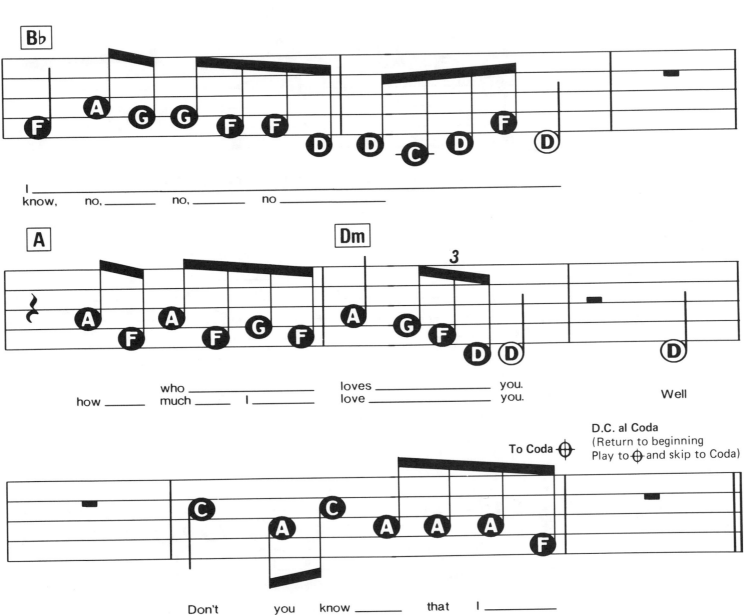

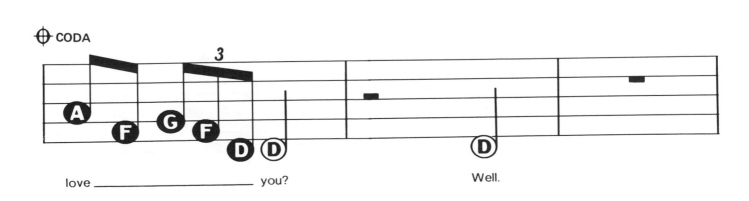

Dm7

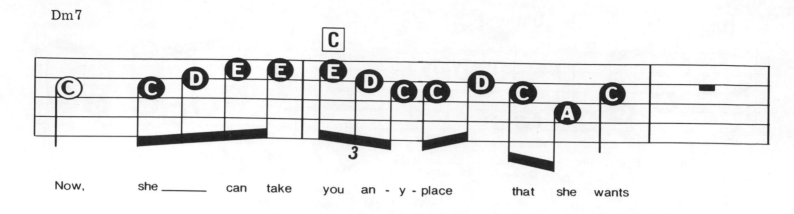

Now,   she _____ can take you an - y - place   that she wants

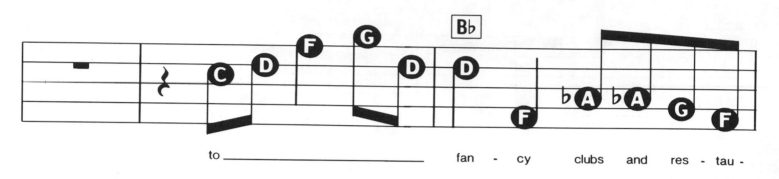

to _____ fan - cy clubs and res - tau -

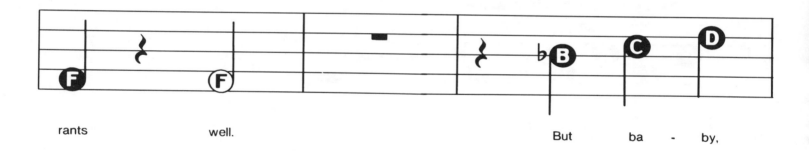

rants   well.   But   ba - by,

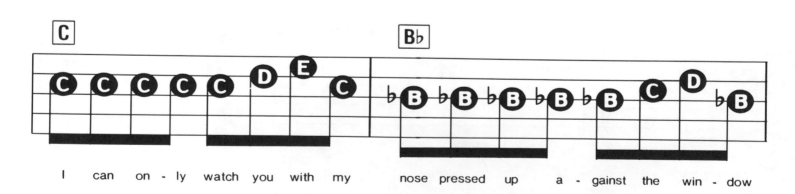

I can on - ly watch you with my   nose pressed up a - gainst the win - dow

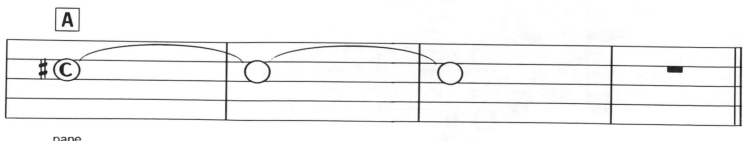

pane. _____

Play 4 times

Love ya, hoo, hoo, hoo. I love ya; love ya'.

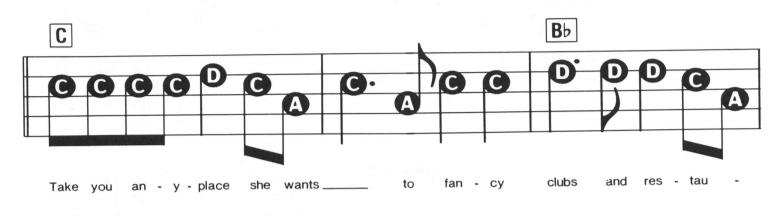

Take you an - y - place she wants _____ to fan - cy clubs and res - tau -

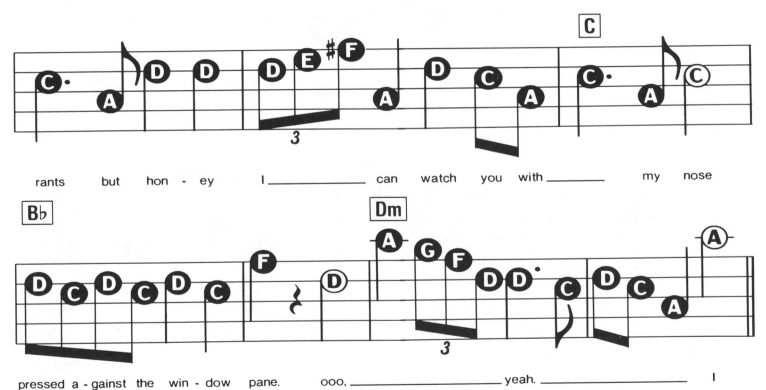

rants but hon - ey I _____ can watch you with _____ my nose

pressed a - gainst the win - dow pane. ooo, _____ yeah. _____ I

Repeat and Fade

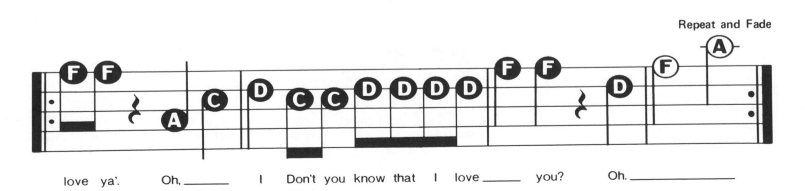

love ya'. Oh, _____ I Don't you know that I love _____ you? Oh. _____

A Gay Ranchero
(Las Altenitas)

Registration 9
Rhythm: Polka or March

Words by Abe Tuvim and Francia Luban
Music by J.J. Espinosa

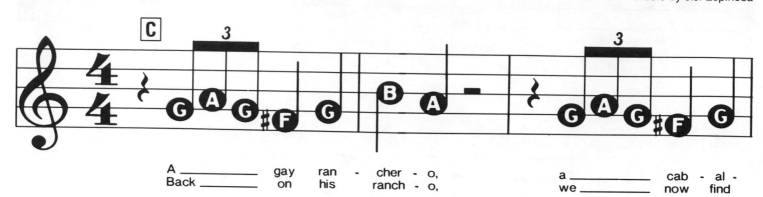

A _____ gay ran - cher - o,   a _____ cab - al -
Back _____ on his ranch - o,   we _____ now find

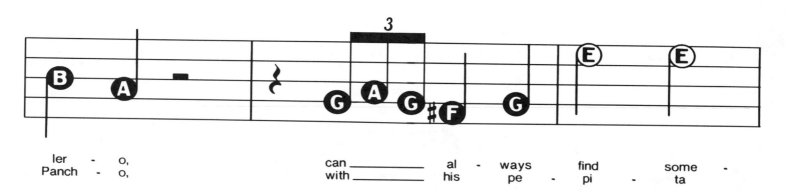

ler - o,   can _____ al - ways find some -
Panch - o,   with _____ his pe - pi - ta

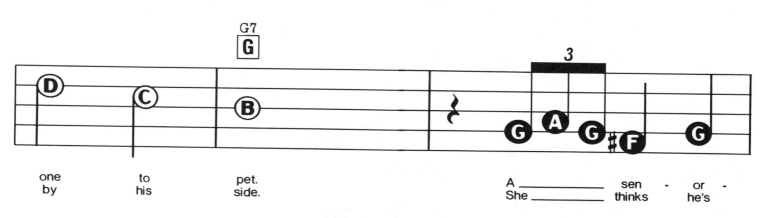

one to pet.   A _____ sen - or -
by his side.   She _____ thinks he's

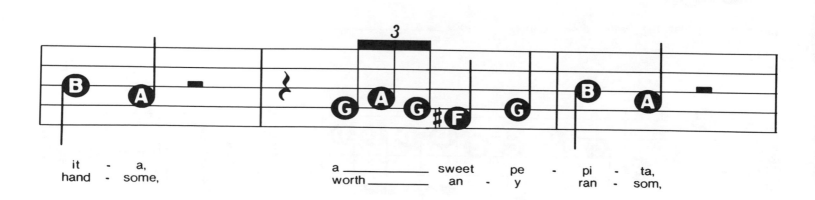

it - a,   a _____ sweet pe - pi - ta,
hand - some,   worth _____ an - y ran - som,

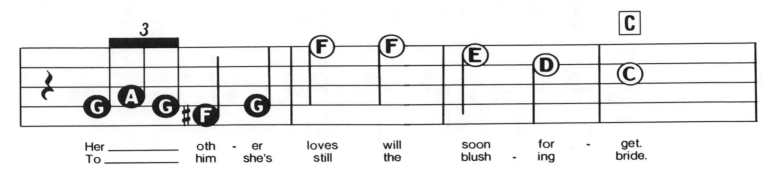

Her _____ oth - er loves will soon for - get.
To _____ him she's still the blush - ing bride.

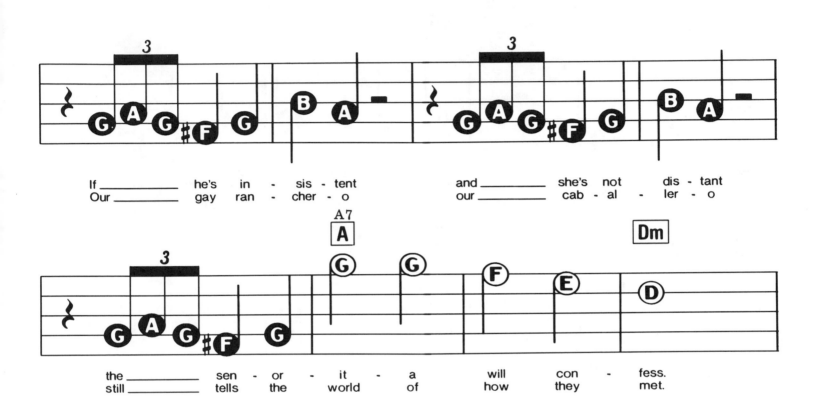

If _____ he's in - sis - tent and _____ she's not dis - tant
Our _____ gay ran - cher - o our _____ cab - al - ler - o

the _____ sen - or - it - a will con - fess.
still _____ tells the world of how they met.

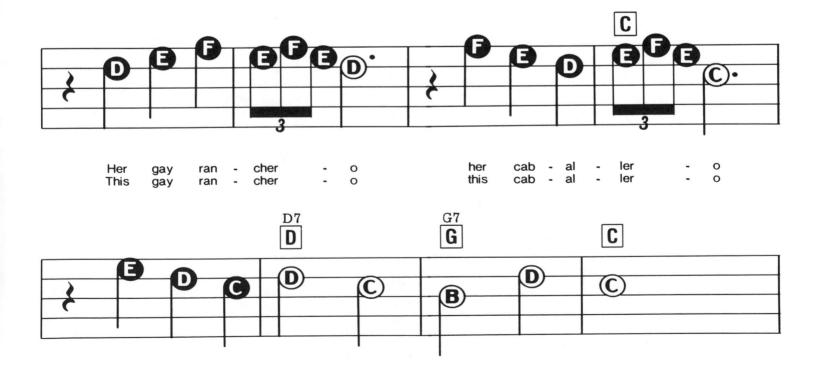

Her gay ran - cher - o her cab - al - ler - o
This gay ran - cher - o this cab - al - ler - o

need on - ly ask and she'll say yes.
says he has noth - ing to re - gret.

I Am...I Said

Registration 3
Rhythm: Fox Trot or March (4/4)

Words and Music by Neil Diamond

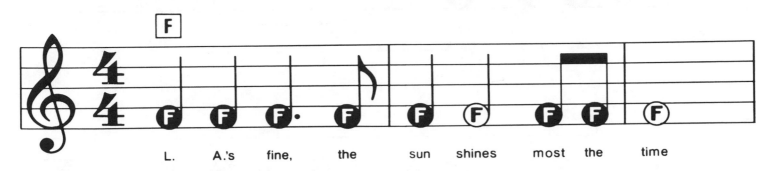

L. A.'s fine, the sun shines most the time

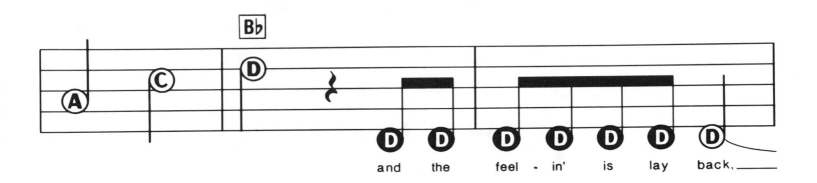

and the feel - in' is lay back, _____

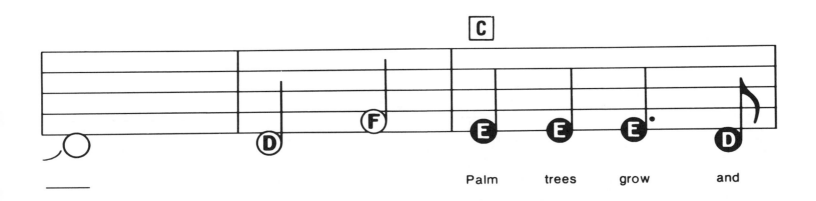

Palm trees grow and

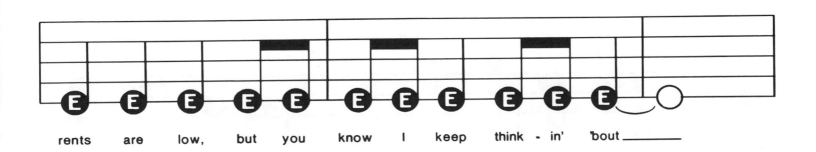

rents are low, but you know I keep think - in' 'bout _____

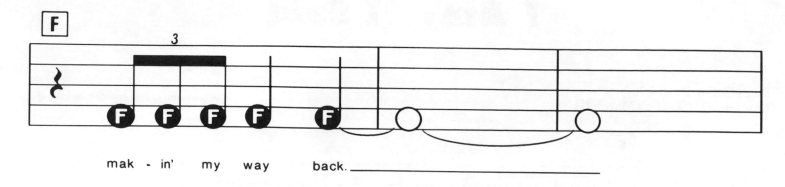

mak - in' my way back._____

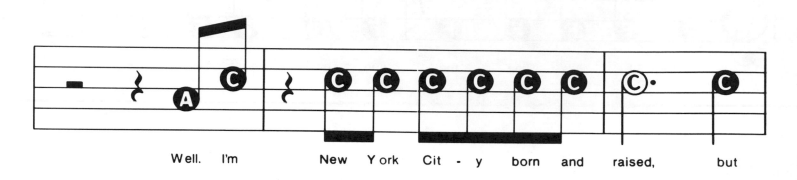

Well. I'm New York Cit - y born and raised, but

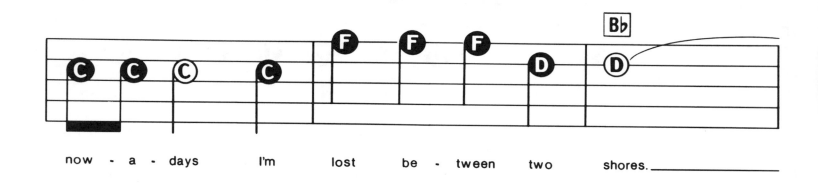

now - a - days I'm lost be - tween two shores._____

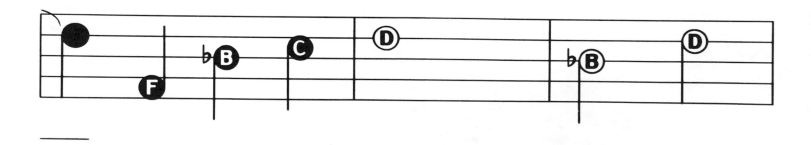

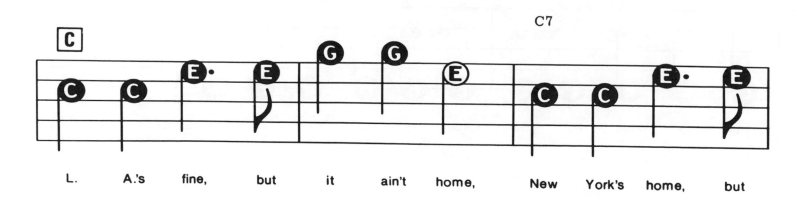

L. A.'s fine, but it ain't home, New York's home, but

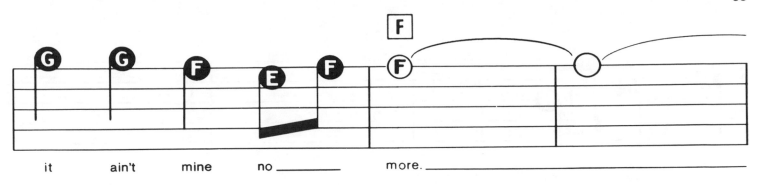

it   ain't   mine   no _____   more. _____

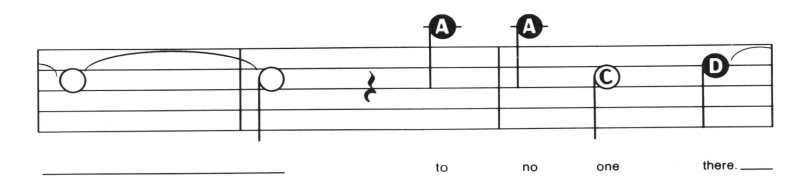

_____   "I   am,"   I   said _____

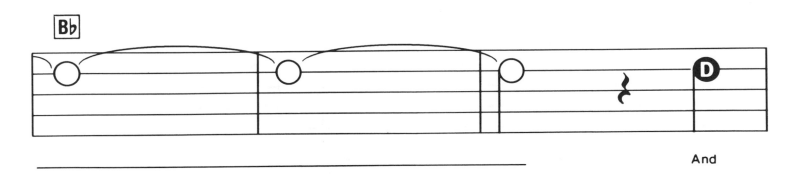

_____   to   no   one   there. ____

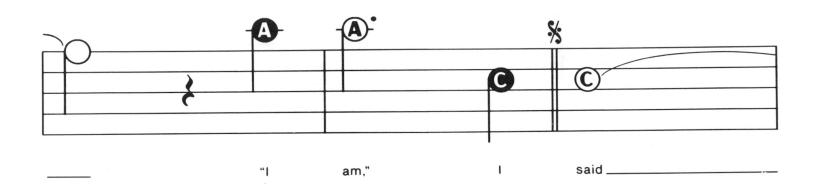

_____   And

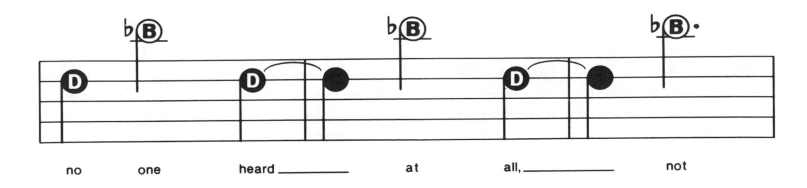

no   one   heard _____   at   all, _____   not

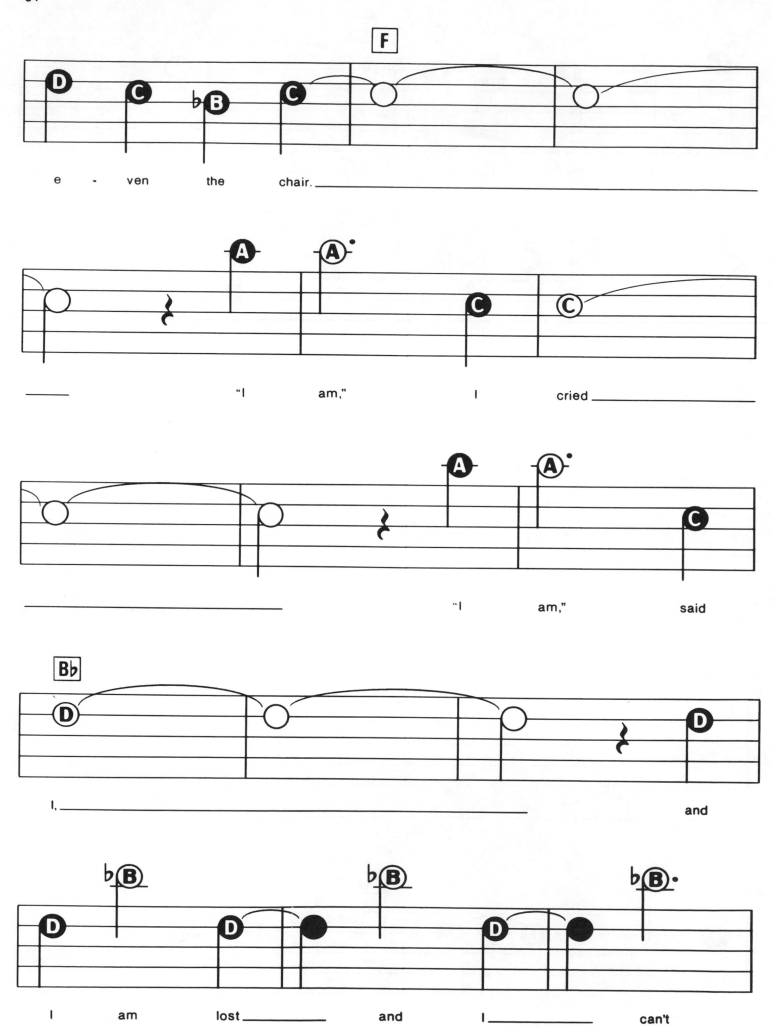

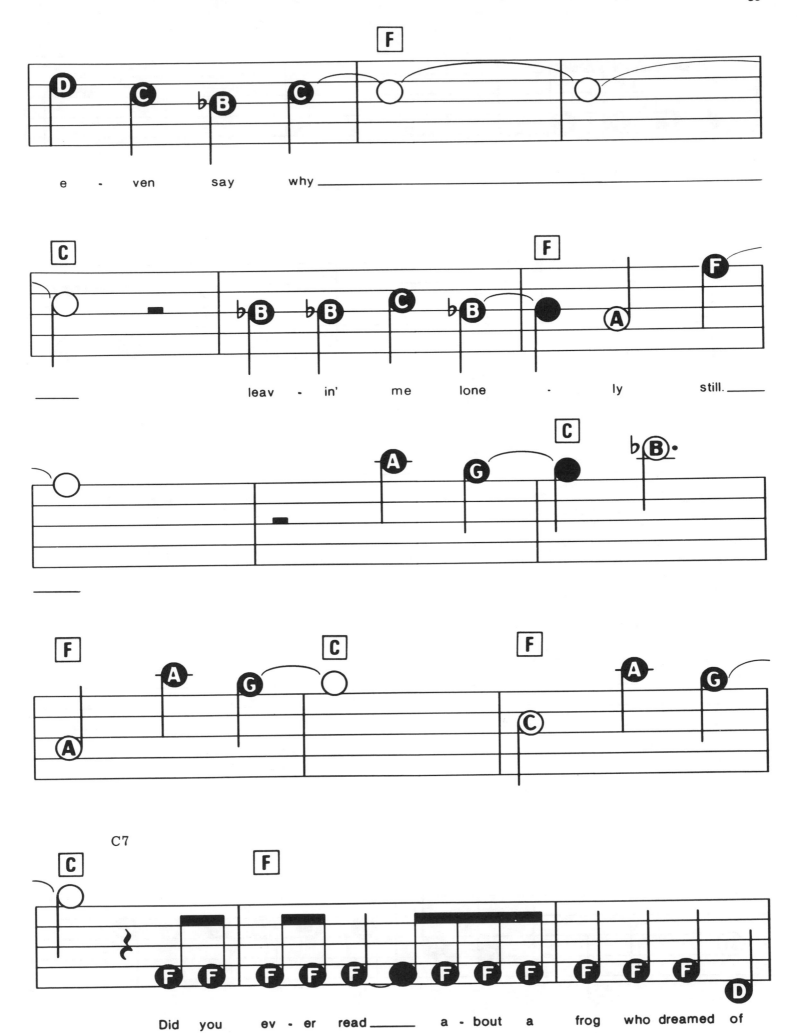

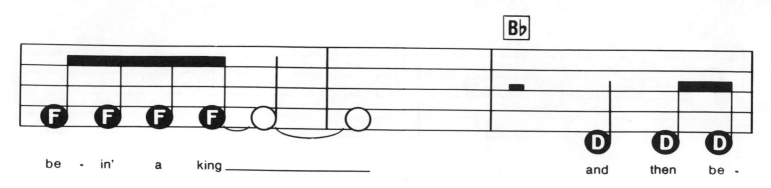

be - in' a king _____ and then be -

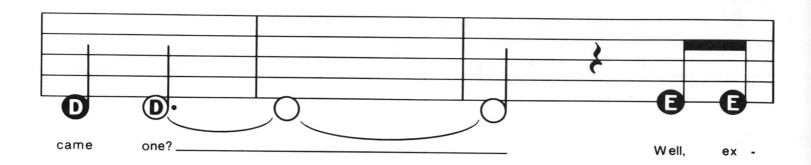

came one? _____ Well, ex -

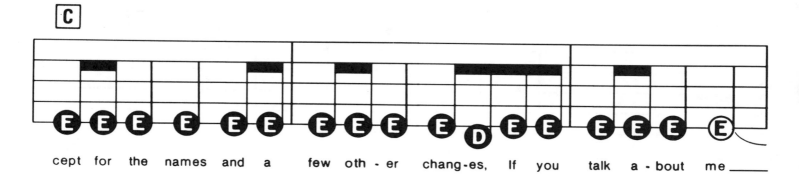

cept for the names and a few oth - er chang-es, If you talk a - bout me ____

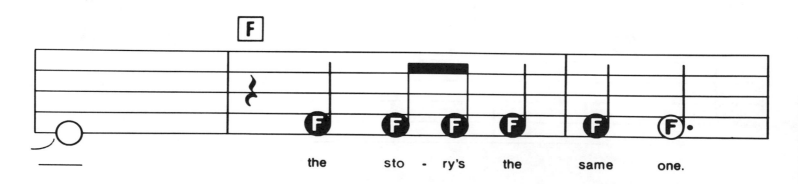

____ the sto - ry's the same one.

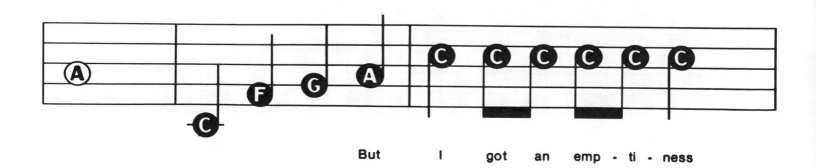

But I got an emp - ti - ness

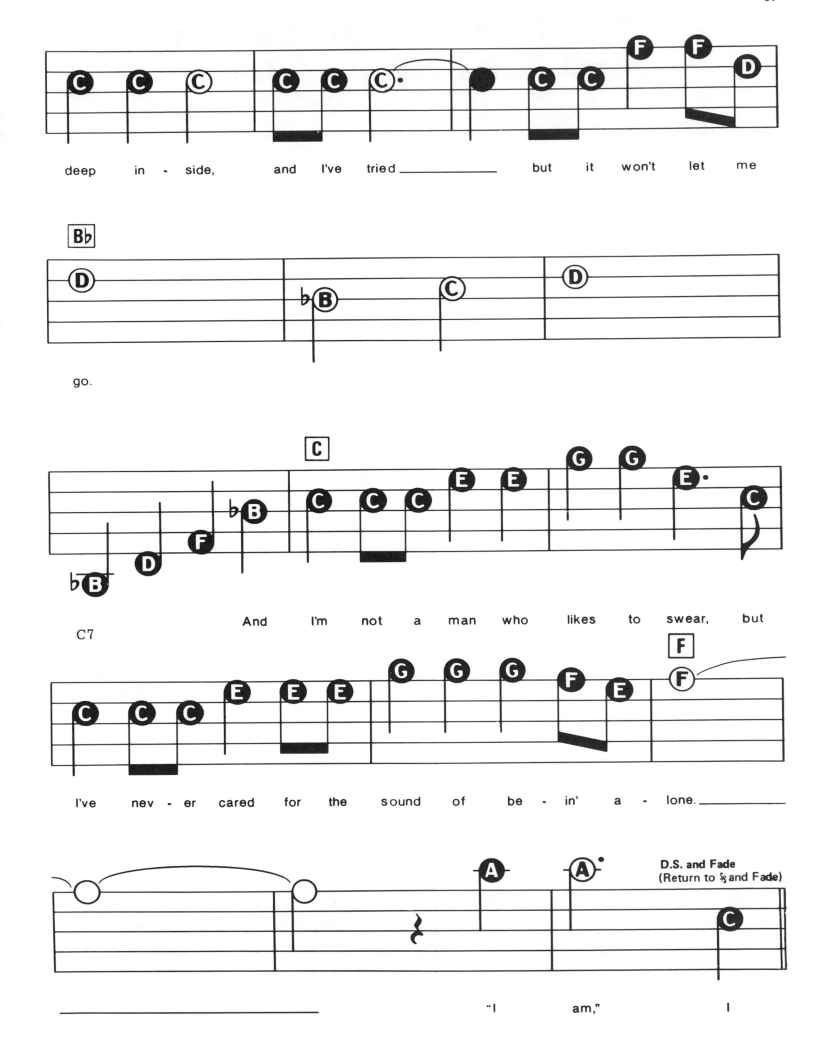

I'm Gonna Sit Right Down And Write Myself A Letter

Registration 3
Rhythm: Shuffle

Words by Joe Young
Music by Fred E. Ahlert

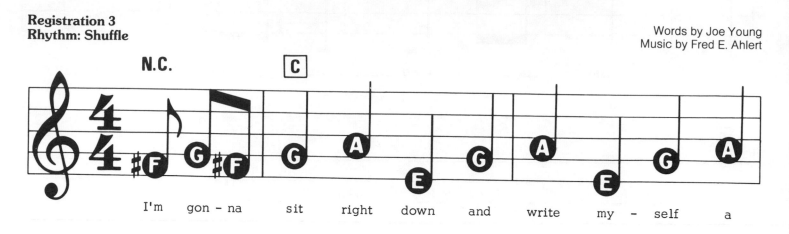

I'm gon - na sit right down and write my - self a

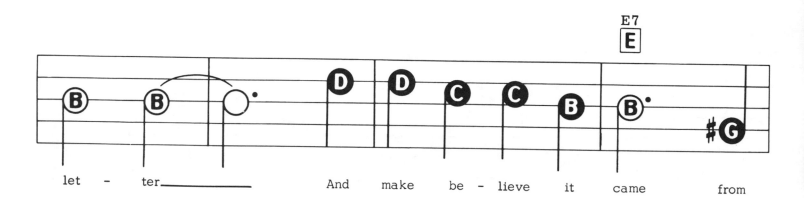

let - ter_____ And make be - lieve it came from

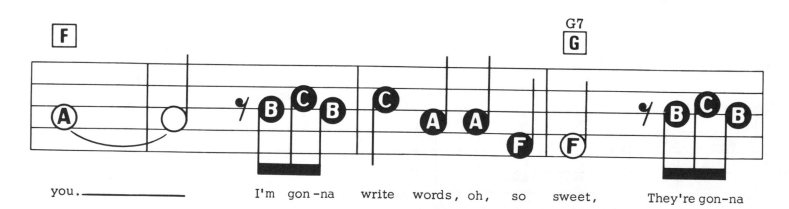

you._____ I'm gon -na write words, oh, so sweet, They're gon-na

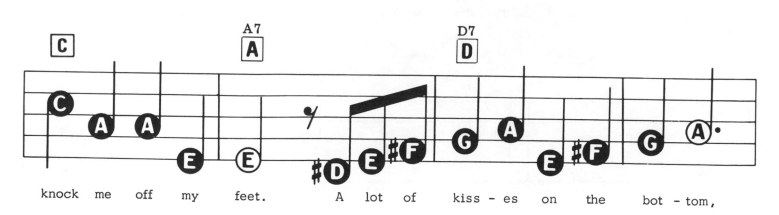

knock me off my feet. A lot of kiss - es on the bot - tom,

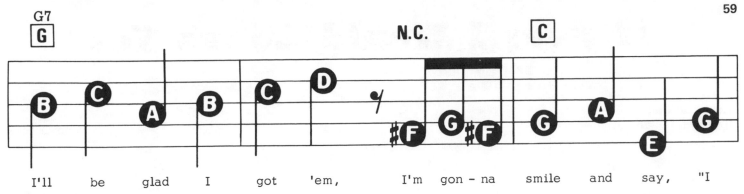

I'll be glad I got 'em, I'm gon-na smile and say, "I

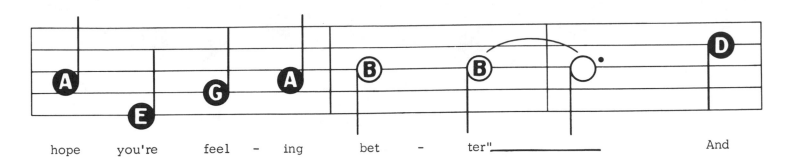

hope you're feel - ing bet - ter"_____ And

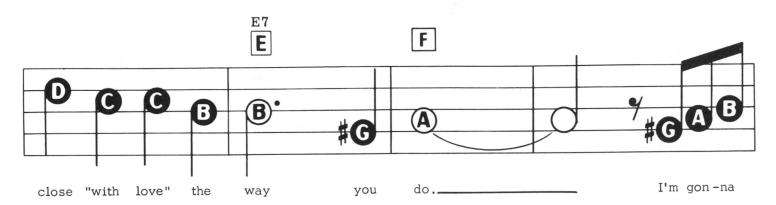

close "with love" the way you do._____ I'm gon-na

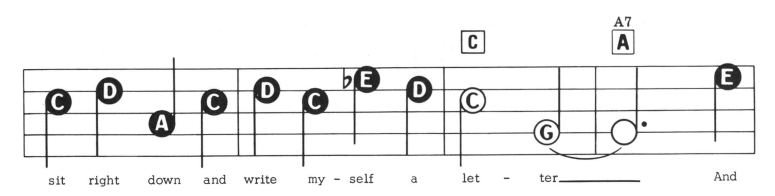

sit right down and write my - self a let - ter_____ And

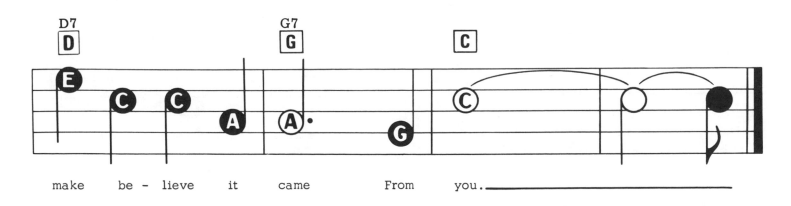

make be - lieve it came From you._____

If Ever I Would Leave You

Registration 5
Rhythm: Ballad

Words by Alan Jay Lerner
Music by Frederick Loewe

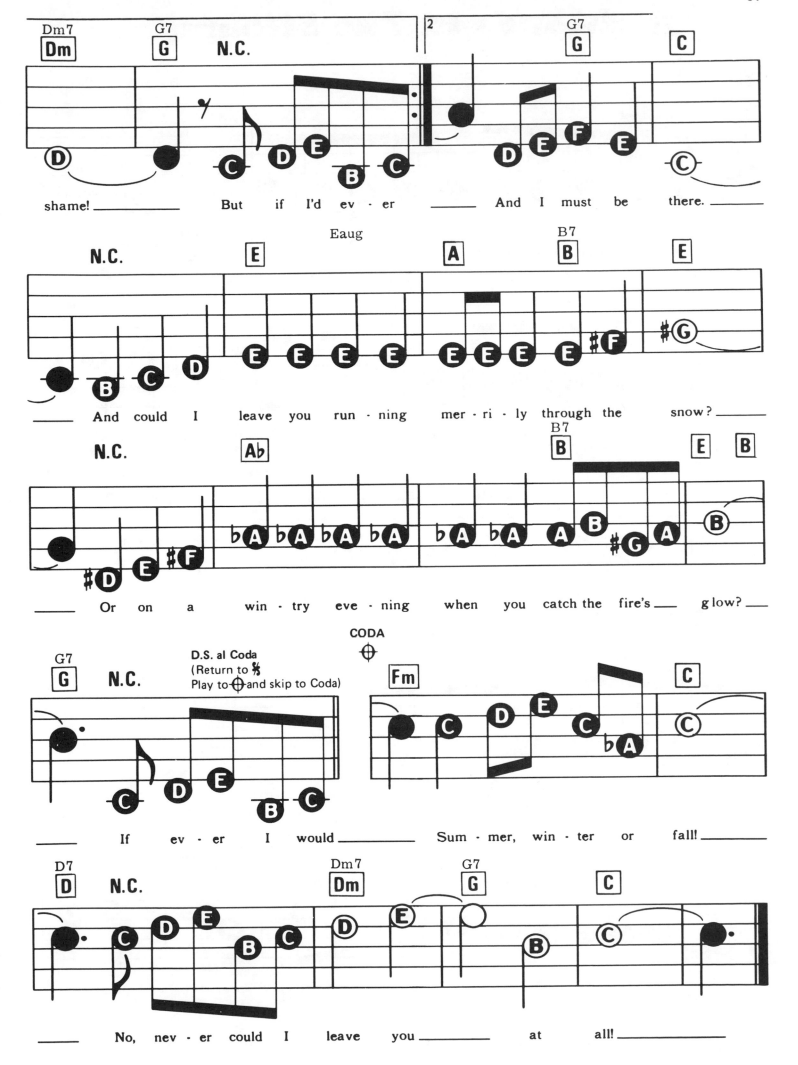

Islands In The Stream

Registration 3
Rhythm: Rock

Words and Music by Barry Gibb,
Maurice Gibb and Robin Gibb

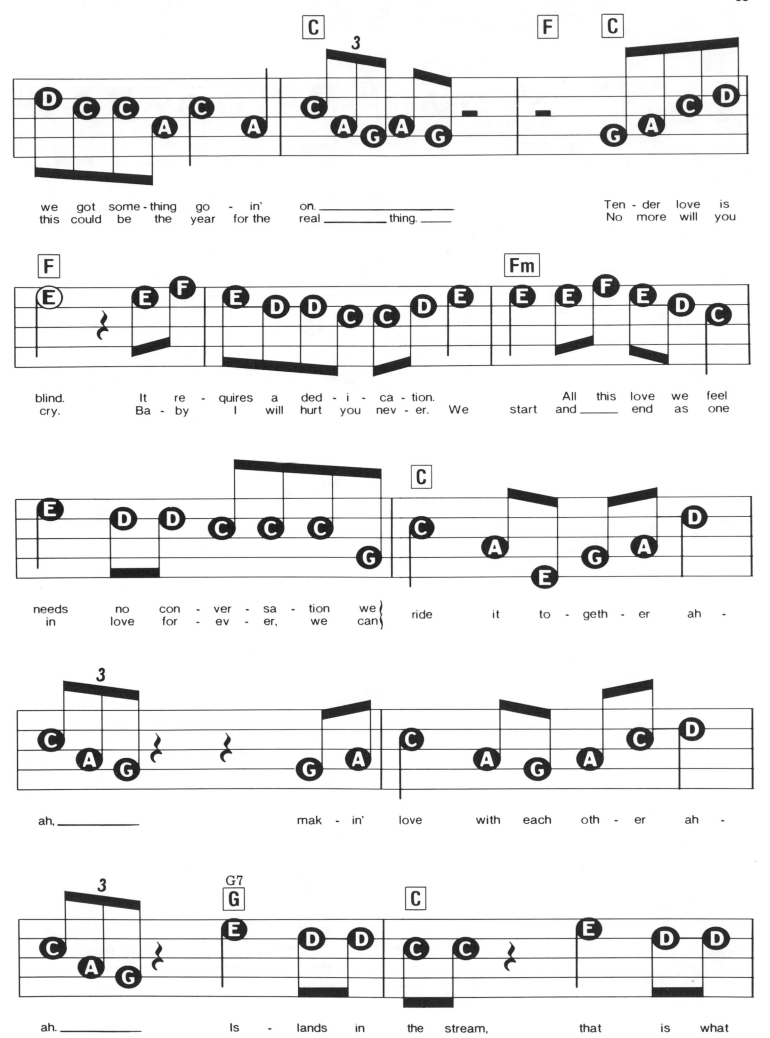

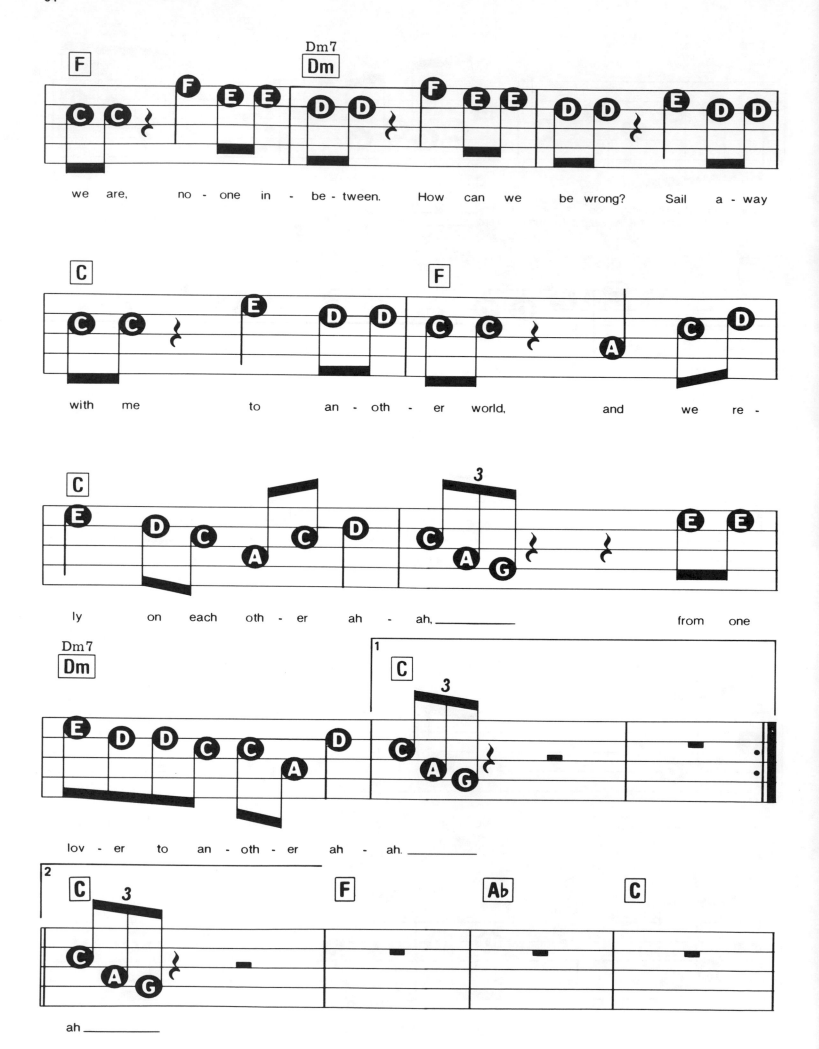

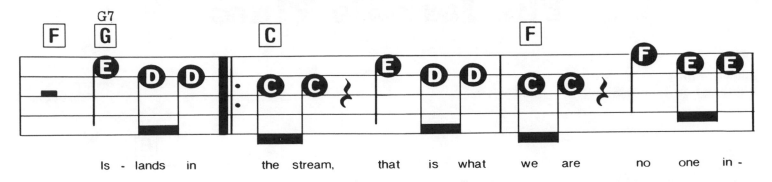

Is - lands in the stream, that is what we are no one in -

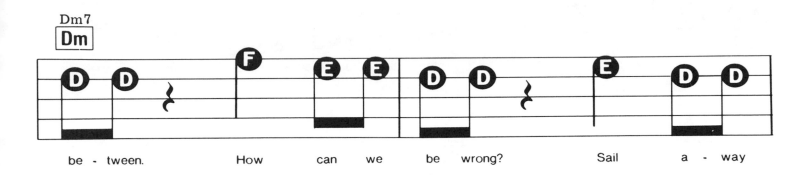

be - tween. How can we be wrong? Sail a - way

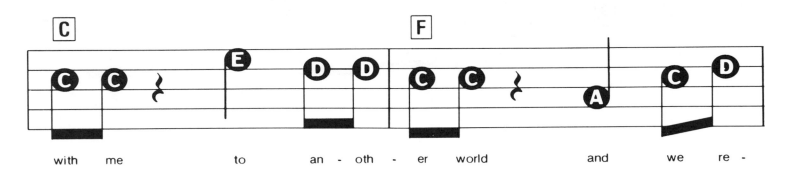

with me to an - oth - er world and we re -

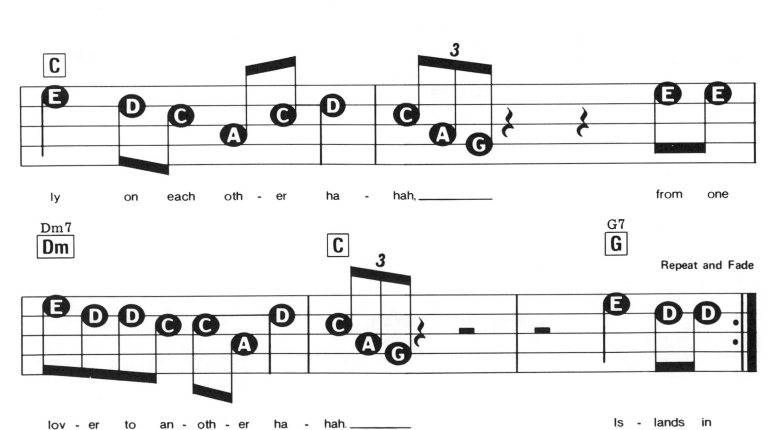

ly on each oth - er ha - hah,_____ from one

Repeat and Fade

lov - er to an - oth - er ha - hah._____ Is - lands in

The Jazz-Me Blues

Registration 4
Rhythm: Fox Trot or Swing

Words and Music by
Tom Delaney

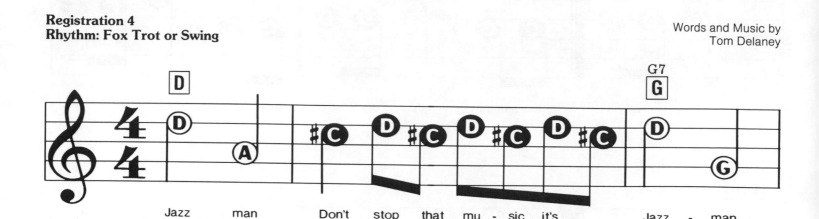

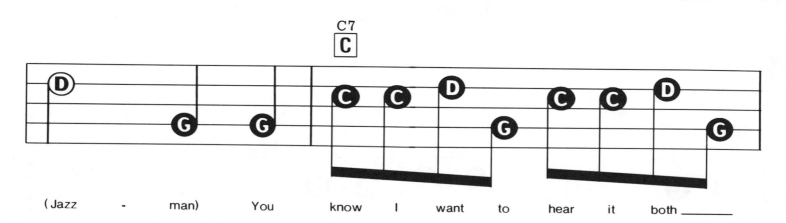

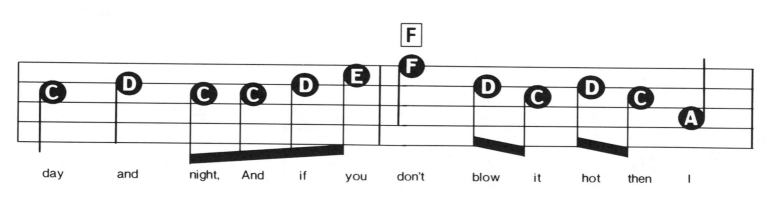

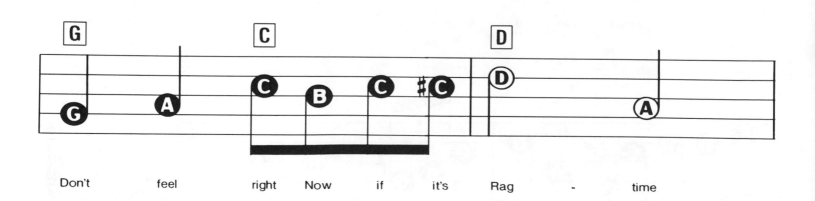

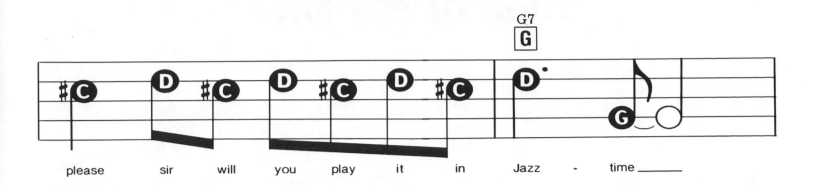

please sir will you play it in Jazz - time ____

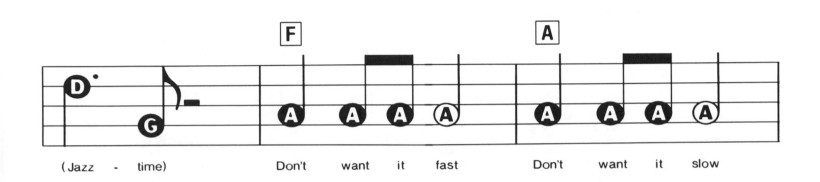

(Jazz - time)   Don't want it fast   Don't want it slow

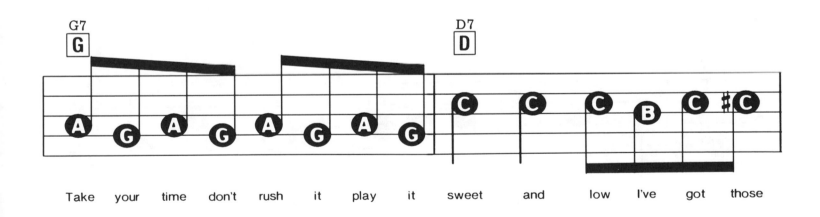

Take your time don't rush it play it sweet and low I've got those

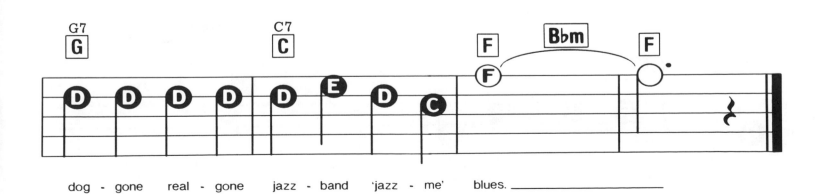

dog - gone real - gone jazz - band 'jazz - me' blues. ____

King Of The Road

Registration 7
Rhythm: Country

Words and Music by
Roger Miller

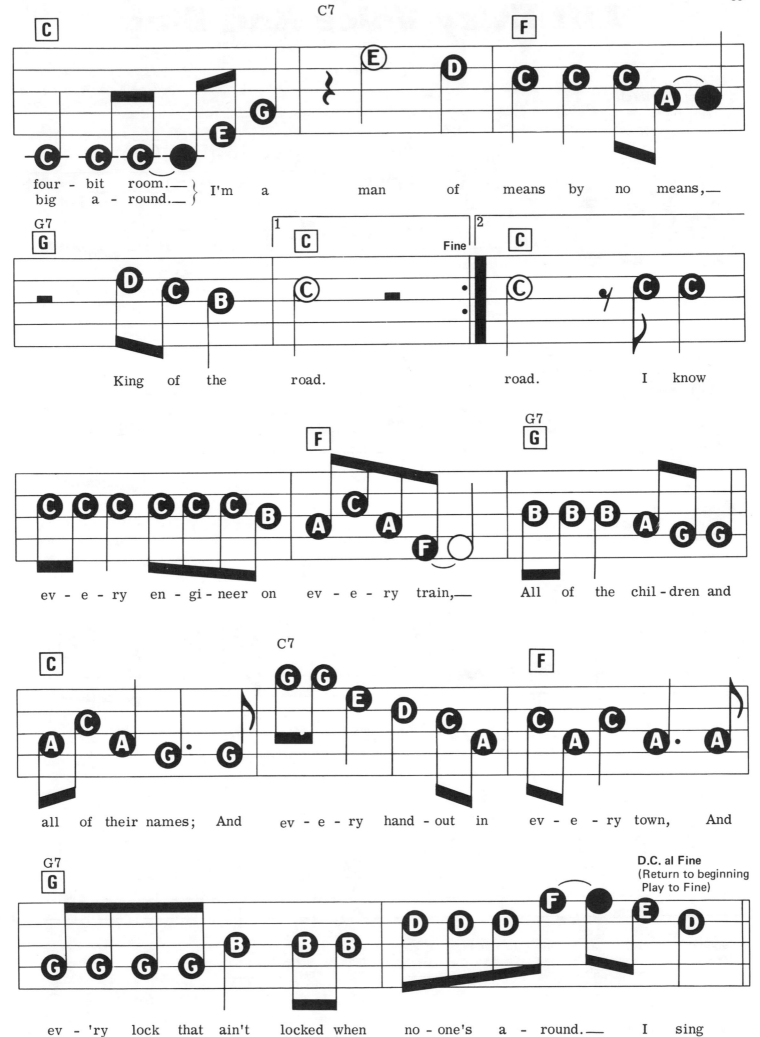

Lift Ev'ry Voice And Sing

Registration 5
Rhythm: 6/8 March

Words by James Weldon Johnson
Music by J. Rosamond Johnson

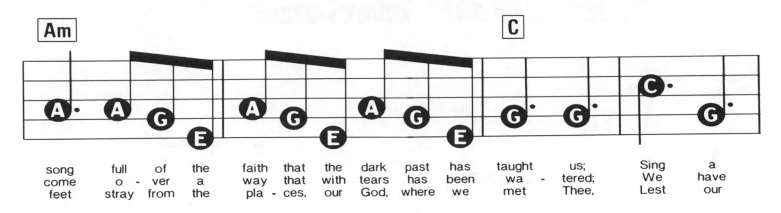

song full of the faith that the dark past has taught us;
come o - ver a way that with tears has been wa - tered;
feet stray from the pla - ces, our God, where we met Thee,

Sing a
We have
Lest our

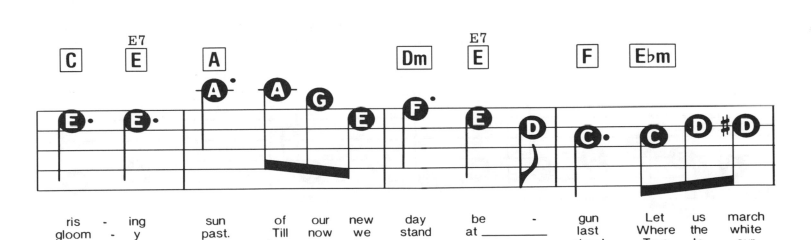

song full of the hope that the pres - ent has brought ___ us;
come, tread - ing our path thro' the blood of the slaugh -
hearts, drunk with the wine of the world we for - get ___

Fac - ing the
tered, Out from the
Thee: Shad - owed be-

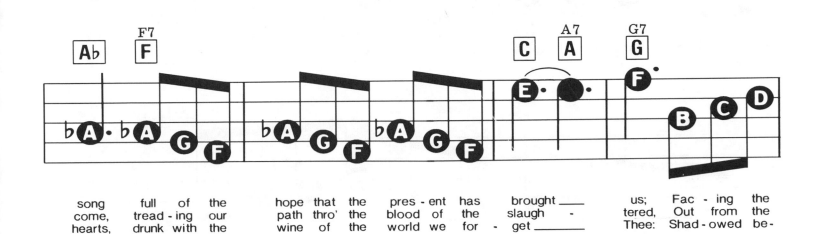

ris - ing sun of our new day be - gun
gloom - y past. Till now we stand at ___ last
neath Thy hand, May we for - ev - er ___ stand.

Let us march
Where the white
True to our

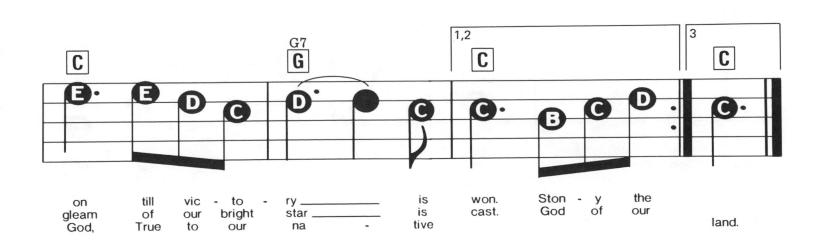

on till vic - to - ry ___ is won.
gleam of our bright star ___ is cast.
God, True to our na - tive

Ston - y the
God of our

land.

Lilli Marlene

Registration 9
Rhythm: Ballad or Fox Trot

German Lyric by Hans Leip
English Lyric by Tommie Connor
Music by Norbert Schultze

Un - der - neath the lan - tern by the bar - rack gate,
Time would come for roll call, time for us to part,

Dar - ling I re - mem - ber the way you used to wait; 'Twas
Dar - ling I'd ca - ress you and press you to my heart; And

there that you whis - pered ten - der - ly, That you lov'd me, You'd
there 'neath that far off lan - tern light, I'd hold you tight, We'd

al - ways be kiss "Good - night," My Lil - li of the lamp - light, My

73

Lollipop

Registration 7
Rhythm: Swing or Jazz

Words and Music by
Beverly Ross and Julius Dixon

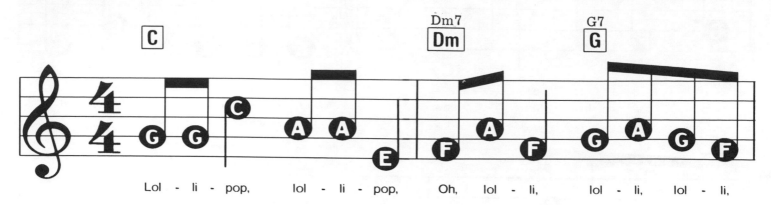

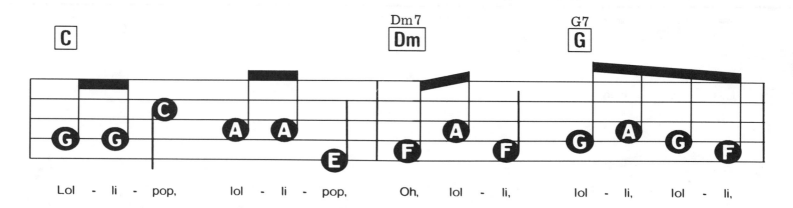

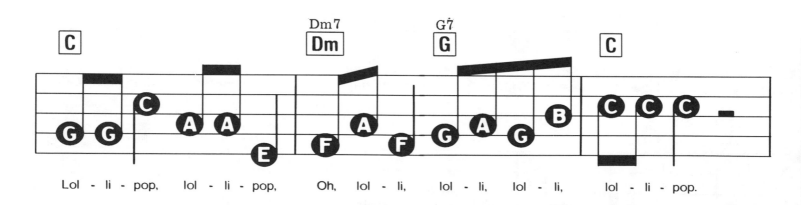

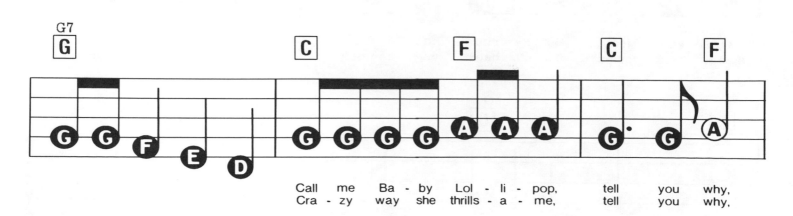

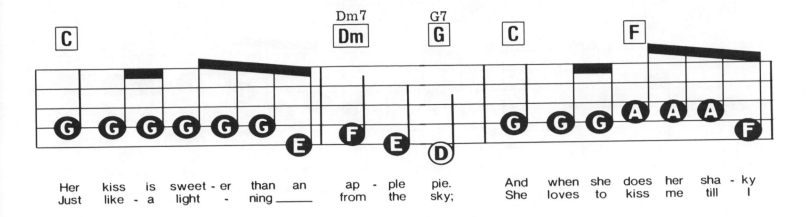

Her kiss is sweet - er than an ap - ple pie.
Just like - a light - ning _____ from the sky;
And when she does her sha - ky
She loves to kiss me till I

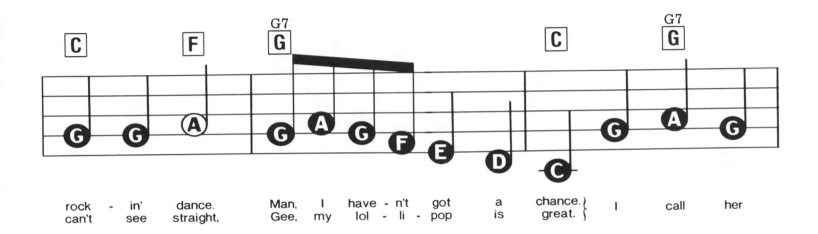

rock - in' dance. Man, I have - n't got a chance.
can't see straight, Gee, my lol - li - pop is great.
I call her

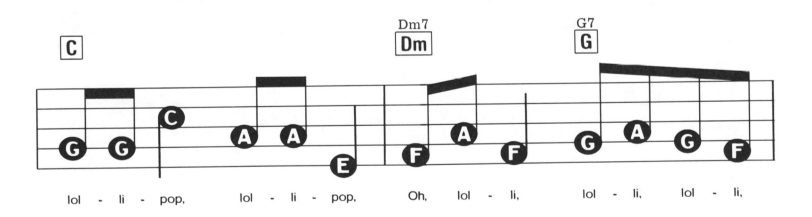

lol - li - pop, lol - li - pop, Oh, lol - li, lol - li, lol - li,

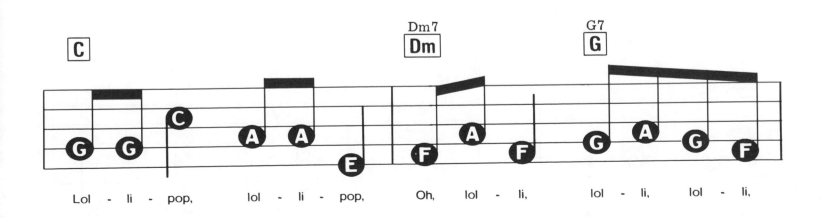

Lol - li - pop, lol - li - pop, Oh, lol - li, lol - li, lol - li,

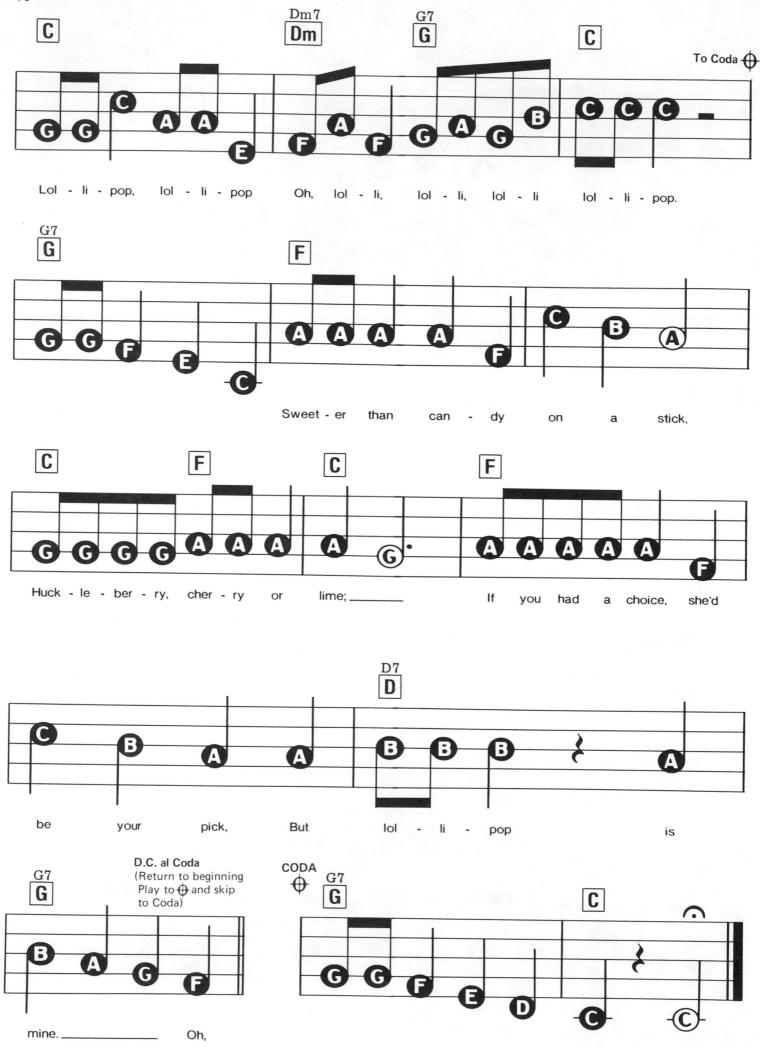

Mama Inez

Words by L. Wolfe Gilbert
Music by Eliseo Grenet

Registration 5
Rhythm: Rhumba or Latin

Manhattan
(From the Broadway Musical "GARRICK GAITIES")

Registration 7
Rhythm: Fox Trot or Swing

Lyric by Lorenz Hart
Music by Richard Rodgers

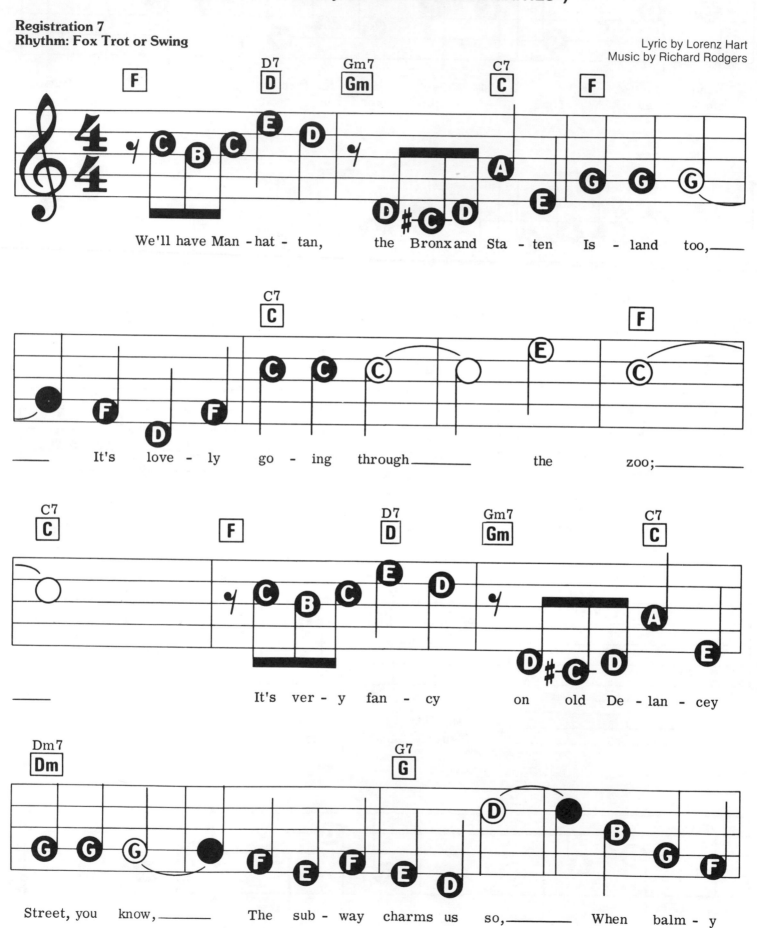

We'll have Man - hat - tan, the Bronx and Sta - ten Is - land too,

It's love - ly go - ing through the zoo;

It's ver - y fan - cy on old De - lan - cey

Street, you know, The sub - way charms us so, When balm - y

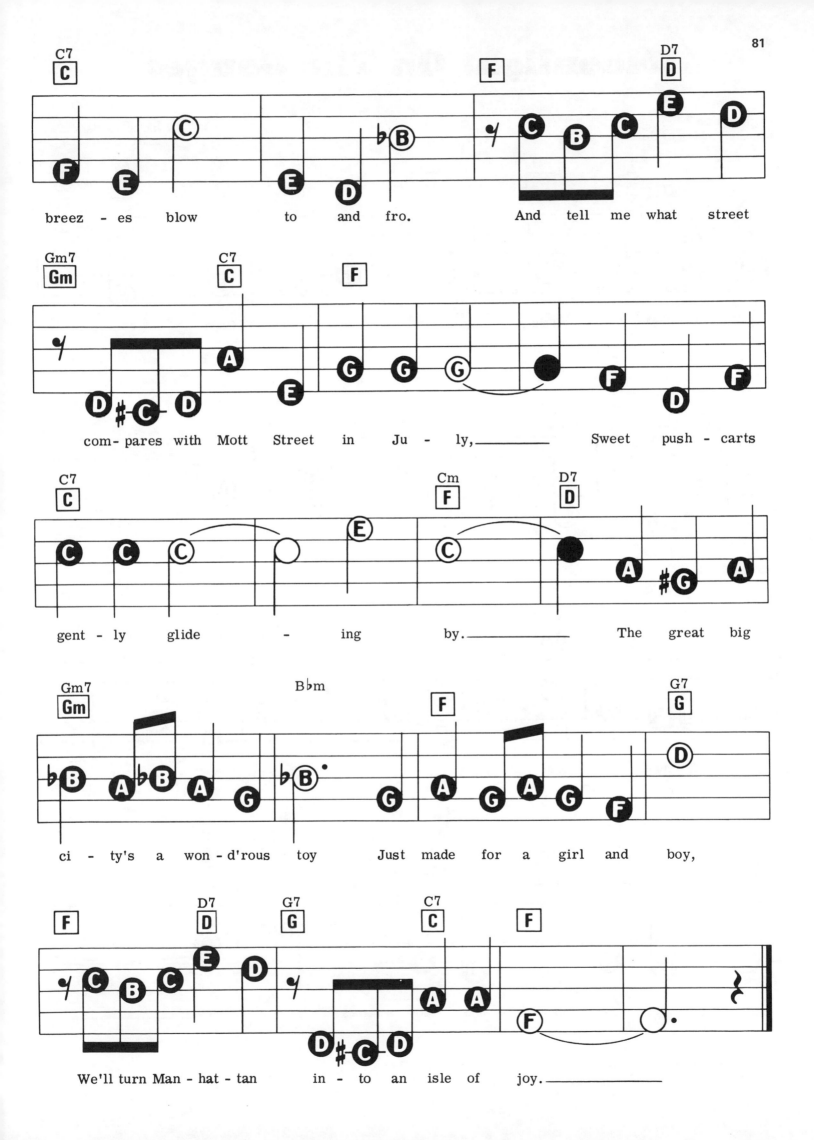

Moonlight On The Ganges

Registration 7
Rhythm: Swing or Jazz

Lyric by Chester Wallace
Music by Sherman Myers

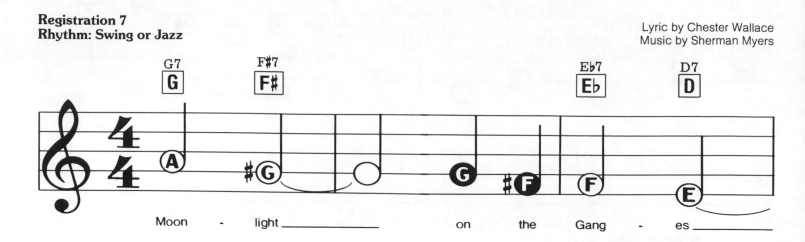

Moon - light _____ on the Gang - es _____

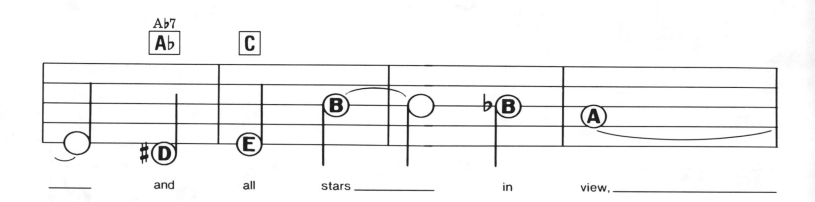

_____ and all stars _____ in view, _____

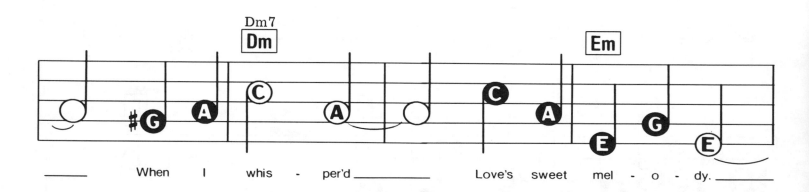

_____ When I whis - per'd _____ Love's sweet mel - o - dy.

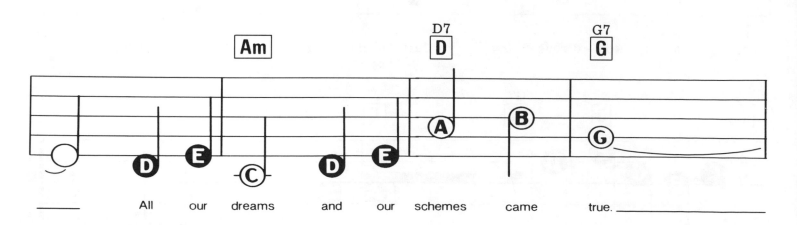

_____ All our dreams and our schemes came true. _____

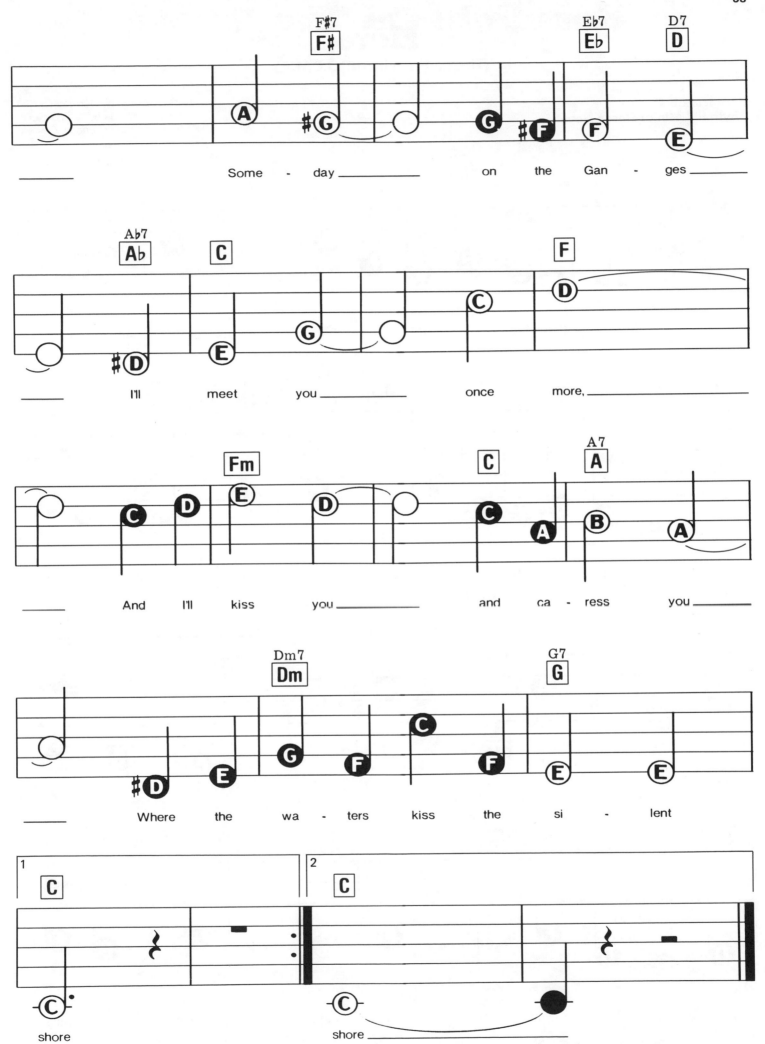

More
(Theme From MONDO CANE)

Registration 4
Rhythm: Latin or Bossa Nova

English Words by Norman Newell
Original Words by M. Ciorciolini
Music by R. Ortolani and N. Oliviero

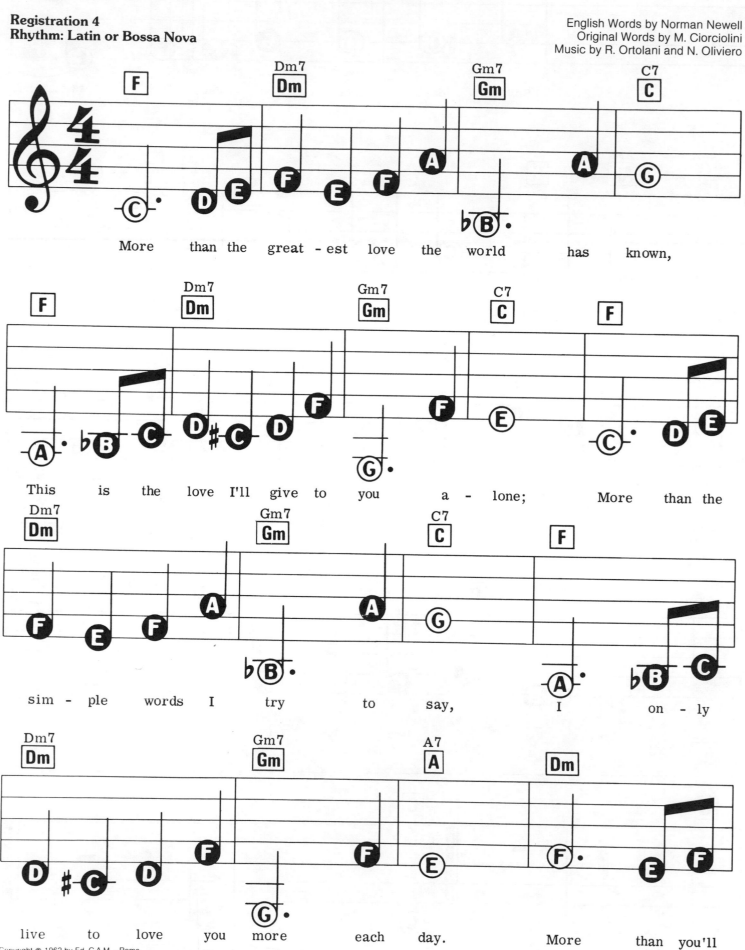

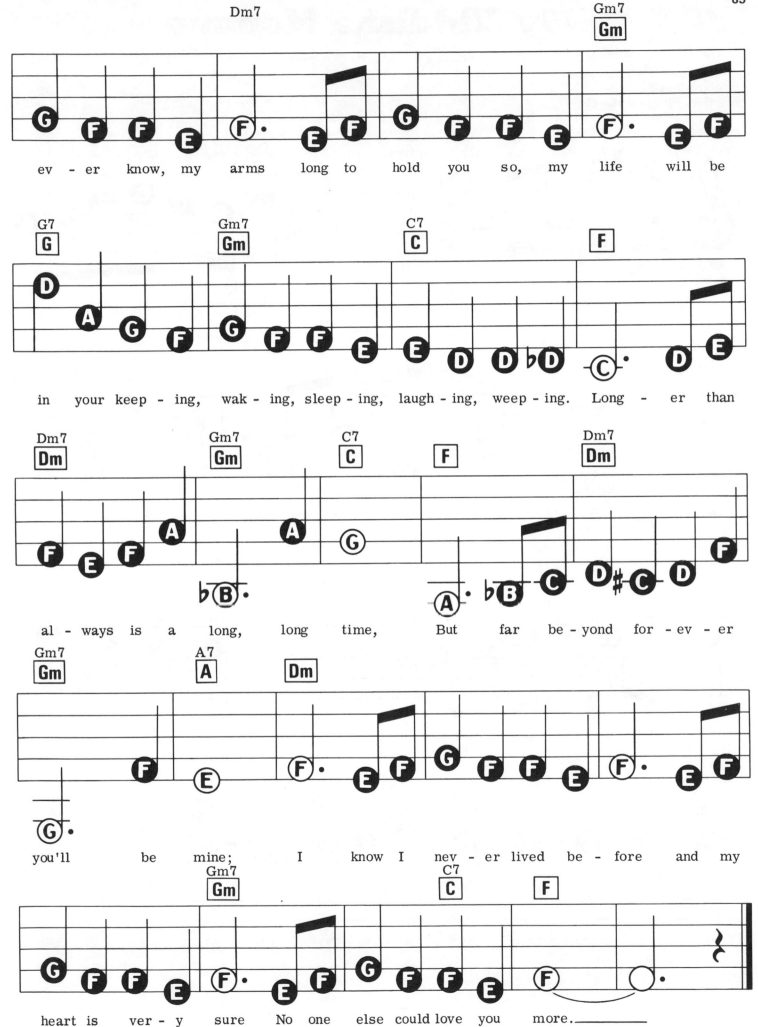

My Yiddishe Momme

Registration 4
Rhythm: Polka or March

Music by Lew Pollack and Jack Yellen
Words by Jack Yellen

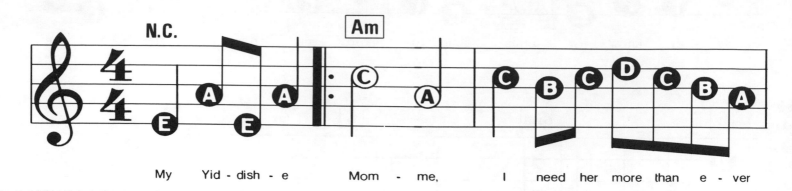

My Yid - dish - e Mom - me, I need her more than e - ver

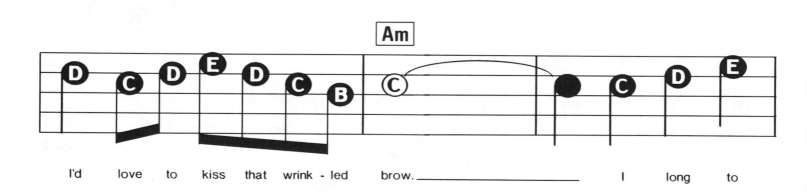

now, _____ My Yid - dish - e Mom - me,

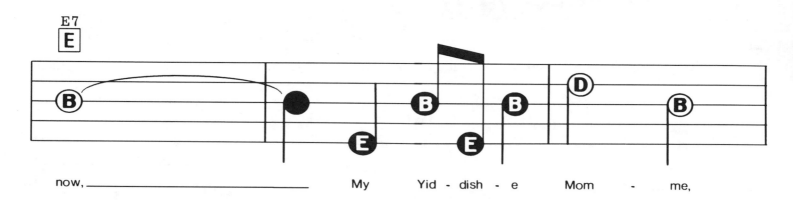

I'd love to kiss that wrink - led brow. _____ I long to

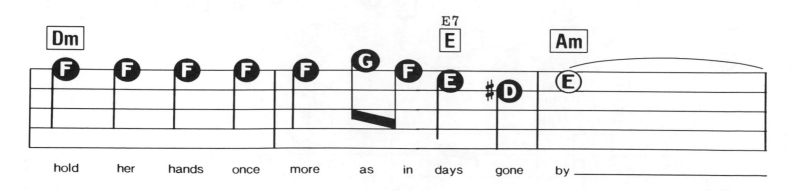

hold her hands once more as in days gone by _____

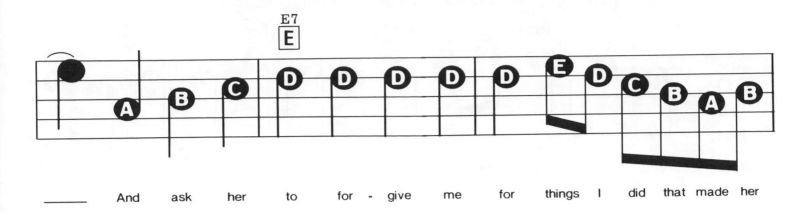

And ask her to for - give me for things I did that made her

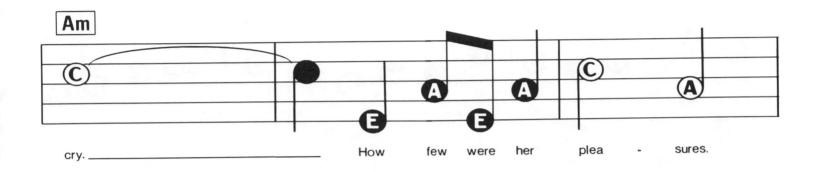

cry. _____ How few were her plea - sures.

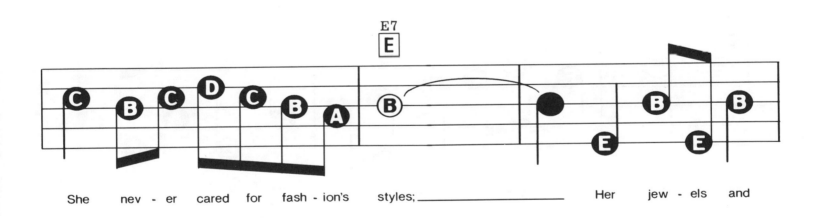

She nev - er cared for fash - ion's styles; _____ Her jew - els and

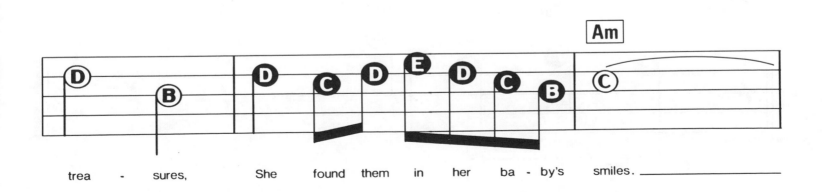

trea - sures, She found them in her ba - by's smiles. _____

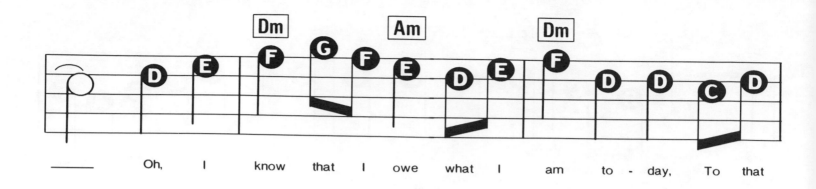

Oh, I know that I owe what I am to - day, To that

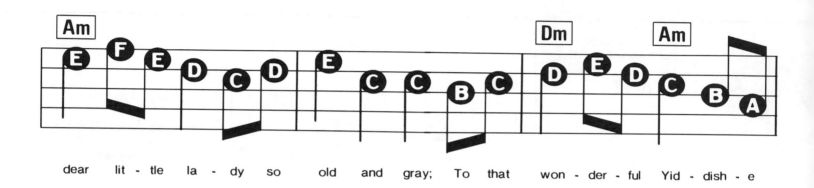

dear lit - tle la - dy so old and gray; To that won - der - ful Yid - dish - e

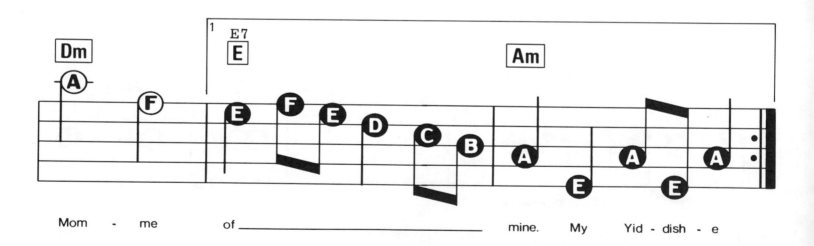

Mom - me of _____ mine. My Yid - dish - e

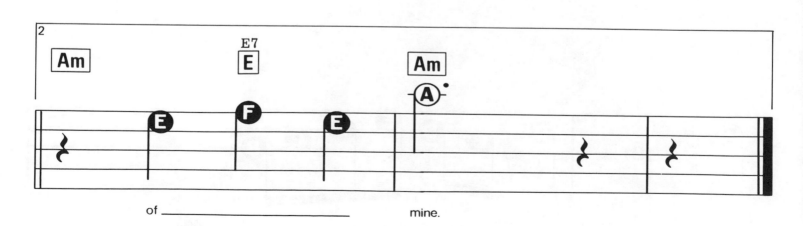

of _____ mine.

Papa, Won't You Dance With Me?

(From "HIGH BUTTON SHOES")

Words by Sammy Cahn
Music by Jule Styne

Registration 4
Rhythm: Polka or March

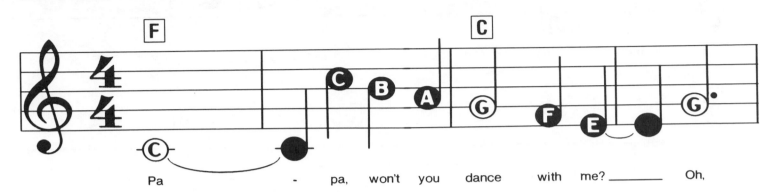

Pa - pa, won't you dance with me? _____ Oh,

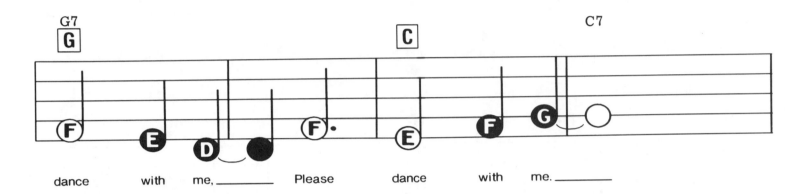

dance with me, _____ Please dance with me. _____

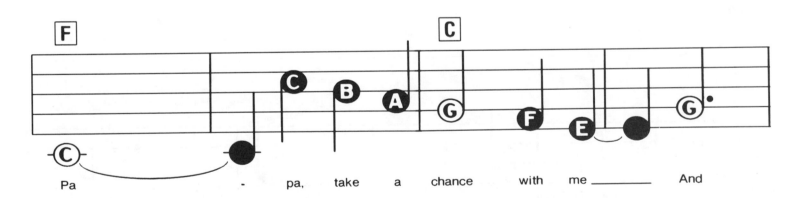

Pa - pa, take a chance with me _____ And

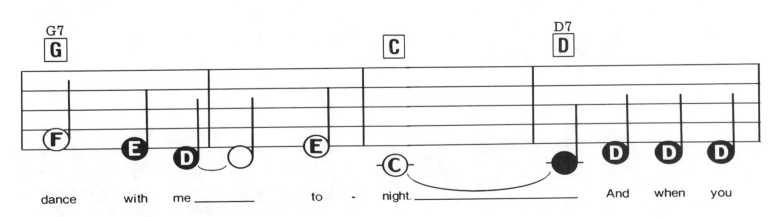

dance with me _____ to - night. _____ And when you

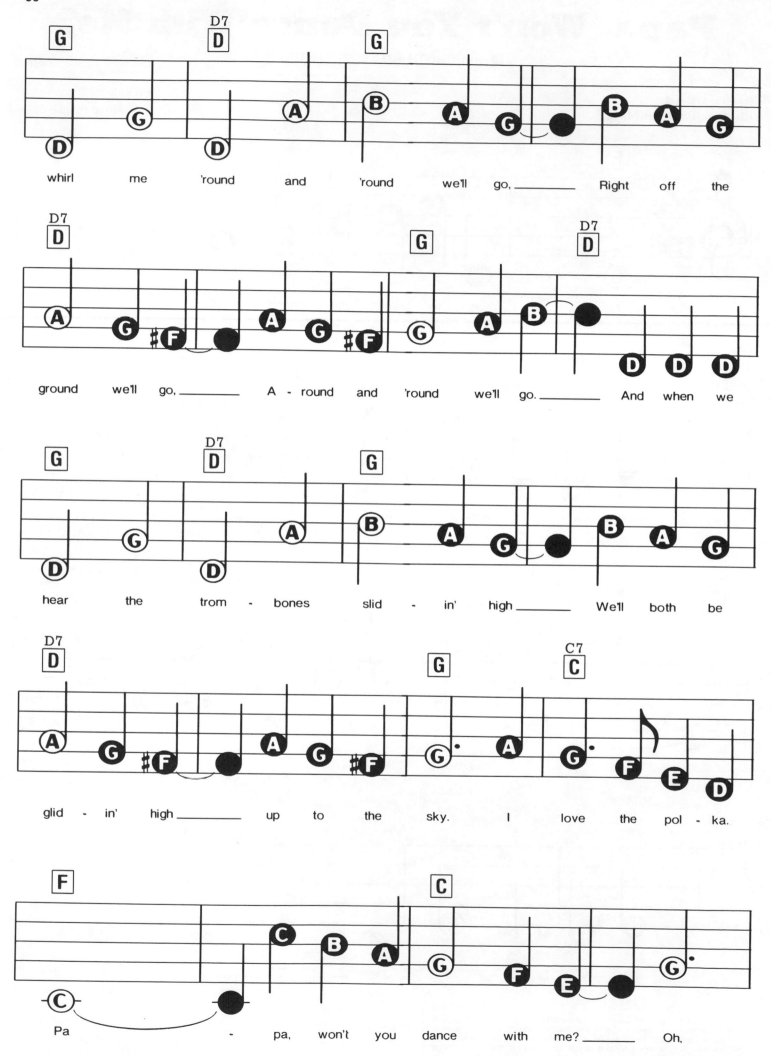

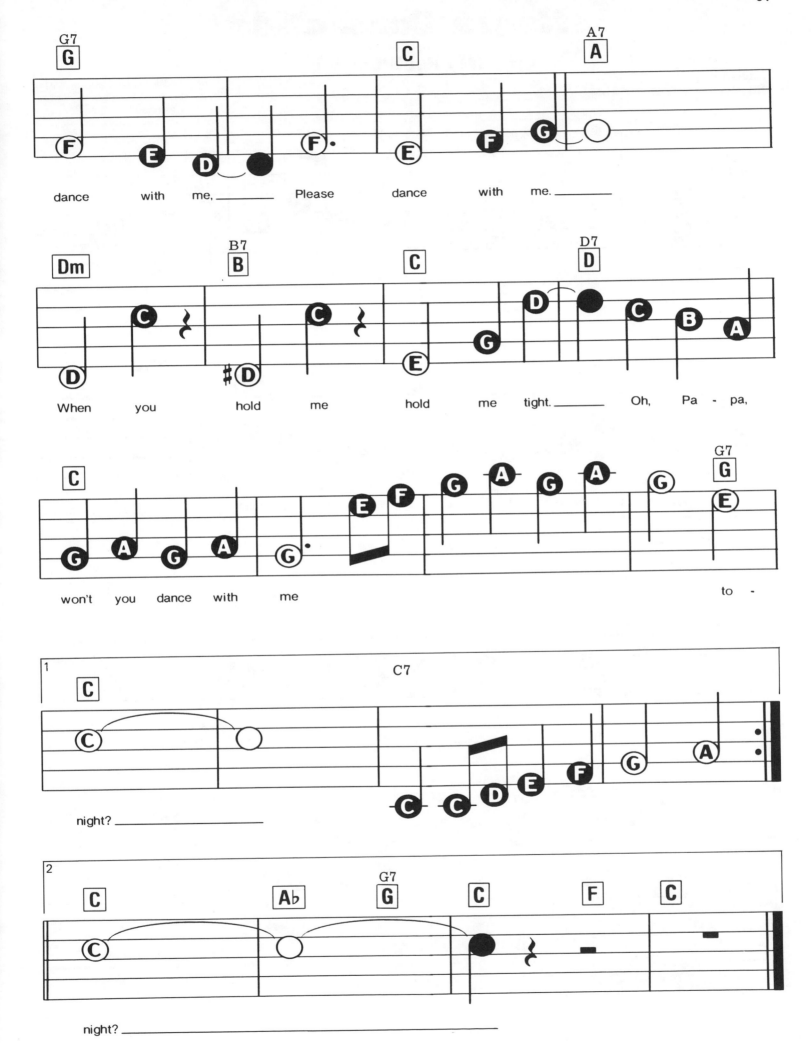

Negra Consentida

(My Pet Brunette)

Registration 7
Rhythm: Fox Trot or Swing

English Words by Marjorie Harper
Spanish Words and Music by Joaquin Pardave
Arranged by Elmer Schoebet

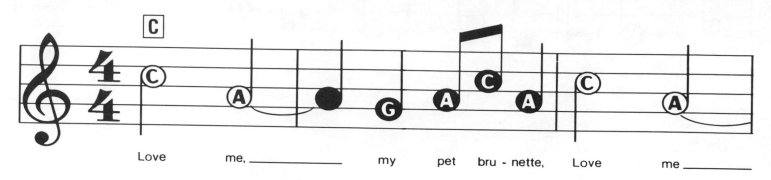

Love me, _____ my pet bru - nette, Love me _____

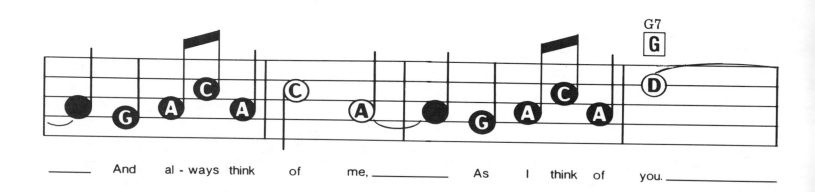

_____ And al - ways think of me, _____ As I think of you. _____

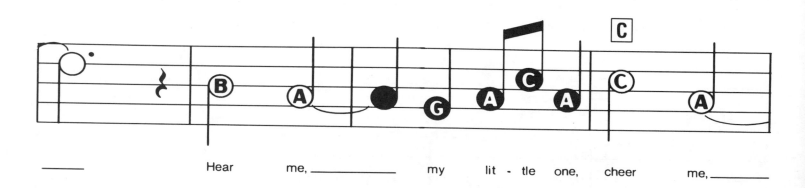

_____ Hear me, _____ my lit - tle one, cheer me, _____

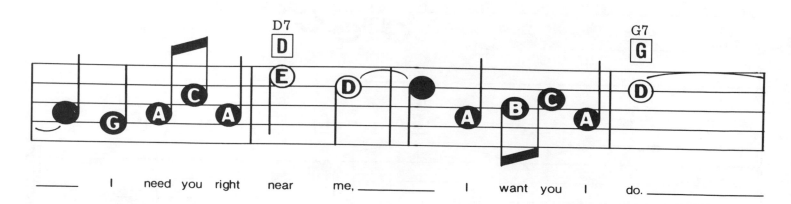

_____ I need you right near me, _____ I want you I do. _____

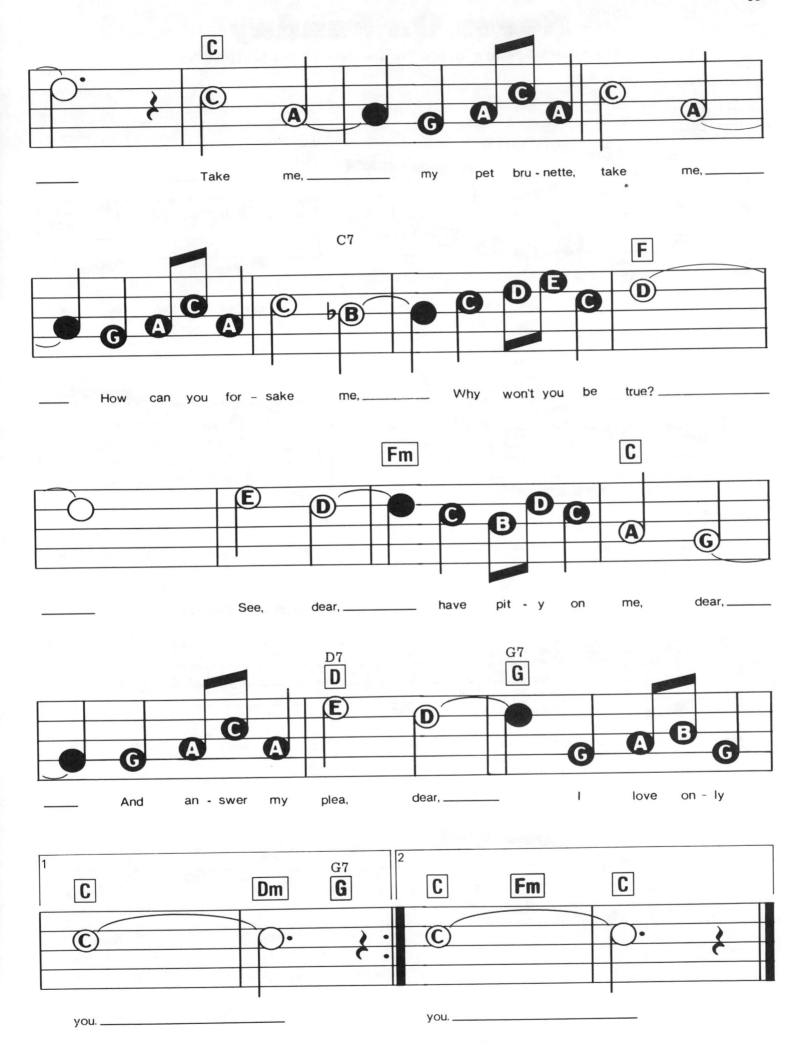

Never On Sunday

(From Jules Dassin's Motion Picture "NEVER ON SUNDAY")

Registration 1
Rhythm: Latin

Words by Billy Towne
Music by Manos Hadjidakis

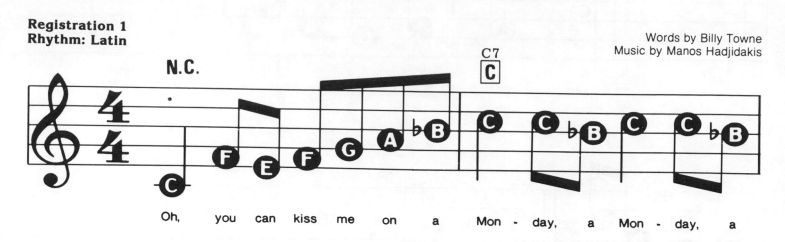

Oh, you can kiss me on a Mon - day, a Mon - day, a

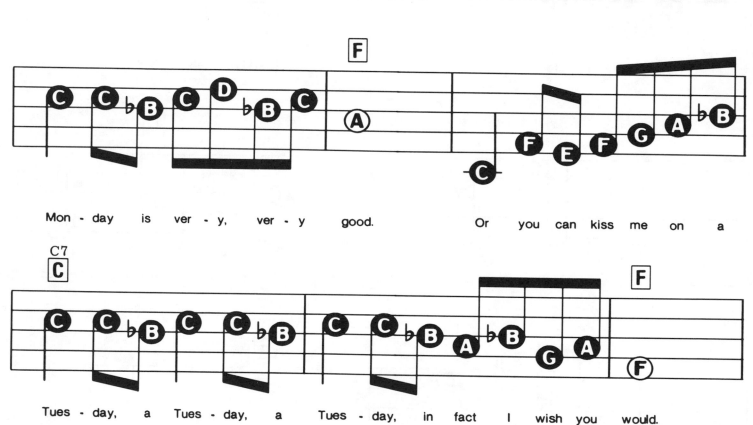

Mon - day is ver - y, ver - y good. Or you can kiss me on a

Tues - day, a Tues - day, a Tues - day, in fact I wish you would.

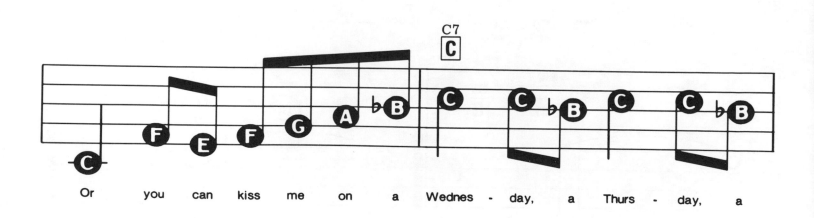

Or you can kiss me on a Wednes - day, a Thurs - day, a

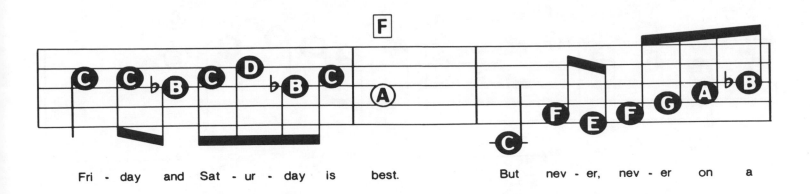

Fri - day and Sat - ur - day is best.   But nev - er, nev - er on a

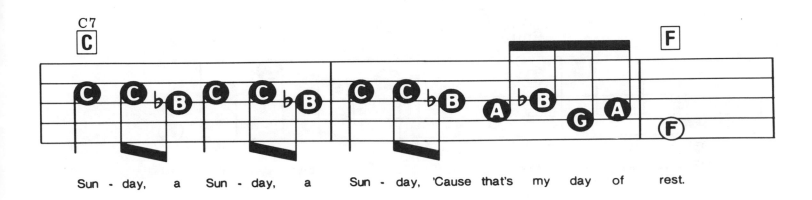

Sun - day, a Sun - day, a   Sun - day, 'Cause that's my day of rest.

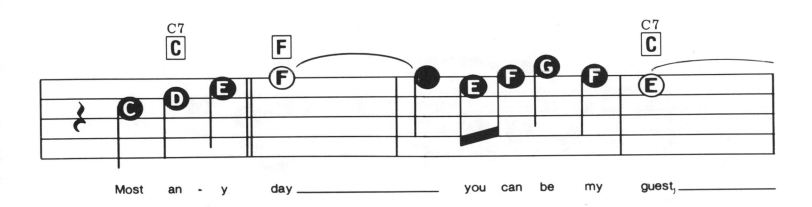

Most an - y day _____ you can be my guest, _____

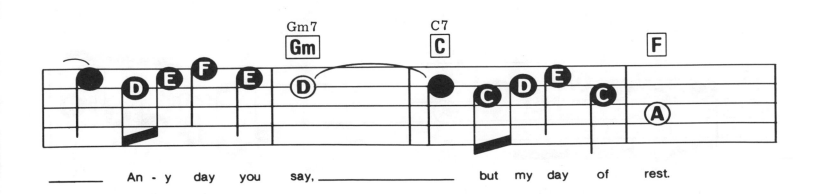

_____ An - y day you say, _____ but my day of rest.

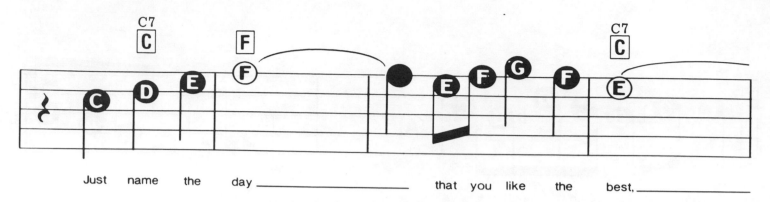

Just name the day _____ that you like the best, _____

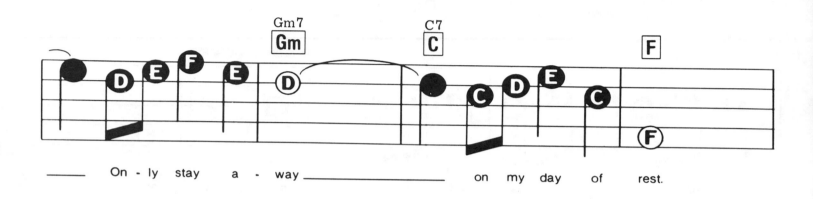

_____ On - ly stay a - way _____ on my day of rest.

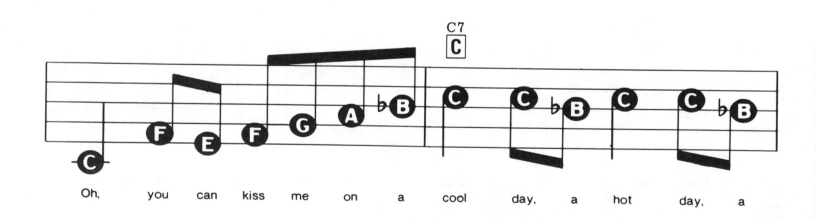

Oh, you can kiss me on a cool day, a hot day, a

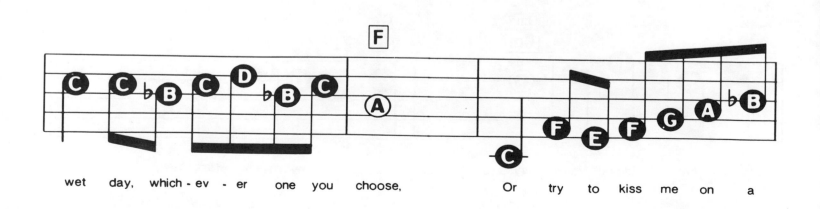

wet day, which - ev - er one you choose, Or try to kiss me on a

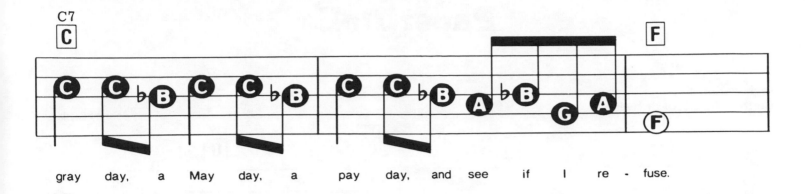

gray day, a May day, a pay day, and see if I re - fuse.

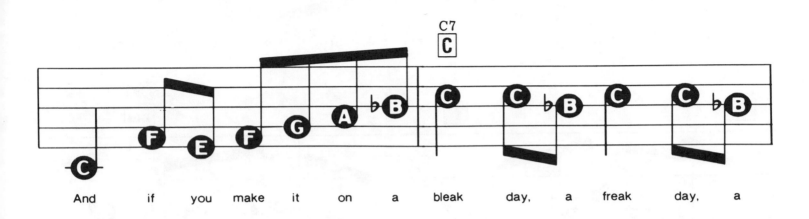

And if you make it on a bleak day, a freak day, a

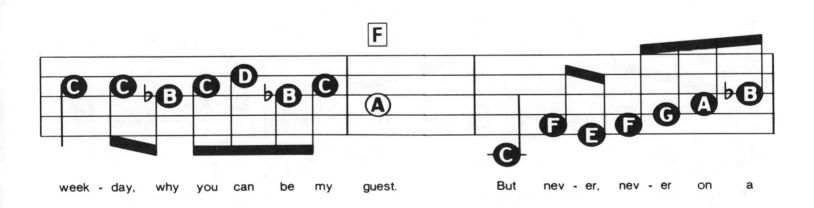

week - day, why you can be my guest. But nev - er, nev - er on a

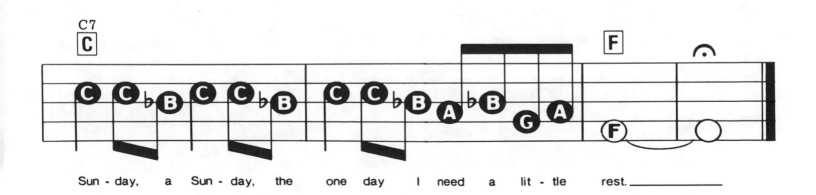

Sun - day, a Sun - day, the one day I need a lit - tle rest.____

Paper Doll

Registration 4
Rhythm: Fox Trot or Swing

By Johnny S. Black

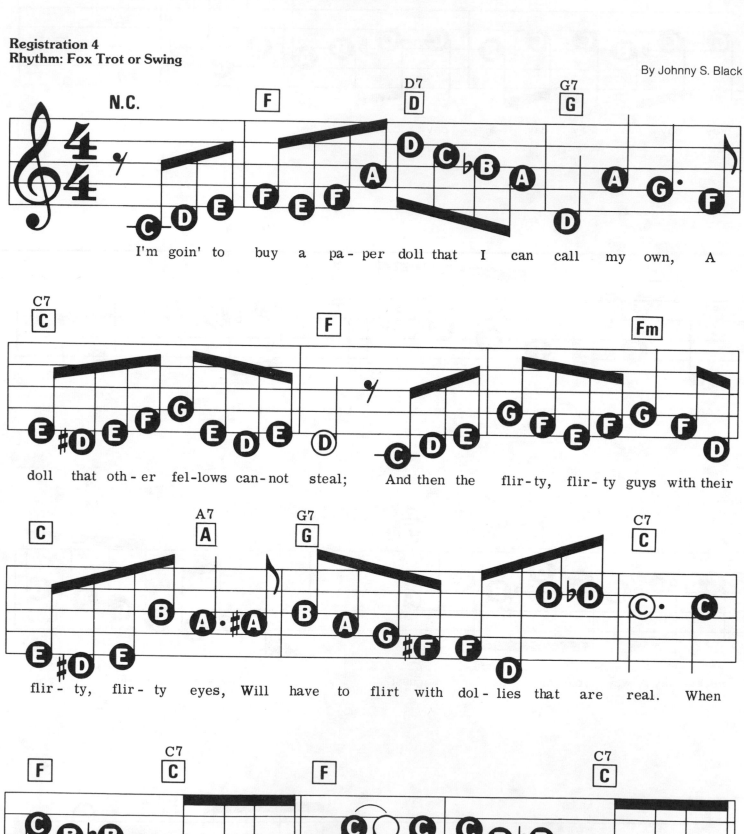

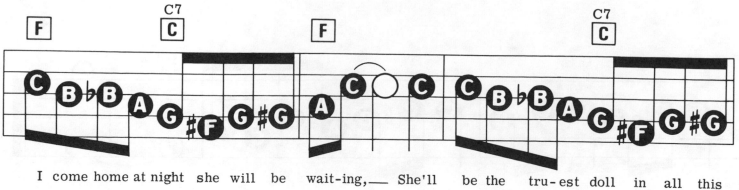

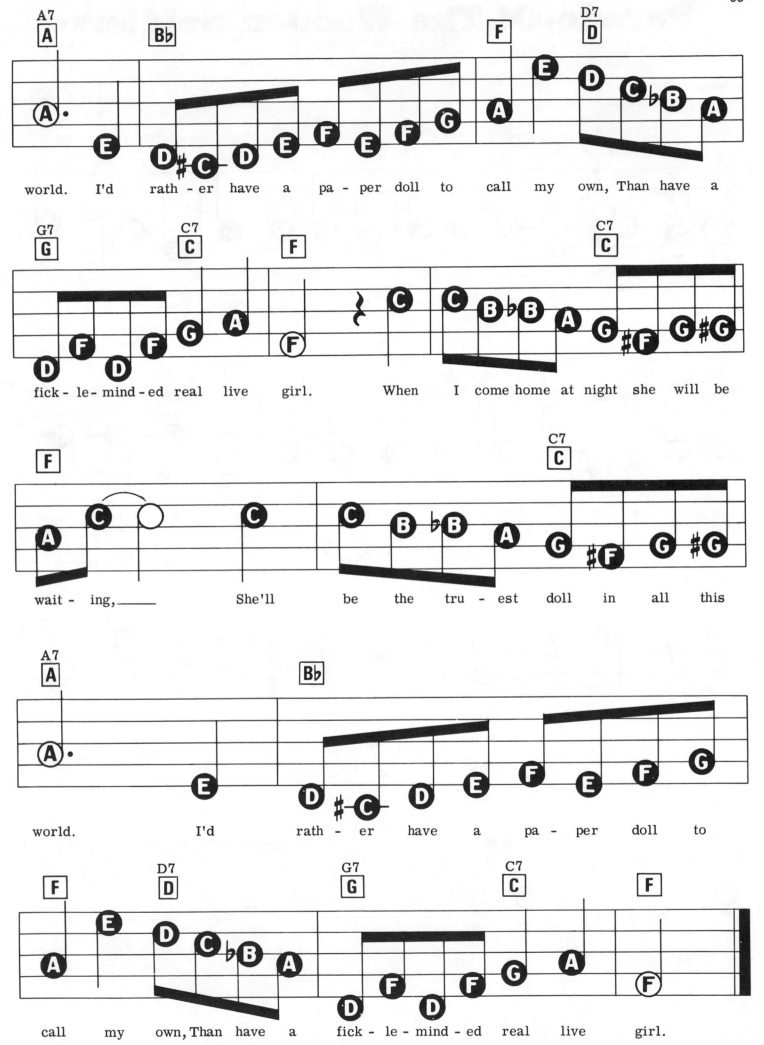

Parade Of The Wooden Soldiers

Registration 5
Rhythm: March or Polka

By Ballard MacDonald
and Leon Jessel

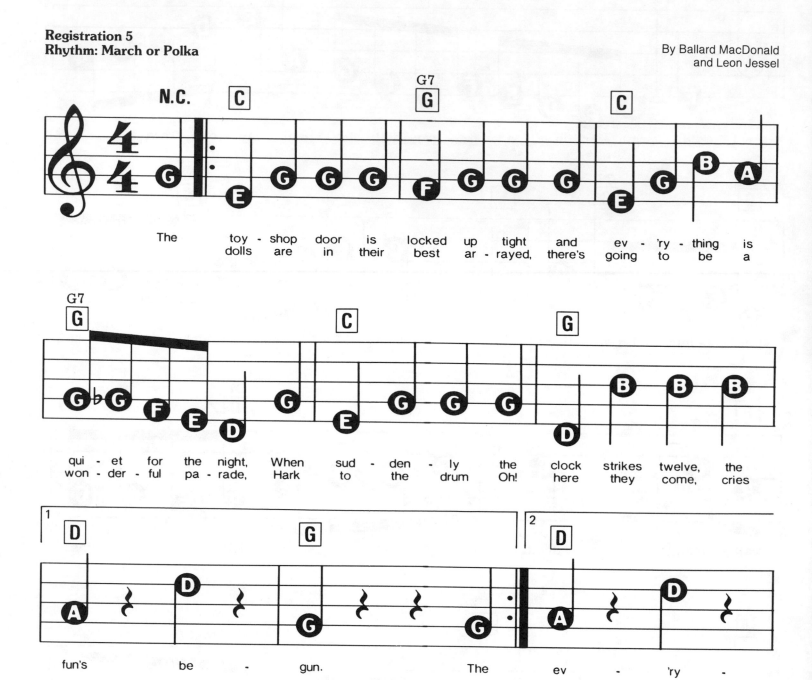

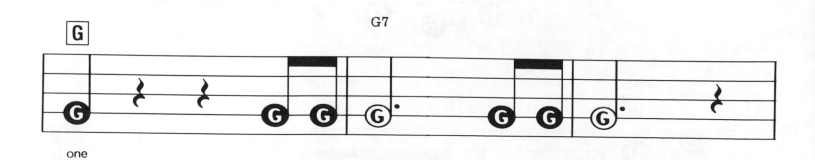

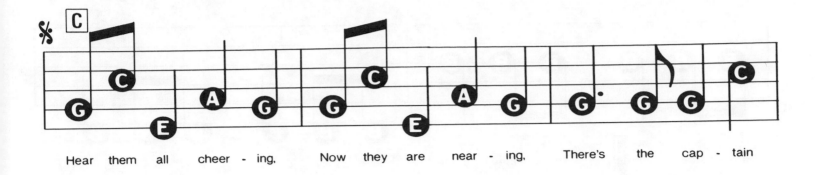

Hear them all cheer - ing, Now they are near - ing, There's the cap - tain

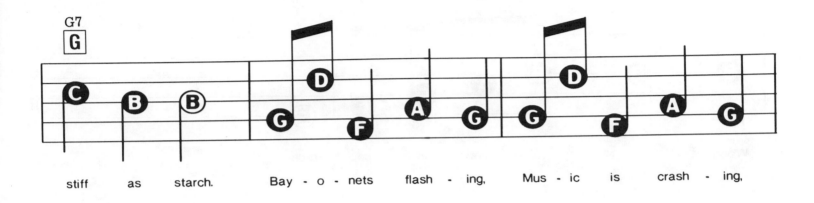

stiff as starch. Bay - o - nets flash - ing, Mus - ic is crash - ing,

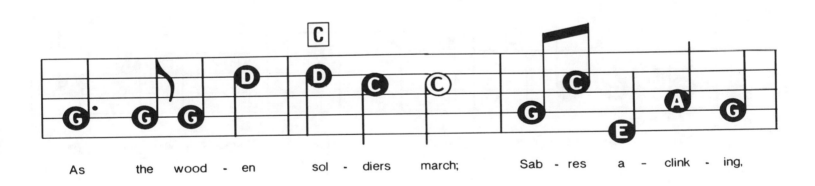

As the wood - en sol - diers march; Sab - res a - clink - ing,

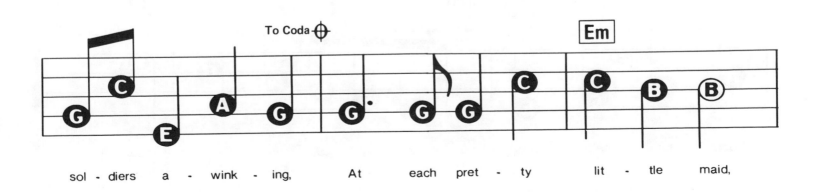

sol - diers a - wink - ing, At each pret - ty lit - tle maid,

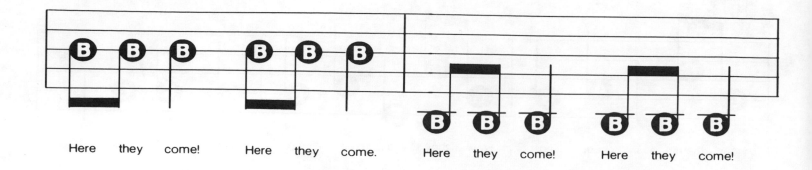

Here they come! Here they come. Here they come! Here they come!

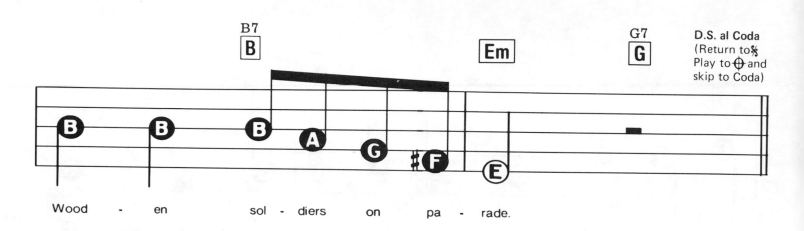

Wood - en sol - diers on pa - rade.

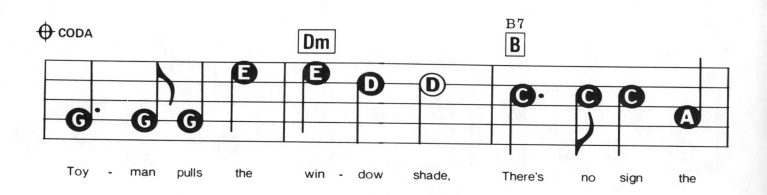

Toy - man pulls the win - dow shade, There's no sign the

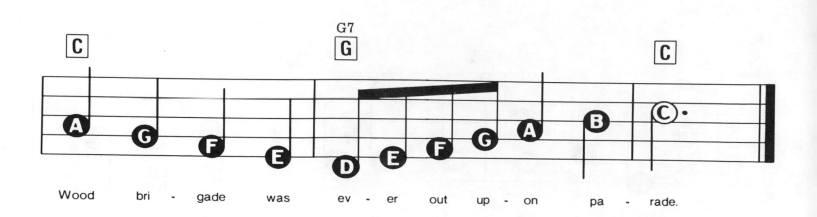

Wood bri - gade was ev - er out up - on pa - rade.

The Peanut Vendor
(El Manisero)

Registration 4
Rhythm: Fox Trot or Swing

English Words by Marion Sunshine and L. Wolfe Gilbert
Music and Spanish Words by Moises Simons

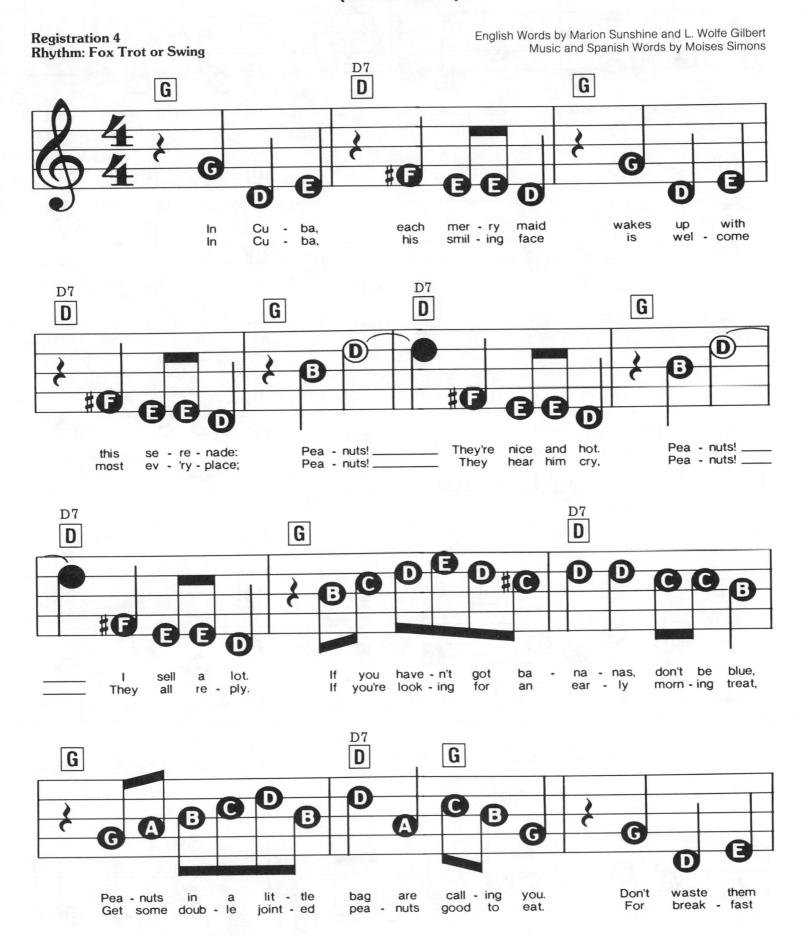

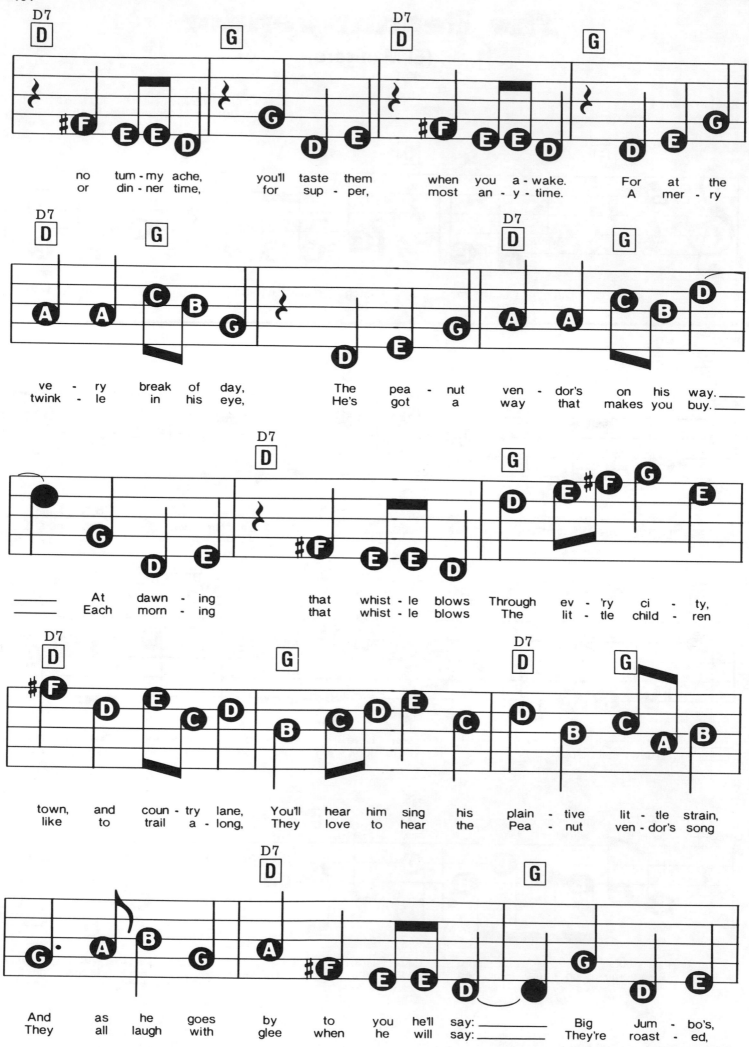

105

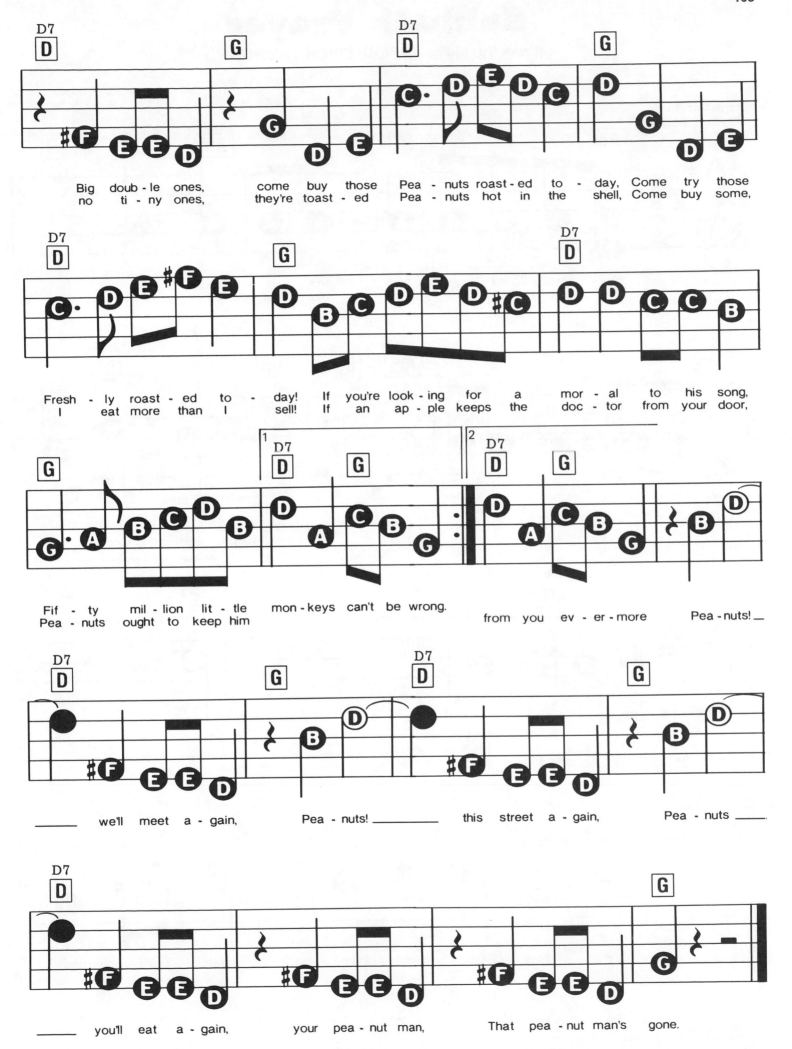

Sabbath Prayer
(From the Musical "FIDDLER ON THE ROOF")

Words by Sheldon Harnick
Music by Jerry Bock

Registration 6
Rhythm: Ballad

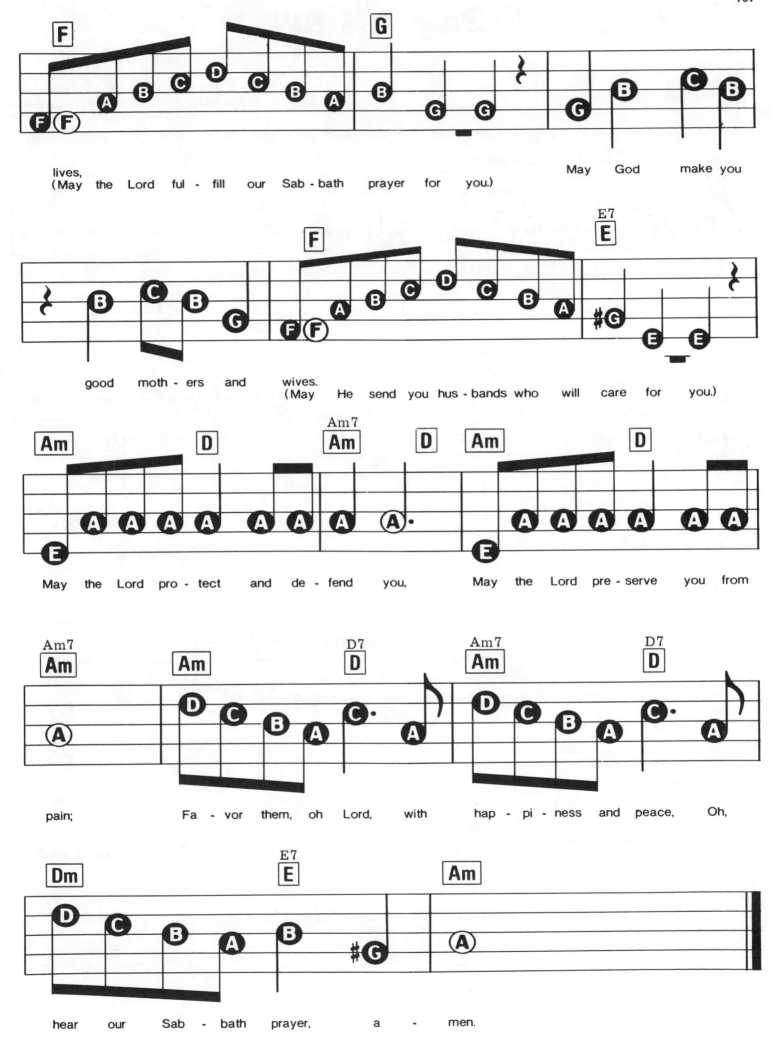

Say "Si Si"

Registration 3
Rhythm: Fox Trot or Swing

Music and Spanish Words by Ernesto Lecuona
English Words by Al Stillman and Francia Luban

In Spain they say ____ "Si, Si;" ____
Hin - du - stan ____ "Ug, Ug;" ____

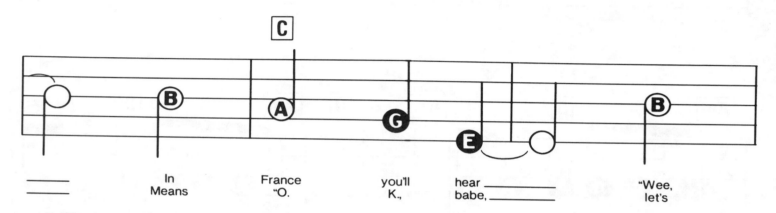

____ In France you'll hear ____ "Wee,
____ Means "O. K., babe, ____ let's

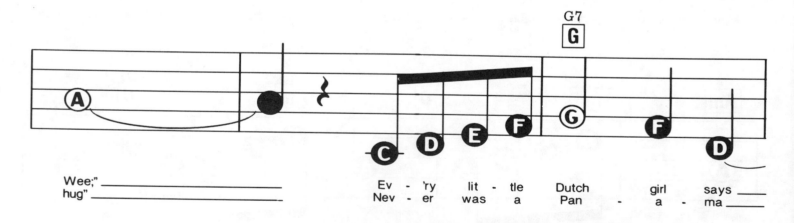

Wee;" ____ Ev - 'ry lit - tle Dutch girl says ____
hug" ____ Nev - er was a Dutch Pan - a - ma ____

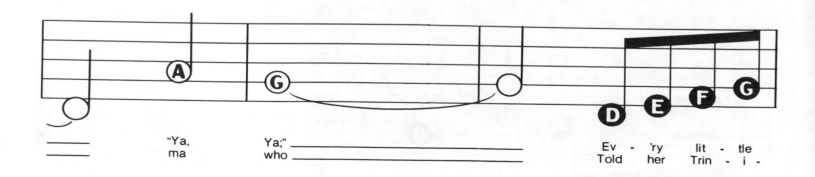

____ "Ya, Ya;" ____ Ev - 'ry lit - tle
ma who ____ Told her Trin - i -

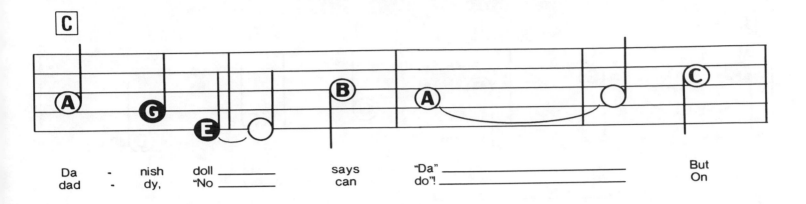

Da - nish doll _____ says "Da" _____ But
dad - dy, "No _____ can do"! _____ On

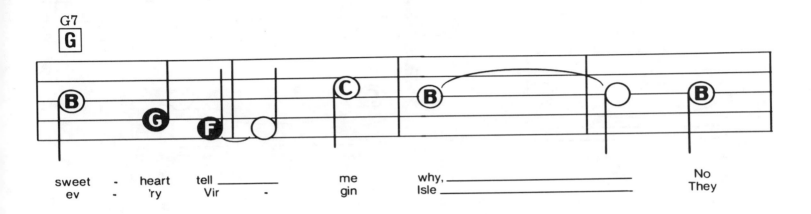

sweet - heart tell _____ me why, _____ No
ev - 'ry Vir - gin Isle _____ They

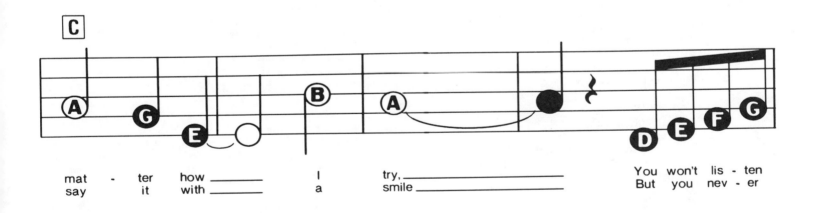

mat - ter how _____ I try, _____ You won't lis - ten
say it with _____ a smile _____ But you nev - er

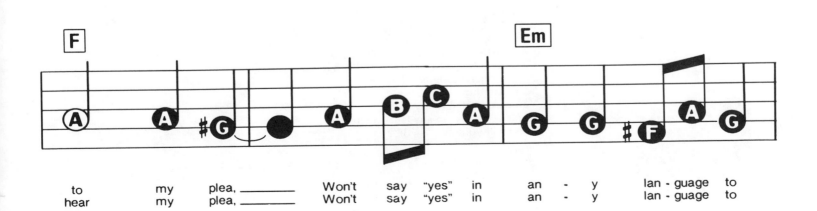

to my plea, _____ Won't say "yes" in an - y lan - guage to
hear my plea, _____ Won't say "yes" in an - y lan - guage to

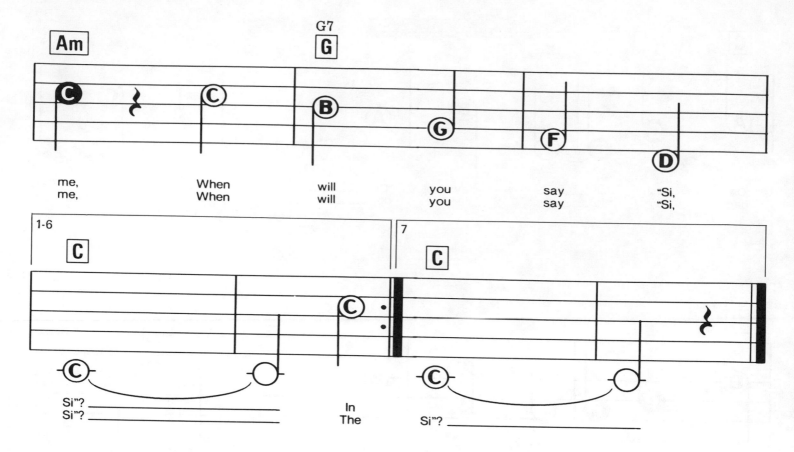

me,
me,
When
When
will
will
you
you
say
say
"Si,
"Si,

1-6 C

7 C

Si"?
Si"?

In
The
Si"?

3rd Chorus

The monkeys in the tree
Don't have to say: "Si, Si",
All they do is wag their little tails;
That's a little gag that never fails.
In darkest Africa
The natives say: "Uh, Huh!"
But you never hear my plea,
Won't say "Yes" in any language to me
When will you say: "Si, Si"?

5th Chorus

In Washington, D.C.,
The yes-men say: "Si, Si";
There are lots of politicians, though
Who can always say both "Yes" and "No".
But sweetheart tell me why,
No matter how I try,
you won't listen to my plea
Won't say "Yes" in any language to me
When will you say "Si, Si"?

4th Chorus

Out West they say: "Wah Hoo!"
That's "O.K., Toots" to you.
Every Southern lady knows her stuff,
'Cause her answer is "Sho Nuff!"
But, sweetheart, tell me why,
No matter how I try.
You won't listen to my plea,
Won't say "Yes" in any language to me
When will you say: "Si, Si"?

6th Chorus

A lady horse, they say,
Means "Yes" when she says: "Neigh!"
Every little gal from Mexico
Hates to give a pal a "No, No, No!"
So, sweetheart, tell me why,
No matter how I try,
You won't listen to my plea
Won't say "Yes" in any language to me
When will you say "Si, Si"?

7th Chorus

In 606 B.C.,
Those gals would mix, Si, Si!
Every little cave man used his dome,
Hit 'em on the head, then dragged 'em home.
So, sweetheart, tell me why,
No matter how I try,
You won't listen to my plea
Won't say "Yes" in any language to me,
When will you say: "Si, Si"?

September Morn

Registration 2
Rhythm: Ballad or Fox Trot

Words and Music by
Neil Diamond and Gilbert Becaud

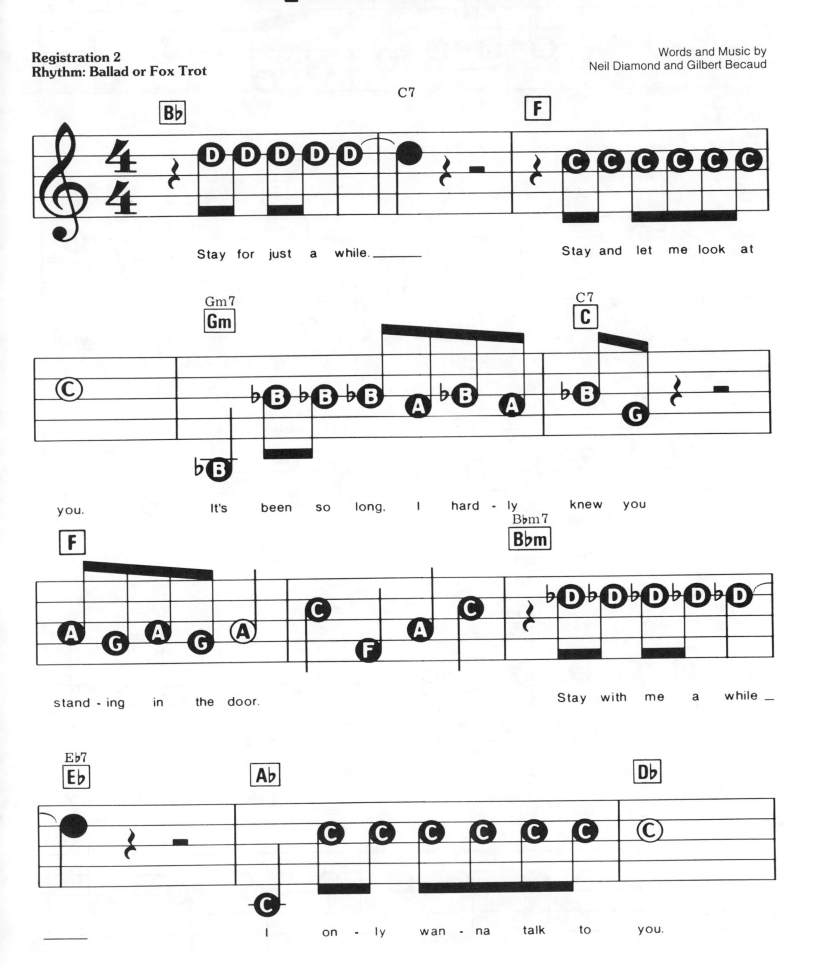

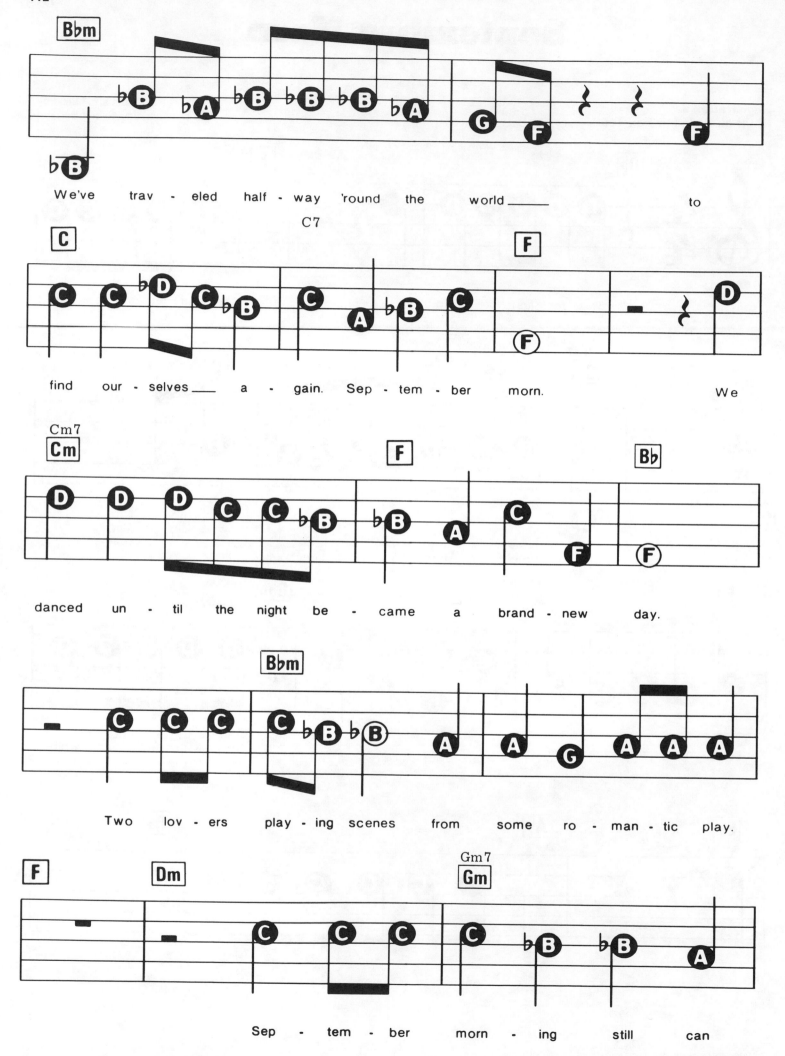

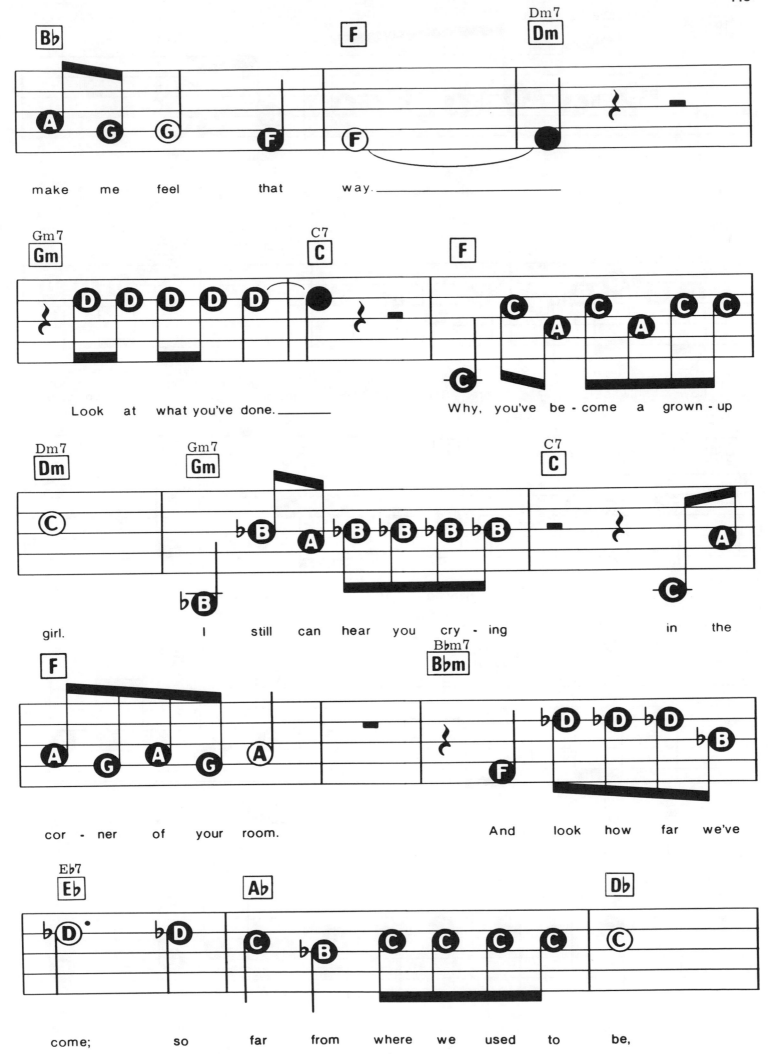

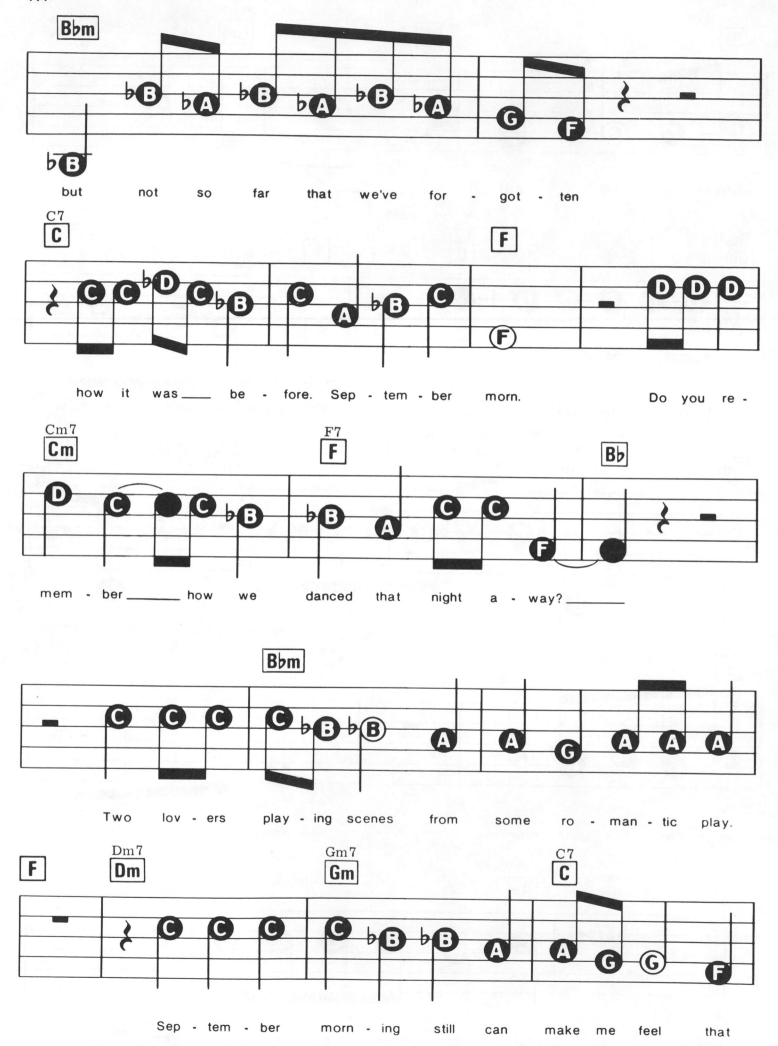

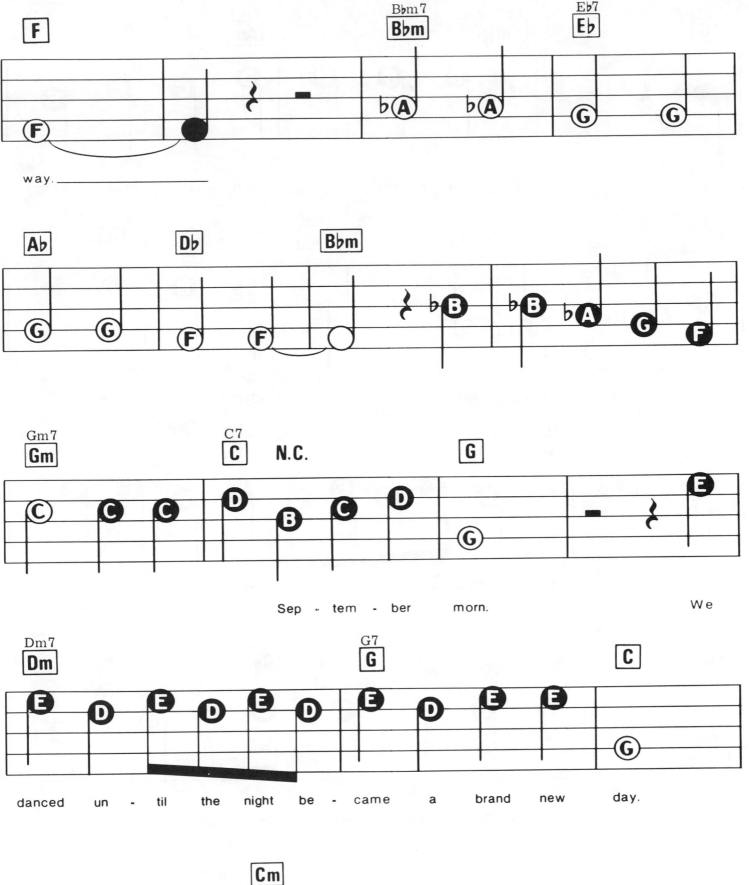

way.

September morn. We

danced until the night became a brand new day.

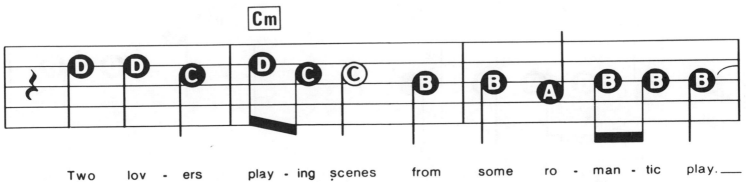

Two lovers playing scenes from some romantic play.

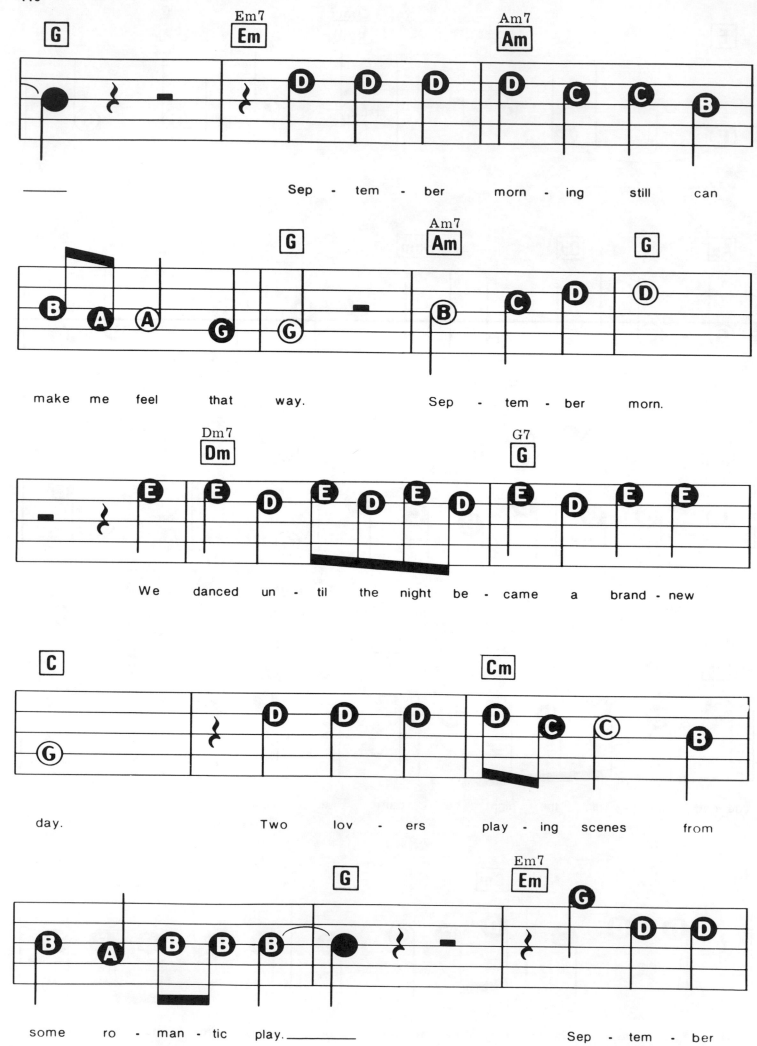

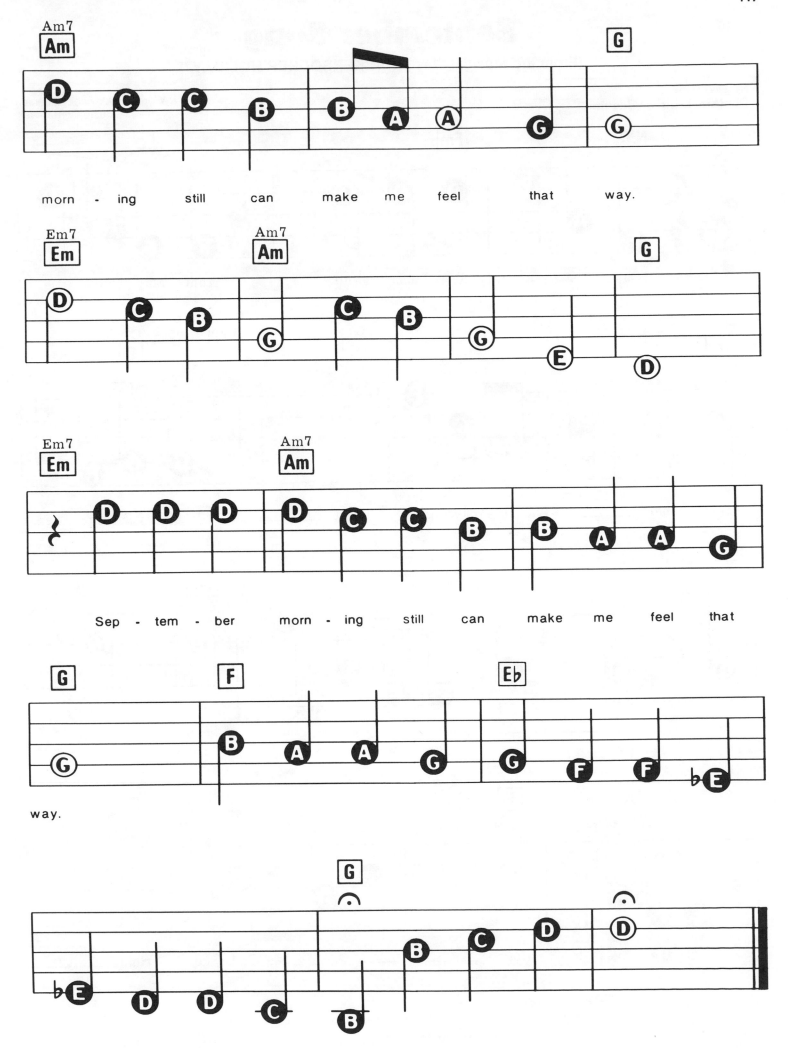

morn - ing still can make me feel that way.

Sep - tem - ber morn - ing still can make me feel that

way.

September Song

(From the Musical Play "KNICKERBOCKER HOLIDAY")

Registration 2
Rhythm: Latin or Beguine

Words by Maxwell Anderson
Music by Kurt Weill

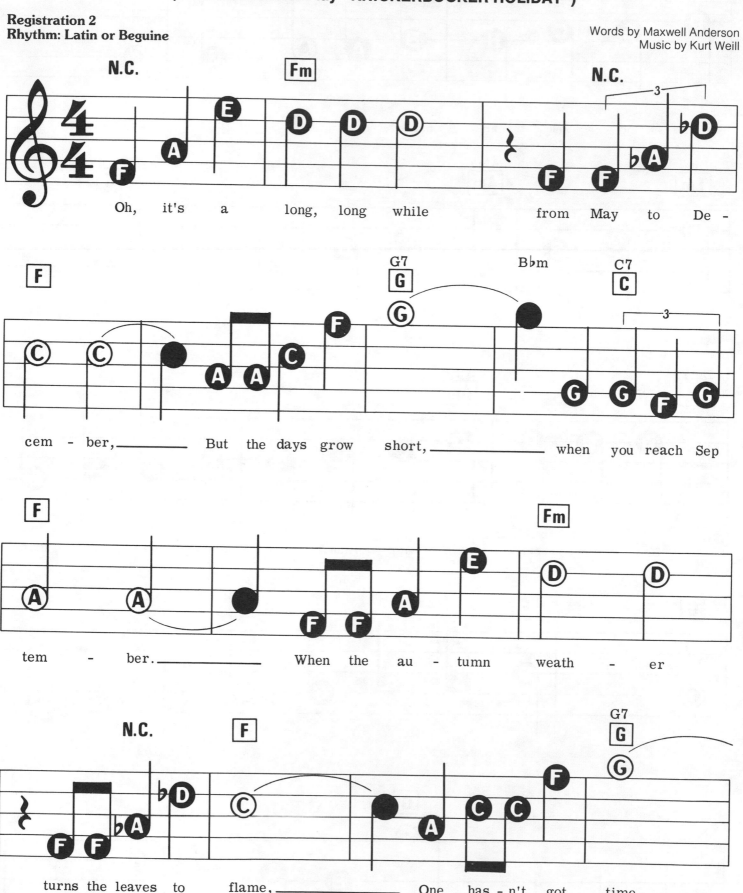

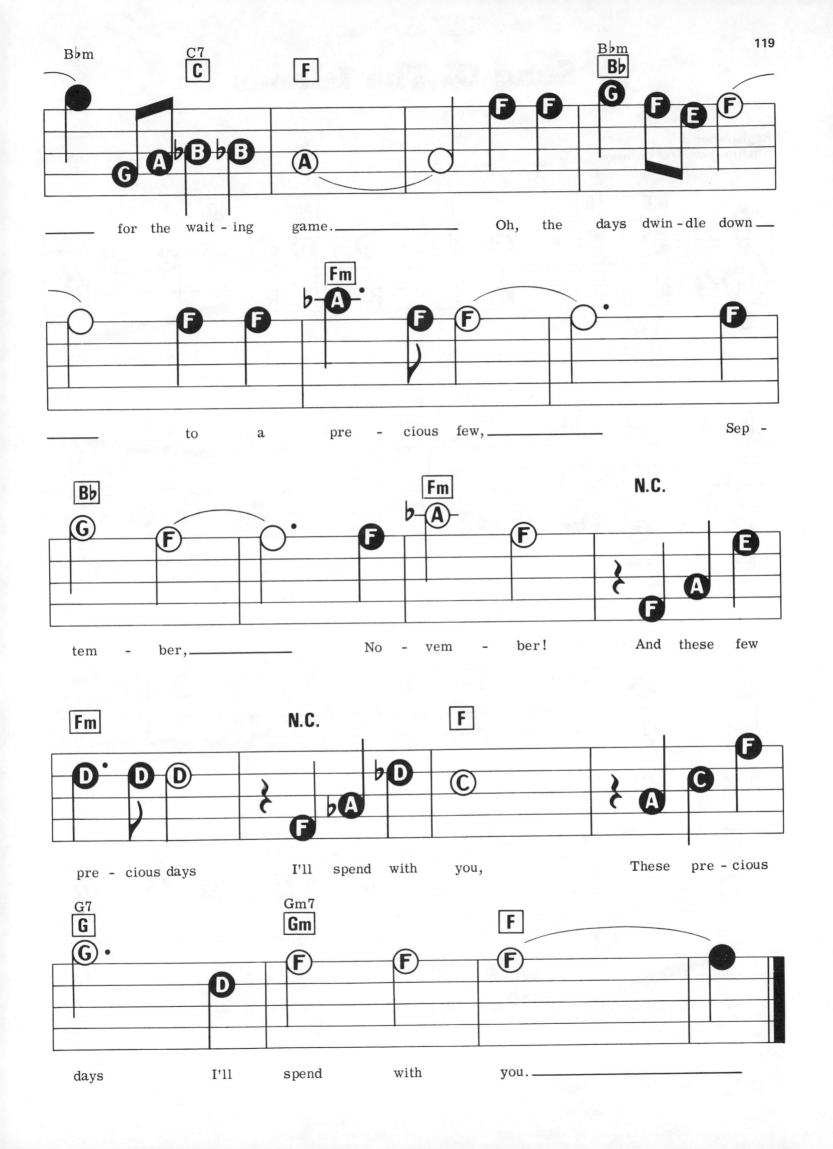

Song Of The Islands

Registration 3
Rhythm: Fox Trot or Swing

Words and Music by
Chas. E. King

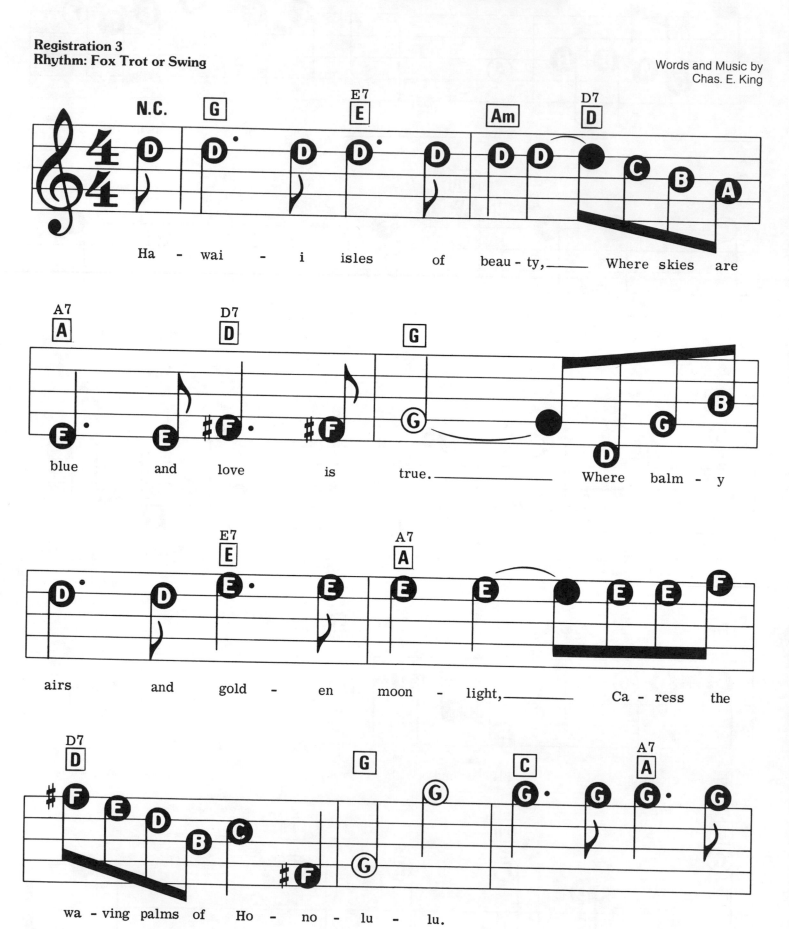

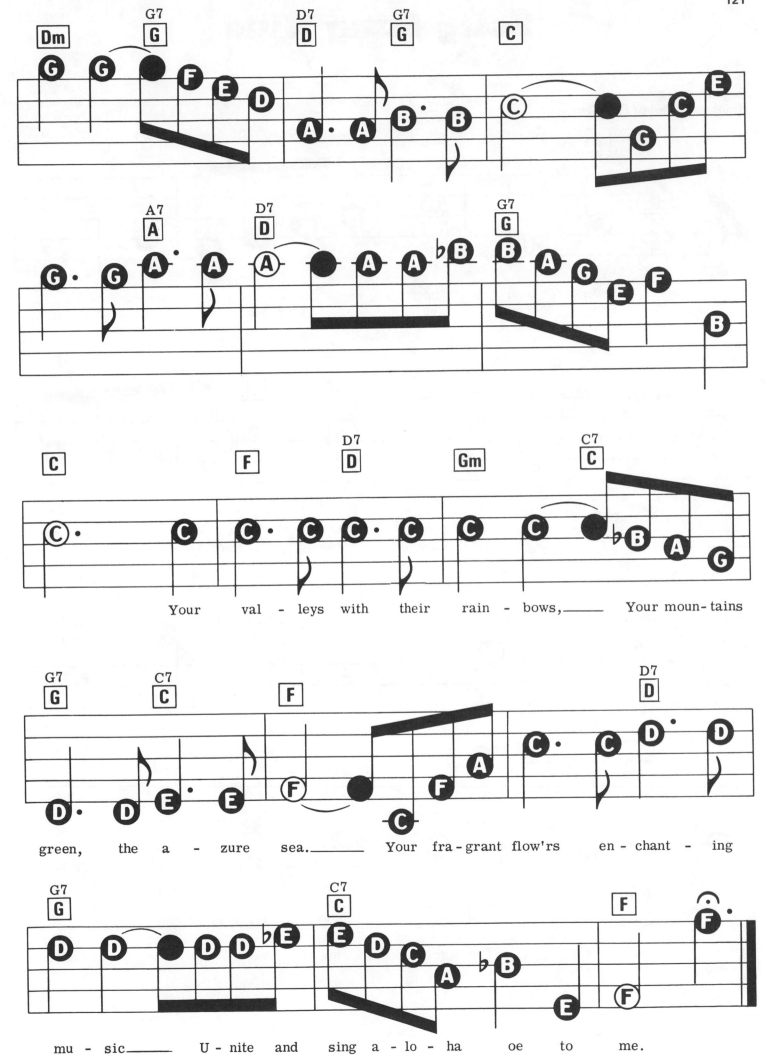

Song Sung Blue

Registration 2
Rhythm: Ballad or Fox Trot

Words and Music by
Neil Diamond

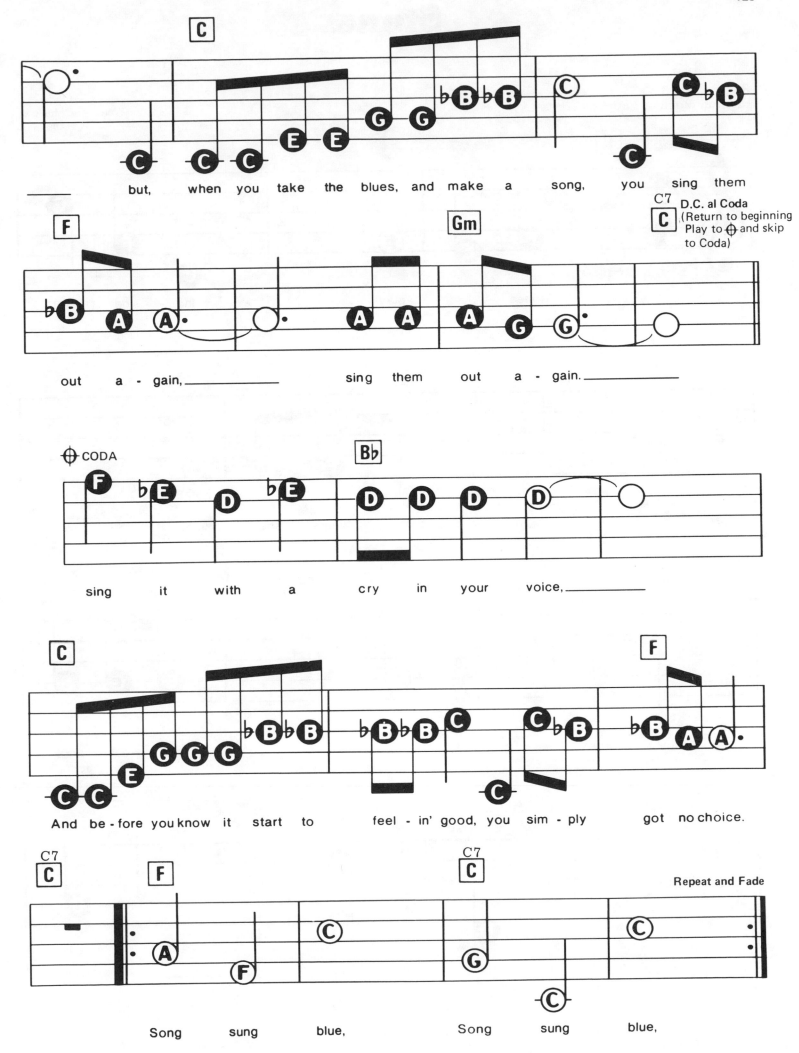

Stones

Registration 3
Rhythm: Rock or Latin

Words and Music by
Neil Diamond

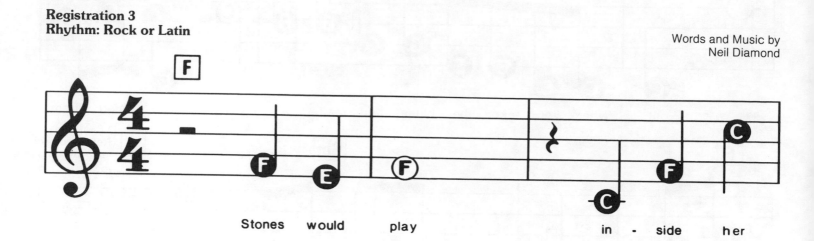

Stones would play in - side her

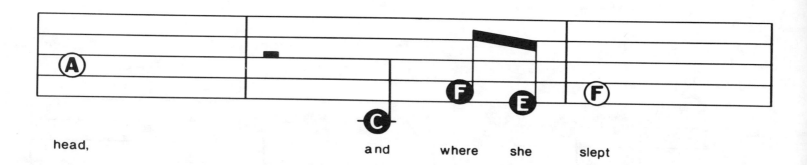

head, and where she slept

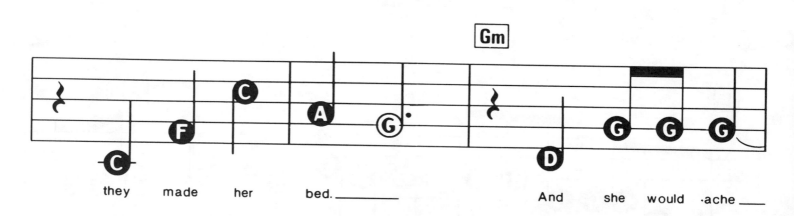

they made her bed._____ And she would ·ache ___

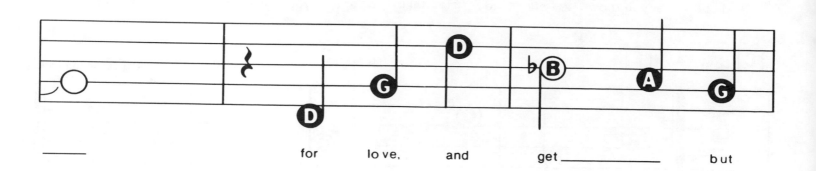

_____ for love, and get _____ but

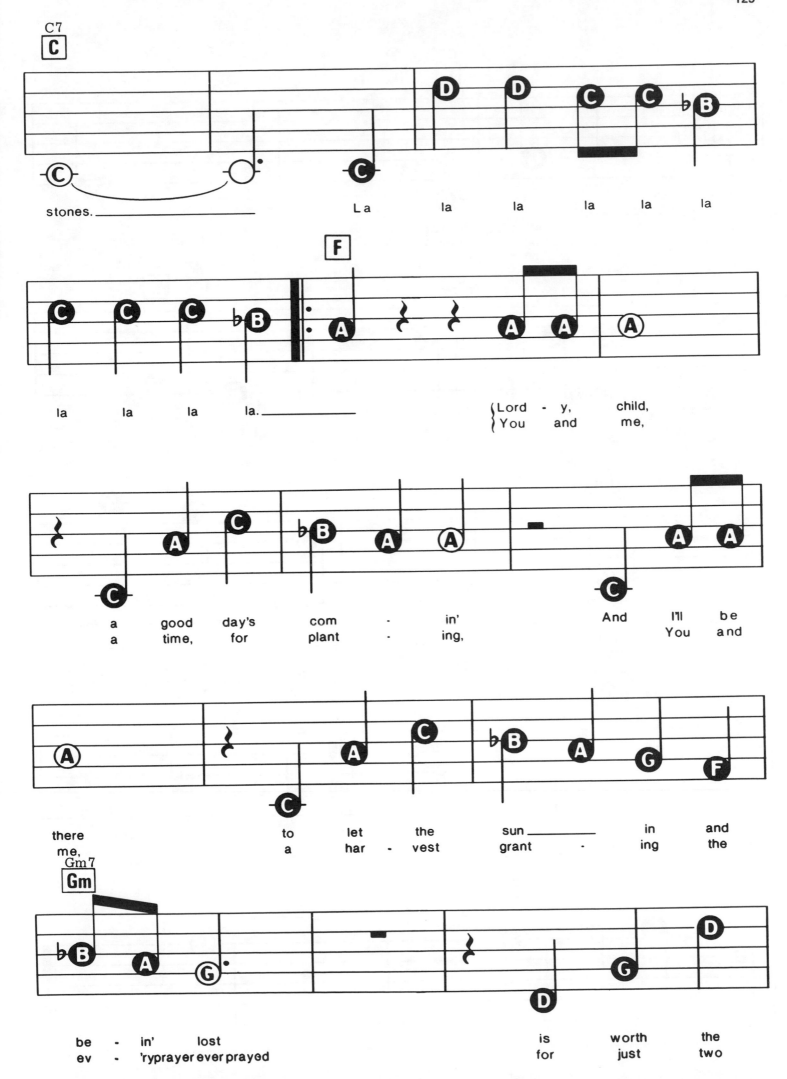

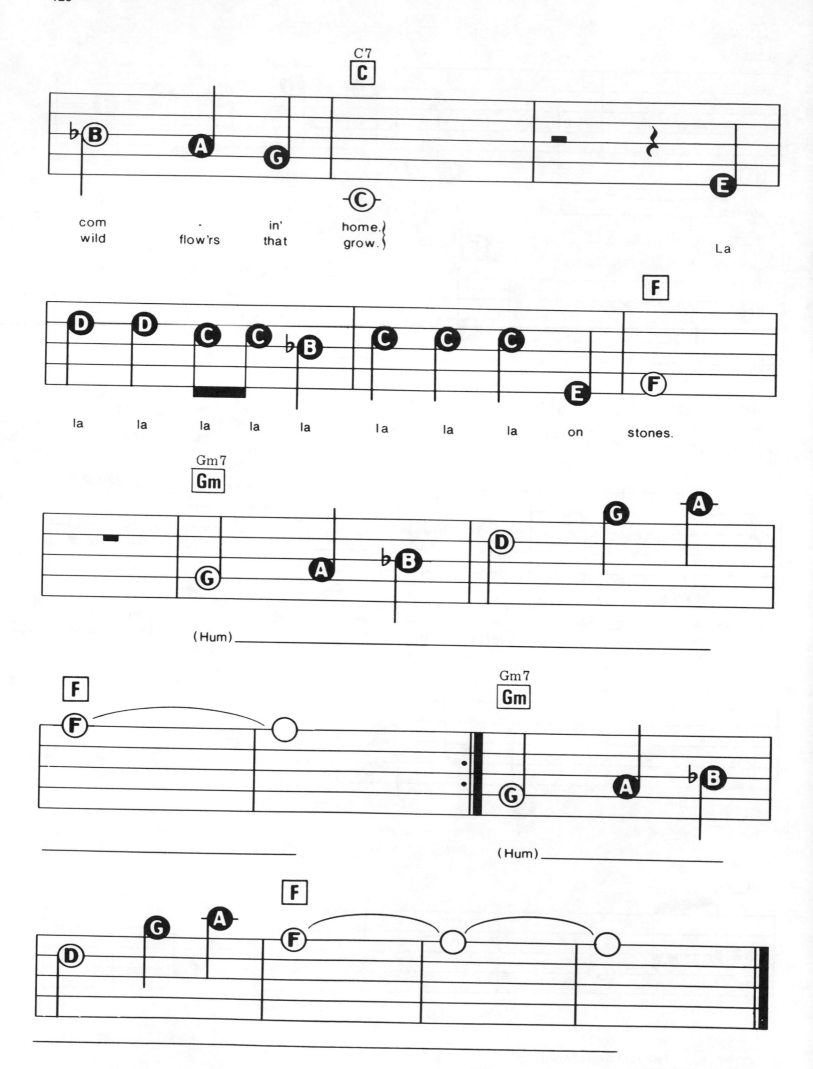

Sweet Caroline

Registration 4
Rhythm: Swing or Fox Trot

Words and Music by
Neil Diamond

Where it be - gan, I can't be -
Was in the spring, and spring be -

gin to know - in', but then I know it's grow - in'
came the sum - mer, who'd have be - lieved you'd come a -

1 strong. _____

2 long? _____

Hands, _____ touch - in' hands, _____ reach - in' out, _____
Warm, _____ touch - in' warm, _____

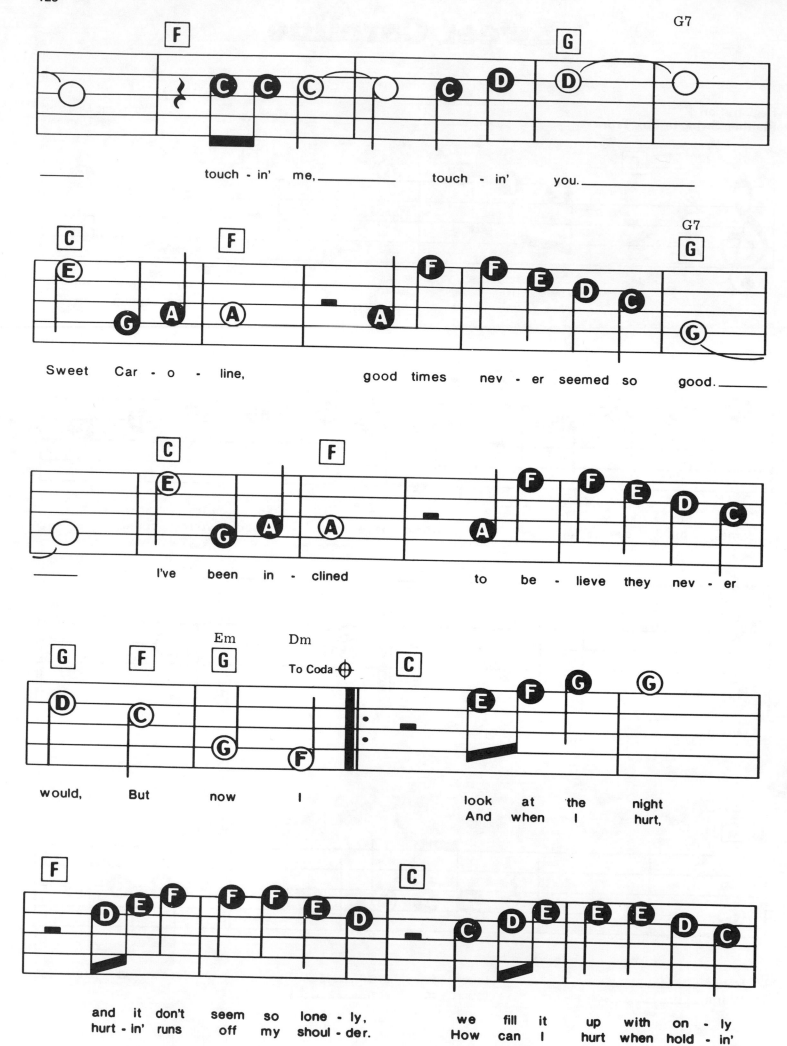

D.S. al Coda
(Return to %
Play to ⊕ and
skip to Coda)

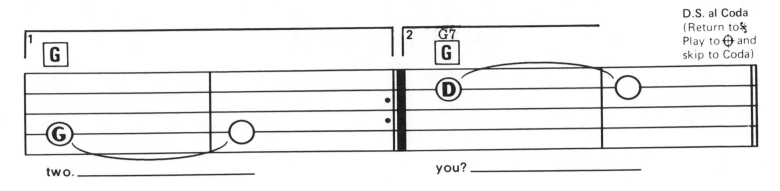

two. _____ you? _____

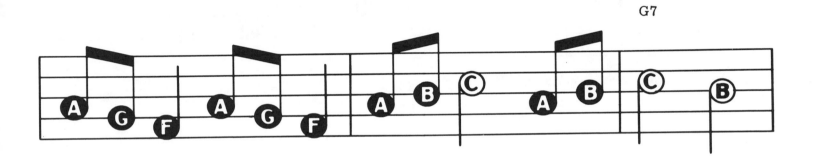

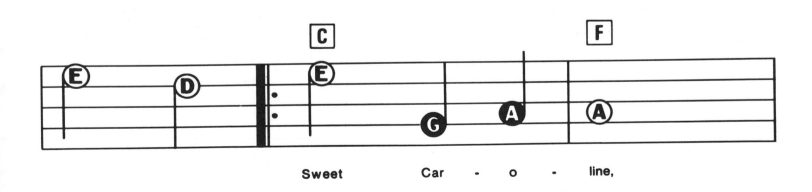

Sweet   Car - o - line,

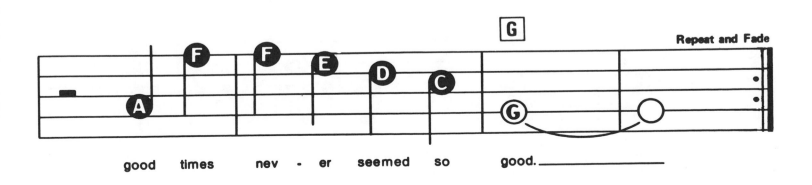

good   times   nev - er   seemed   so   good. _____

Summertime

Registration 10
Rhythm: Ballad

Words by DuBose Heyward
Music by George Gershwin

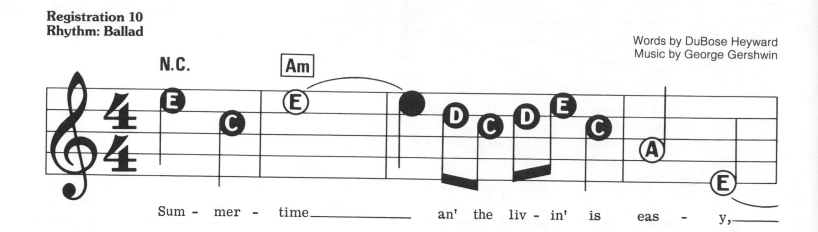

Sum - mer - time_____ an' the liv - in' is eas - y,_____

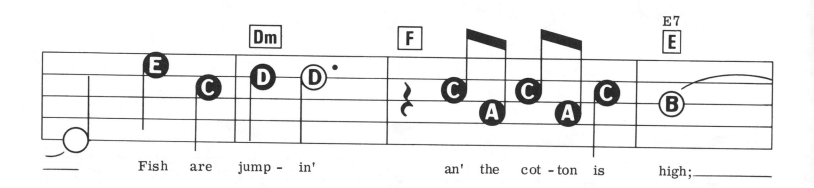

Fish are jump - in' an' the cot - ton is high;_____

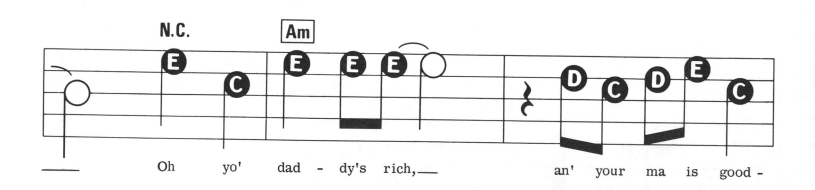

Oh yo' dad - dy's rich,___ an' your ma is good -

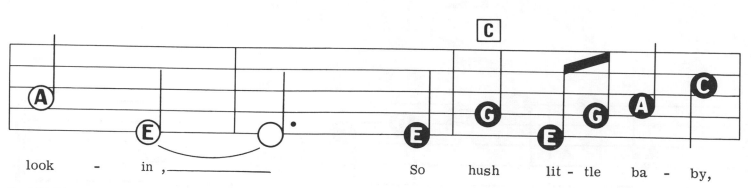

look - in ,_____ So hush lit - tle ba - by,

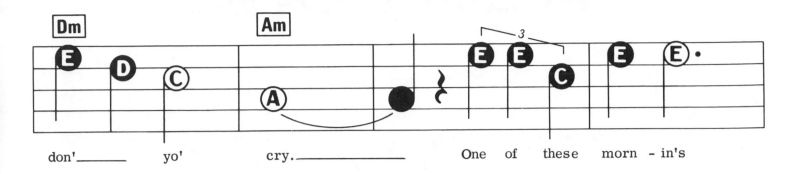

don'_____ yo'   cry._____   One   of   these   morn - in's

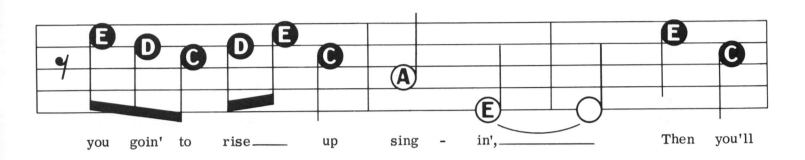

you   goin'   to   rise____   up   sing - in',_____   Then   you'll

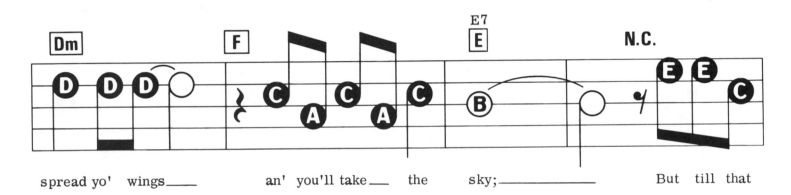

spread yo' wings____   an' you'll take____ the   sky;_____   But   till   that

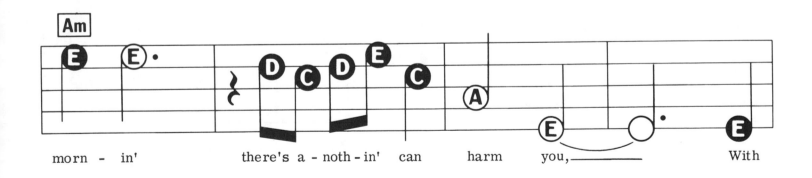

morn - in'   there's a - noth - in' can   harm   you,_____   With

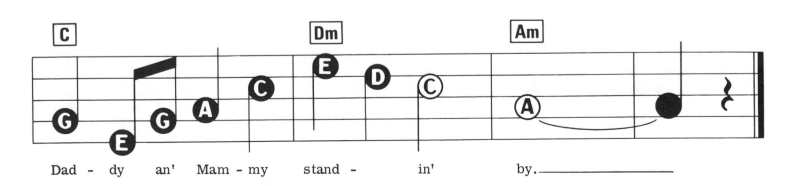

Dad - dy an' Mam - my   stand -   in'   by._____

Tell Laura I Love Her

Registration 4
Rhythm: Country or Shuffle

Words and Music by
Jeff Barry and Ben Raleigh

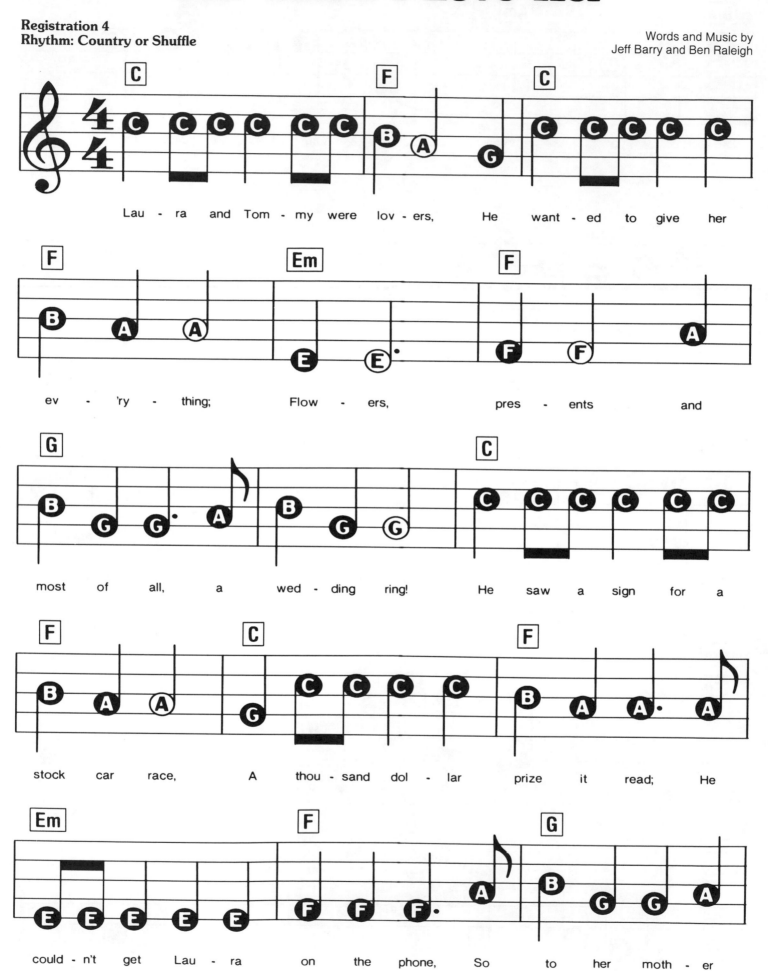

Lau - ra and Tom - my were lov - ers, He want - ed to give her ev - 'ry - thing; Flow - ers, pres - ents and most of all, a wed - ding ring! He saw a sign for a stock car race, A thou - sand dol - lar prize it read; He could - n't get Lau - ra on the phone, So to her moth - er

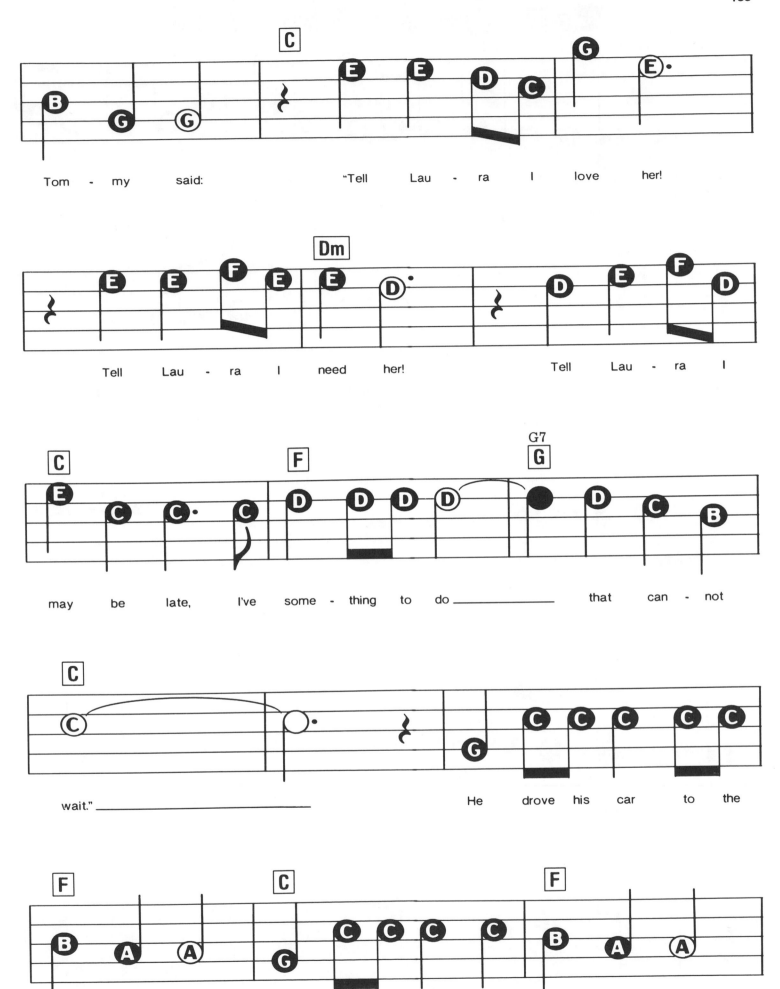

134

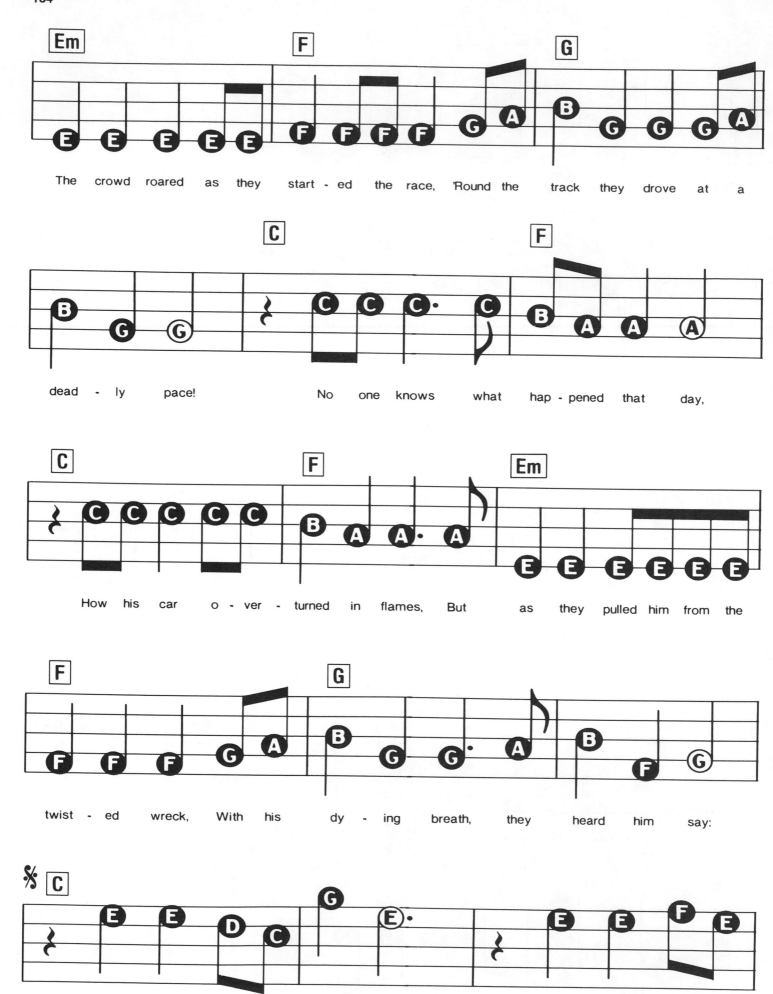

The crowd roared as they start-ed the race, 'Round the track they drove at a

dead-ly pace! No one knows what hap-pened that day,

How his car o-ver-turned in flames, But as they pulled him from the

twist-ed wreck, With his dy-ing breath, they heard him say:

"Tell Lau-ra I love her! Tell Lau-ra I

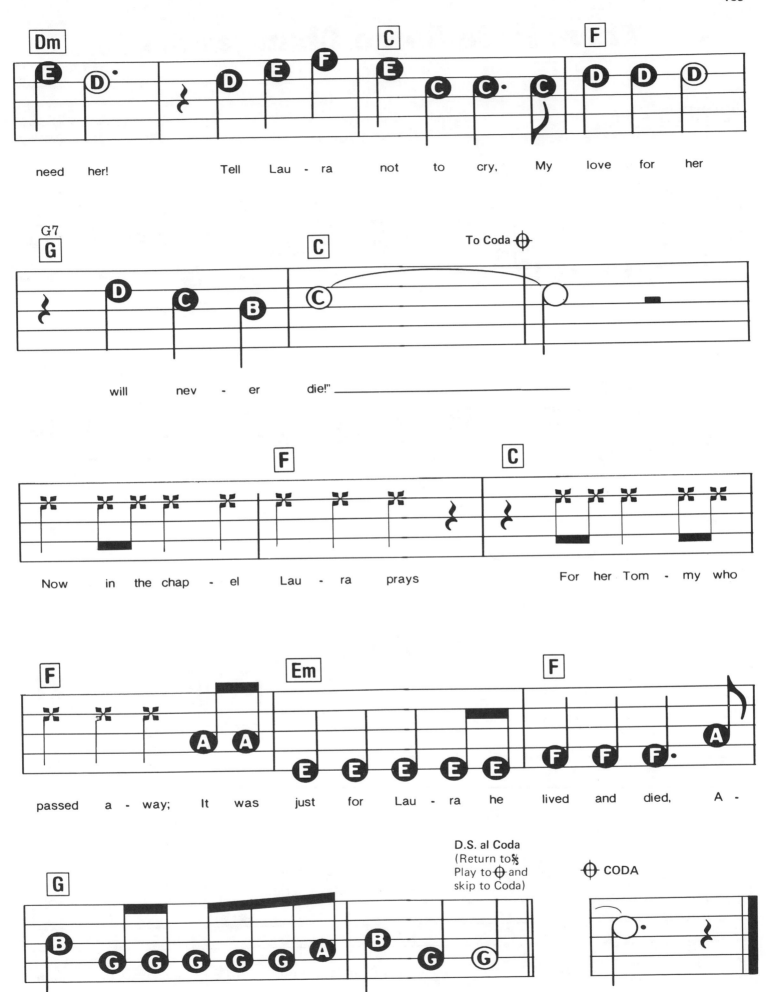

There'll Be Some Changes Made

Registration 7
Rhythm: Swing or Jazz

Words by Billy Higgins
Music by W. Benton Overstreet

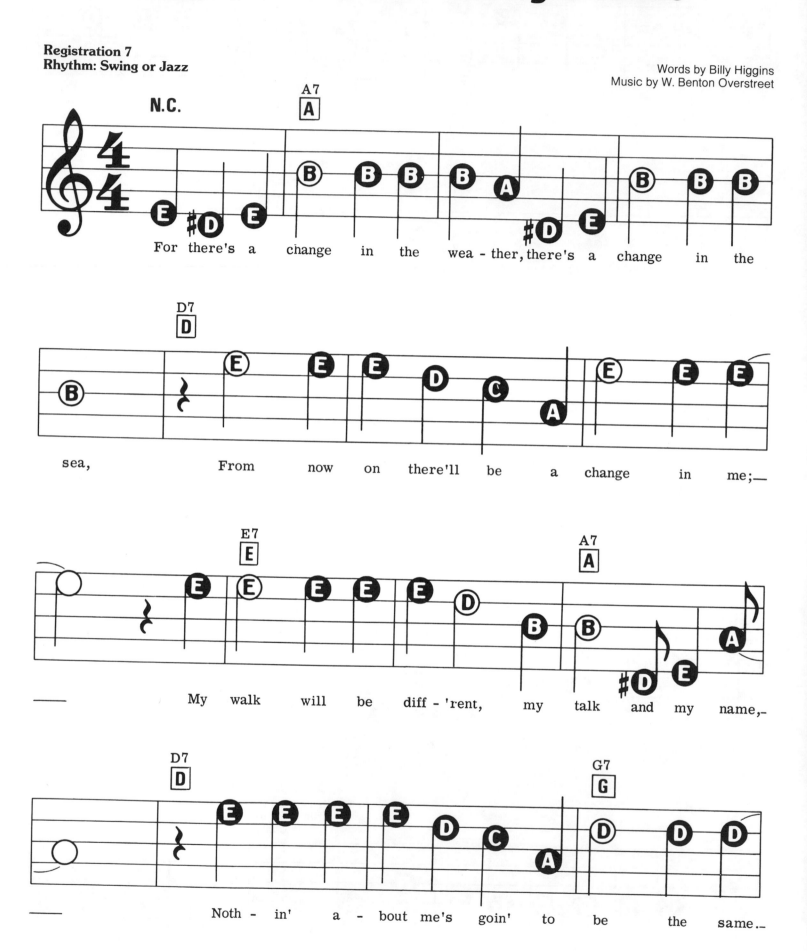

137

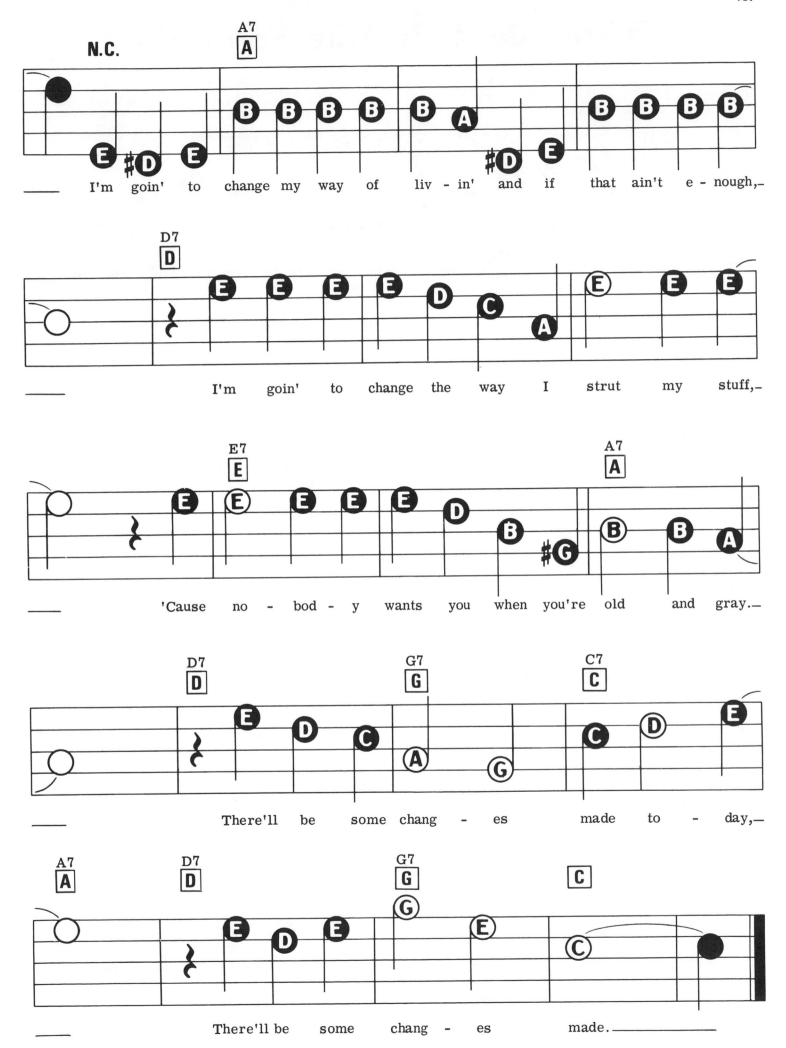

Three Coins In The Fountain

Registration 3
Rhythm: Fox Trot or Swing

Words by Sammy Cahn
Music by Jule Styne

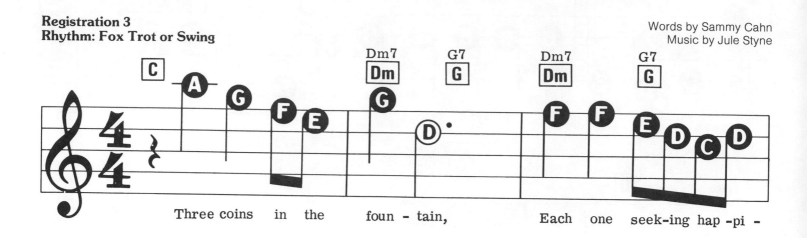

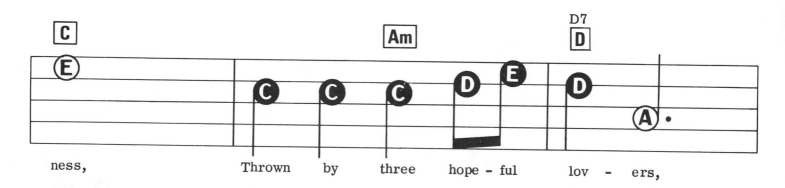

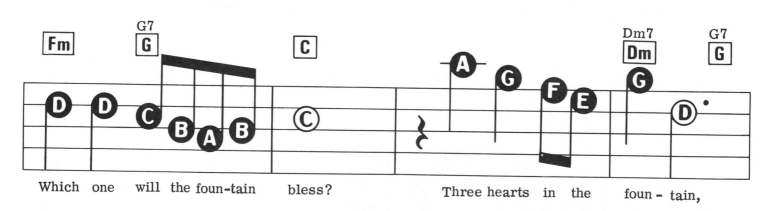

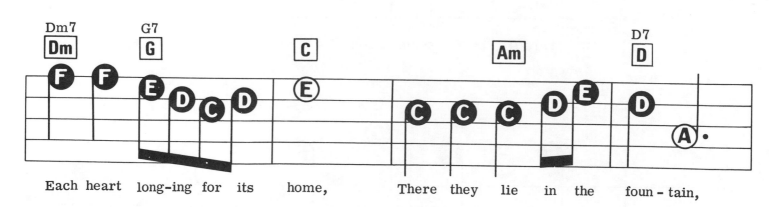

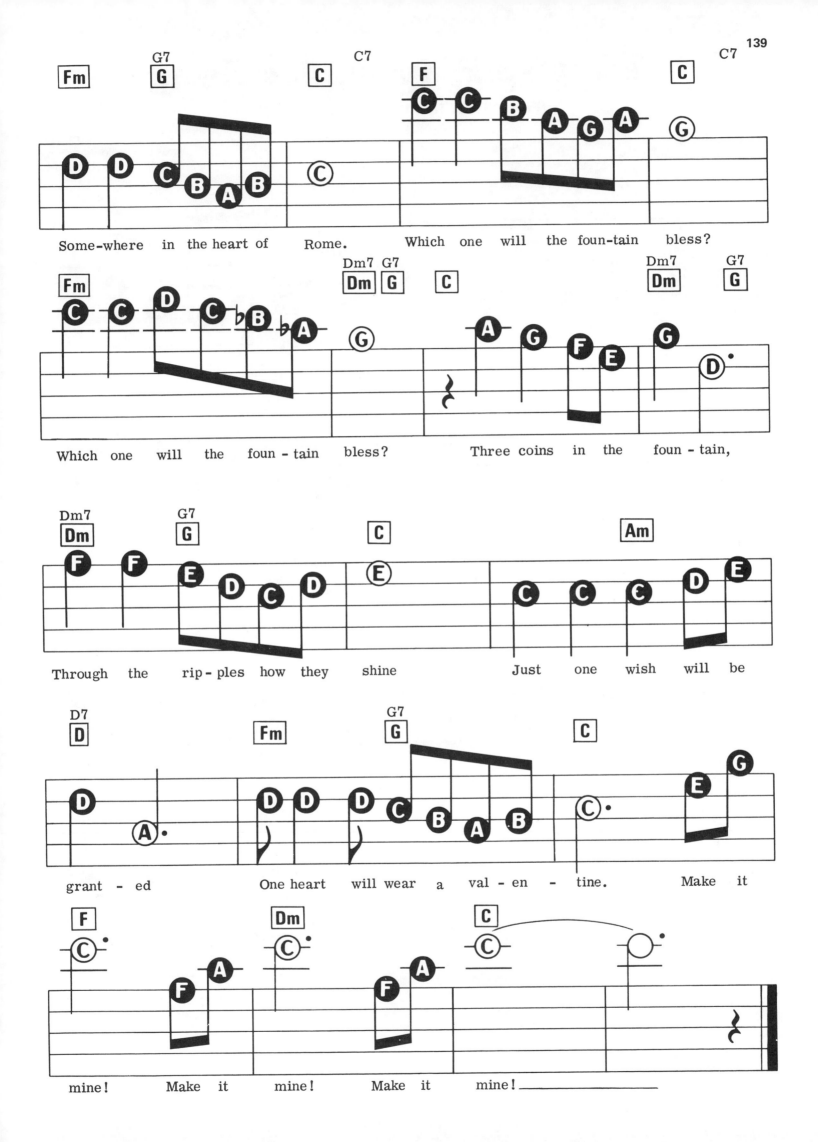

They're Playing My Song

(From "THEY'RE PLAYING OUR SONG")

Registration 5
Rhythm: Disco or Rock

Words by Carole Bayer Sager
Music by Marvin Hamlisch

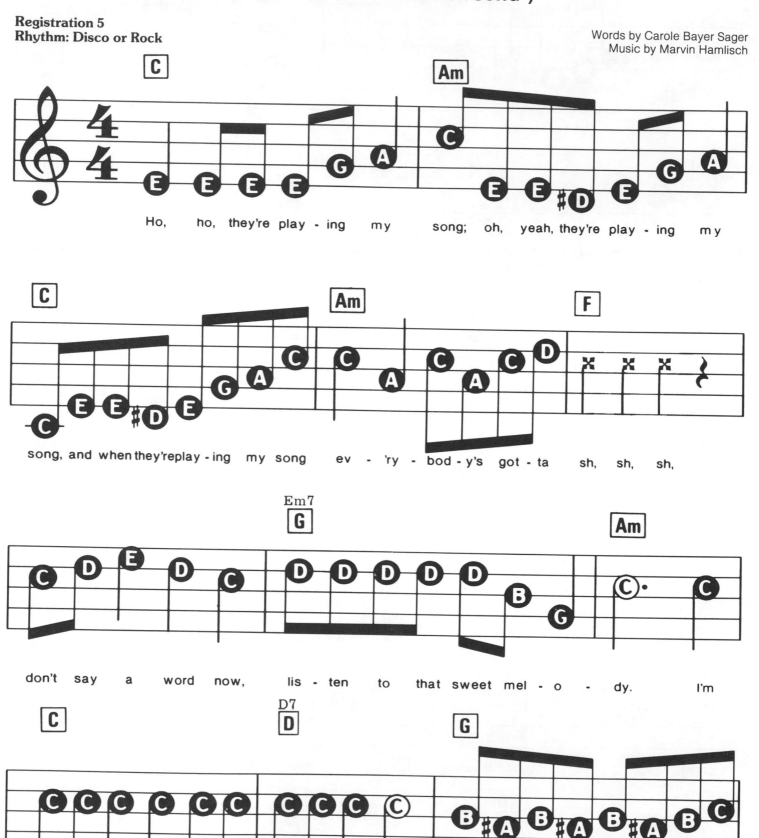

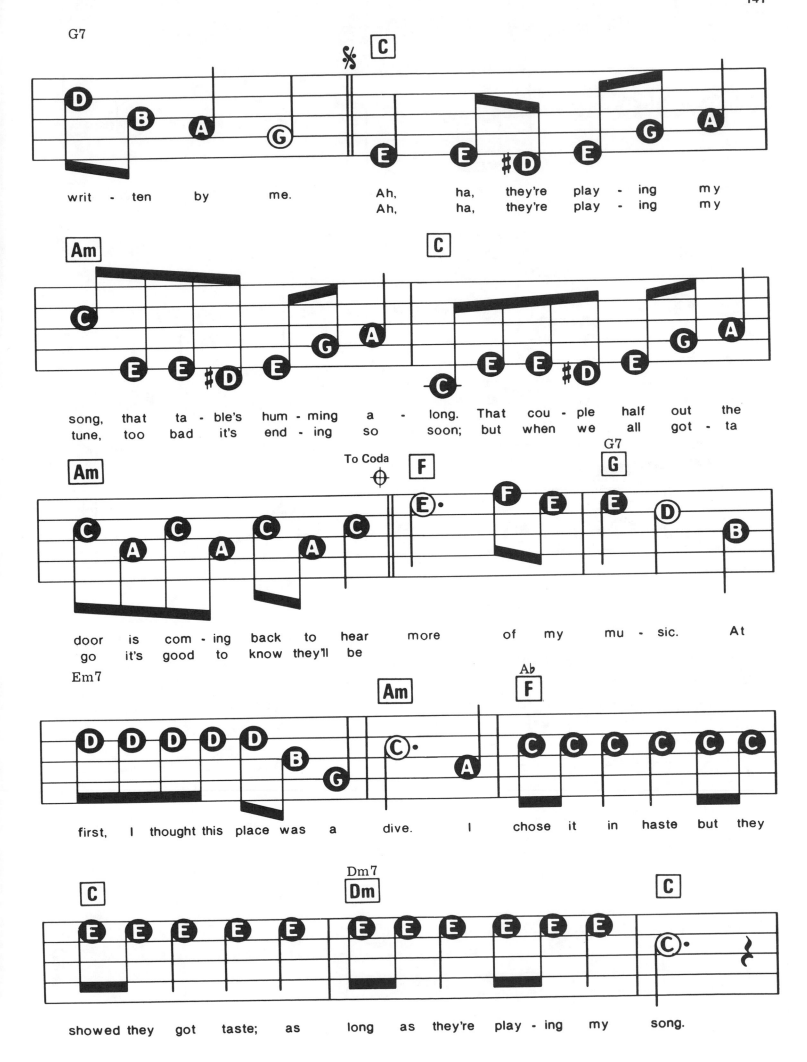

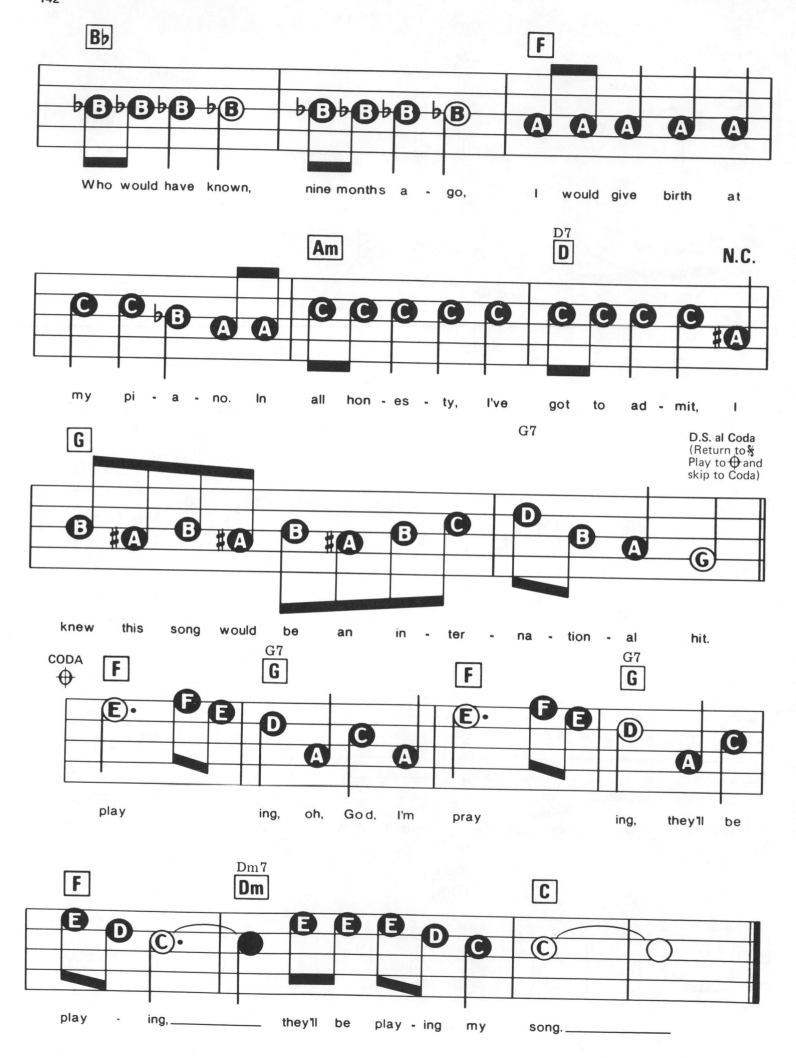

Tot l Eclipse Of T e Heart

Registration 5
Rhythm: Rock

Words and Music by
Jim Steinman

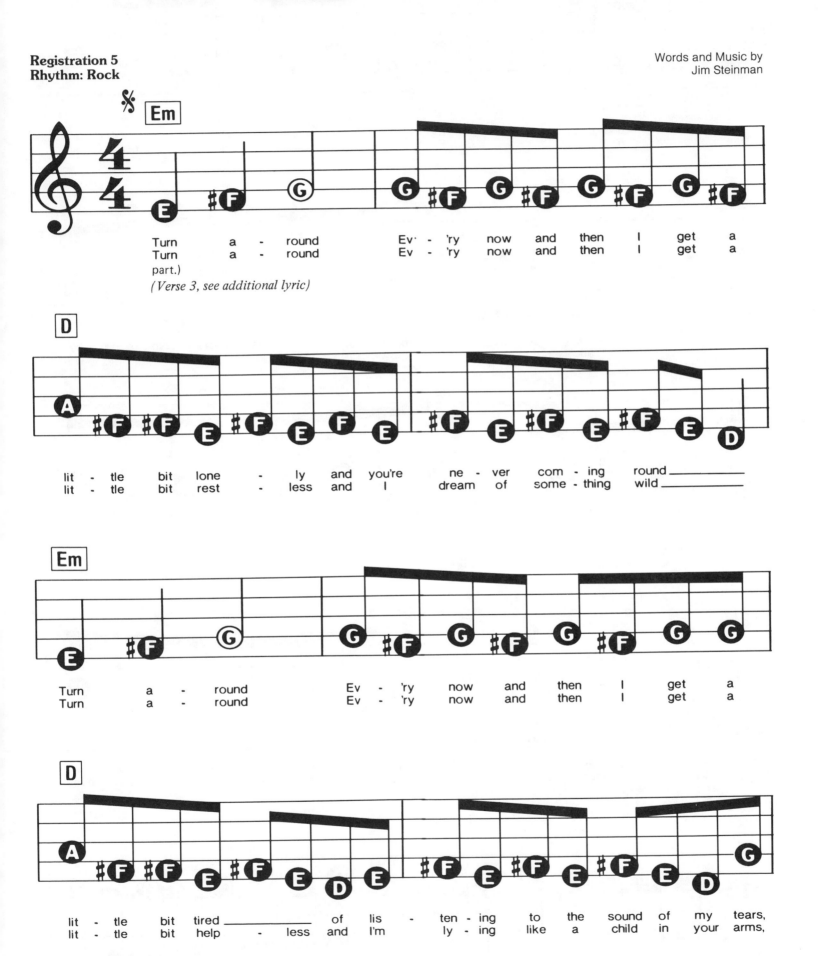

Turn a - round Ev - 'ry now and then I get a
Turn a - round Ev - 'ry now and then I get a
part.)
(Verse 3, see additional lyric)

lit - tle bit lone - ly and you're ne - ver com - ing round ___
lit - tle bit rest - less and I dream of some - thing wild ___

Turn a - round Ev - 'ry now and then I get a
Turn a - round Ev - 'ry now and then I get a

lit - tle bit tired ___ of lis - ten - ing to the sound of my tears,
lit - tle bit help - less and I'm ly - ing like a child in your arms,

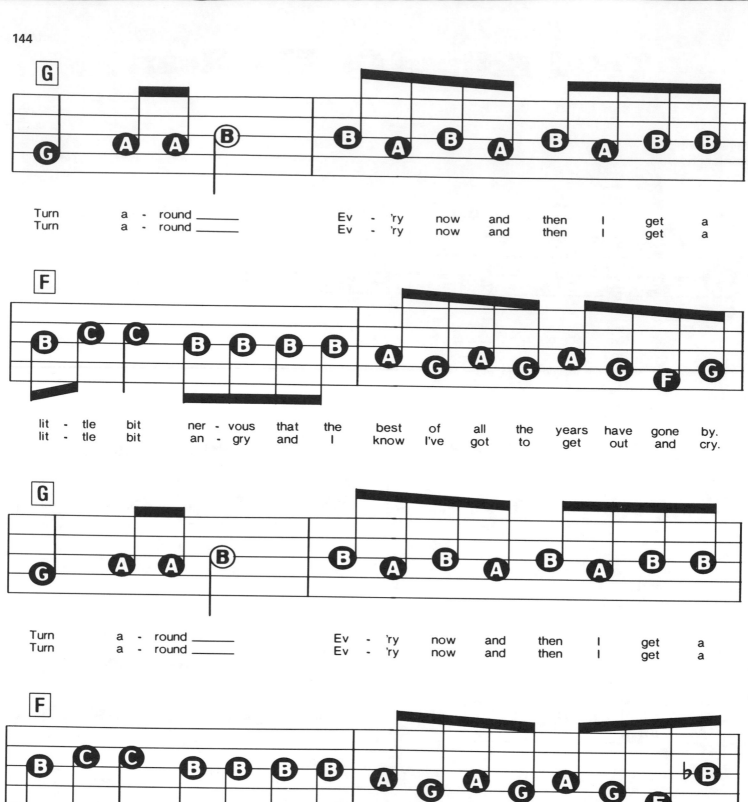

Turn   a - round _____   Ev - 'ry   now   and   then   I   get   a
Turn   a - round _____   Ev - 'ry   now   and   then   I   get   a

lit - tle   bit   ner - vous   that   the   best   of   all   the   years   have   gone   by.
lit - tle   bit   an - gry   and   I   know   I've   got   to   get   out   and   cry.

Turn   a - round _____   Ev - 'ry   now   and   then   I   get   a
Turn   a - round _____   Ev - 'ry   now   and   then   I   get   a

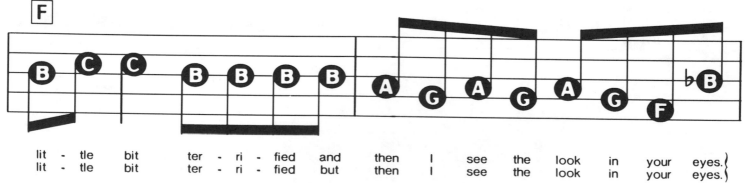

lit - tle   bit   ter - ri - fied   and   then   I   see   the   look   in   your   eyes.⎫
lit - tle   bit   ter - ri - fied   but   then   I   see   the   look   in   your   eyes.⎭

CHORUS

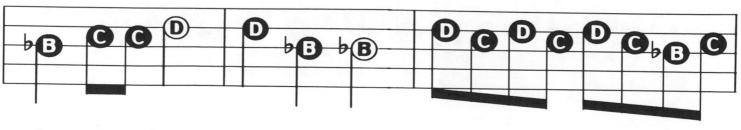

Turn   a - round _____   Bright _____ eyes   Ev - 'ry   now   and   then   I   fall   a-

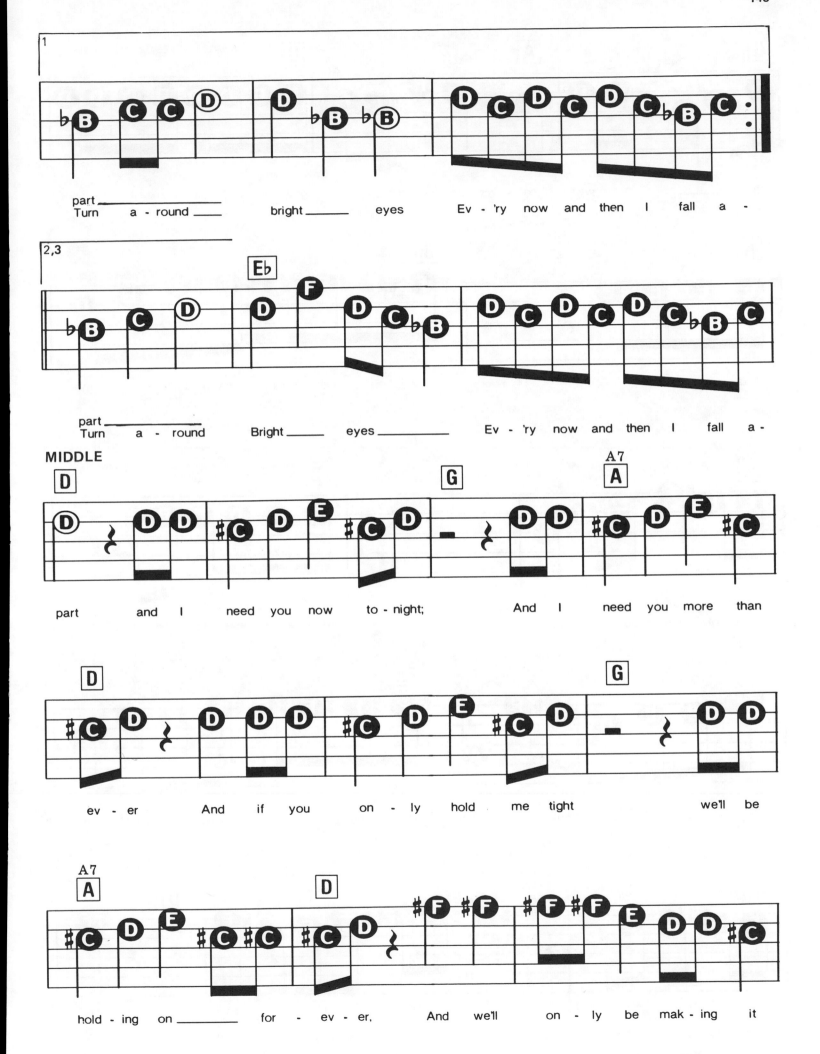

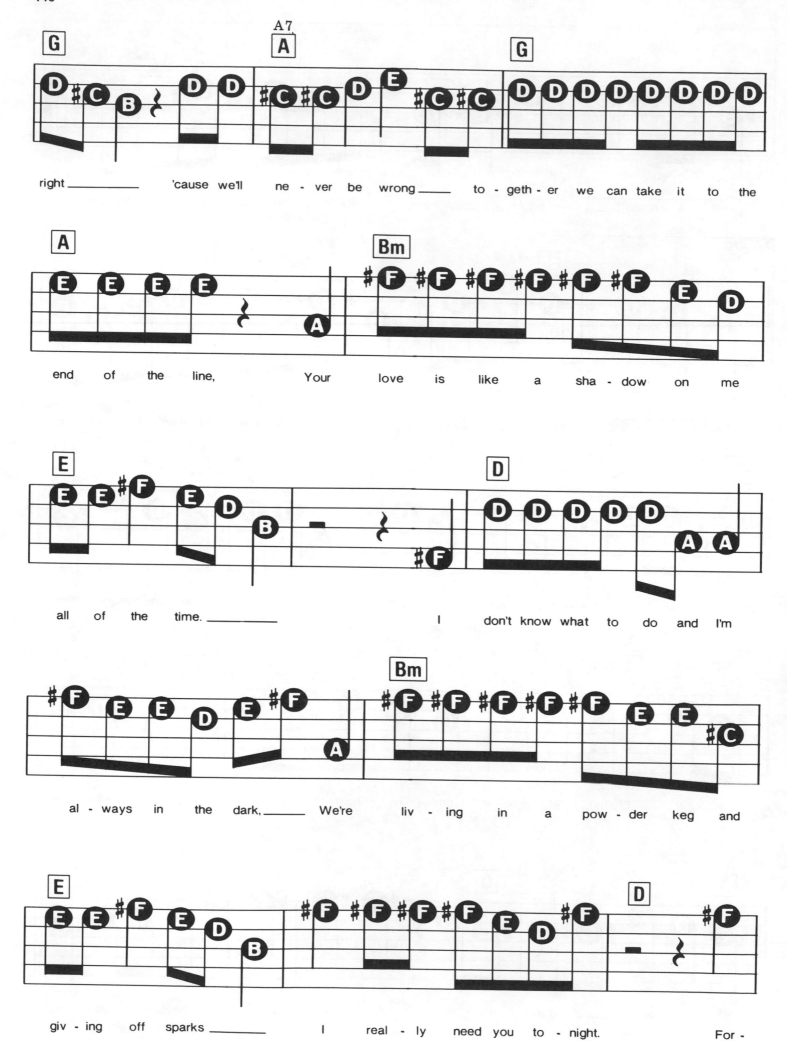

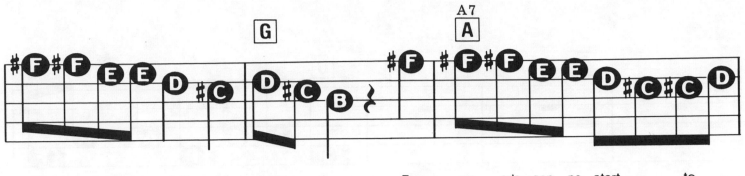

e - ver's gon - na start to - night _____ For - ev - er's gon - na start ____ to -

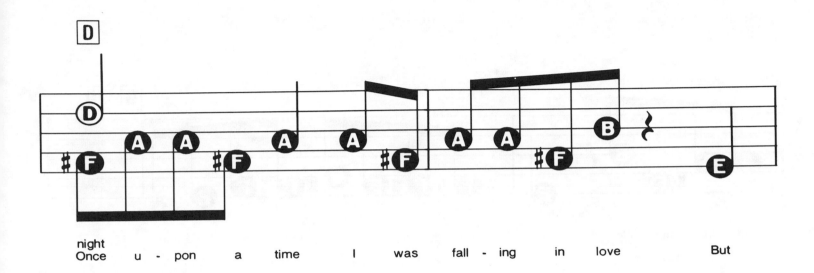

night
Once u - pon a time I was fall - ing in love But

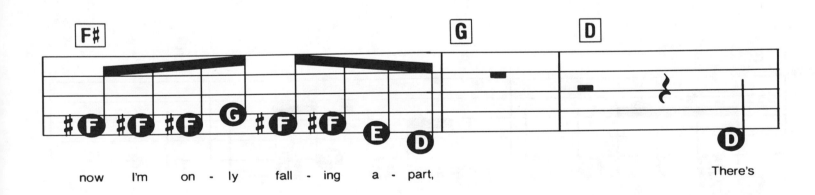

now I'm on - ly fall - ing a - part, There's

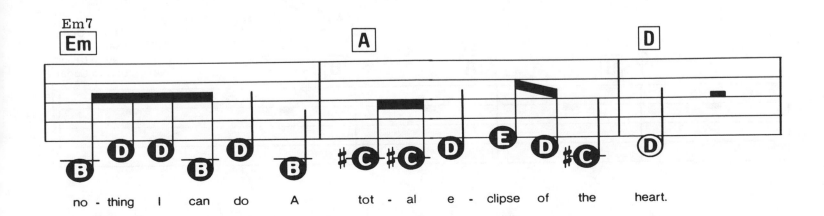

no - thing I can do A tot - al e - clipse of the heart.

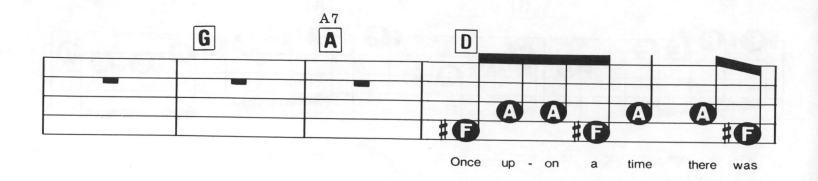

Once up - on a time there was

light in my life, but now there's on - ly love in the dark.

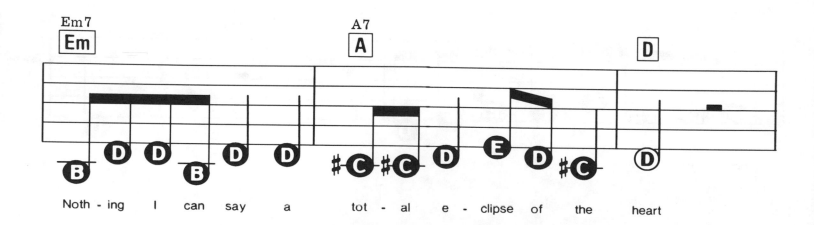

Noth - ing I can say a tot - al e - clipse of the heart

D.S. al Coda
(Return to 𝄋
Play to ⊕ and
skip to Coda)

To Coda ⊕

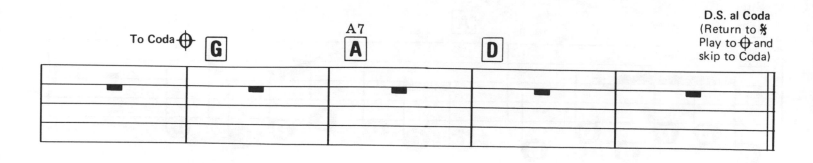

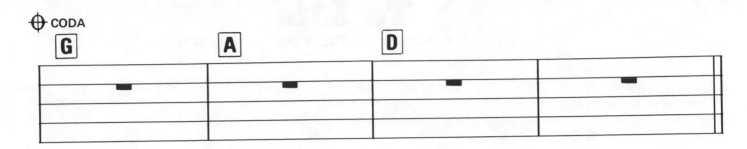

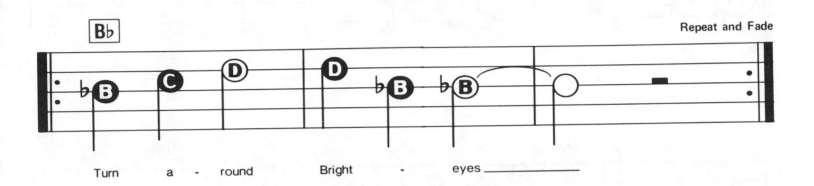

Turn   a - round   Bright - eyes _____

Verse 3.

Turn around
Every now and then I know you'll never be the boy you
always wanted to be
Turn around.
But every now and then I know you'll always be the only boy
who wanted me the way that I am
Turn around.
Every now and then I know there's no-one in the universe as
magical and wonderous as you
Turn around.
Every now and then I know there's nothing any better there's
nothing that I just wouldn't do

Chorus:

Turn around bright eyes
Every now and then I fall apart
Turn around bright eyes
Every now and then I fall apart

Middle:

And I need you now tonight, and I need you more than ever
And if you'll only hold me tight we'll be holding on forever
And we'll only be making it right cause we'll never be
wrong together
We can take it to the end of the line.
Your love is like a shadow on me all the time
I don't know what to do and I'm always in the dark
We're living in a powder keg and giving off sparks
I really need you tonight, forever's gonna start tonight,
forever's gonna start tonight
Once upon a time I was falling in love, but now I'm only
falling apart
Nothing I can do, a total eclipse of the heart
Once upon a time there was light in my life, but now
there's only love in the dark
Nothing I can say, a total eclipse of the heart
A total eclipse of the heart
Turn around bright eyes
Turn around bright eyes
Turn around.

To Life
(From the Musical "FIDDLER ON THE ROOF")

Registration 9
Rhythm: Polka or March

Words by Sheldon Harnick
Music by Jerry Bock

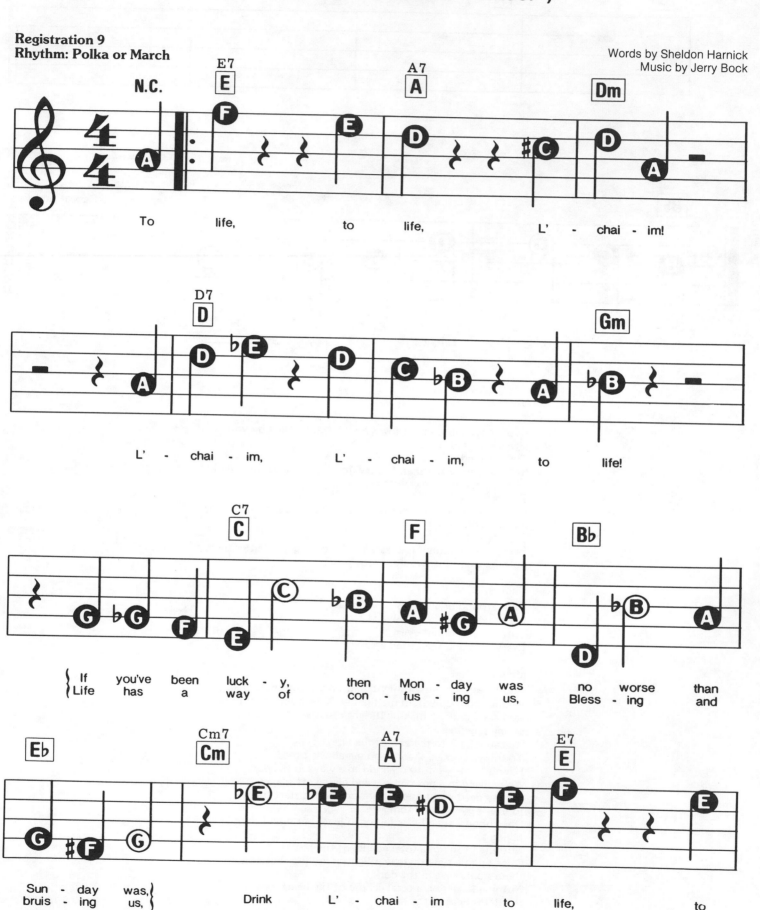

life, L' - chai - im! L' - chai - im, L'-

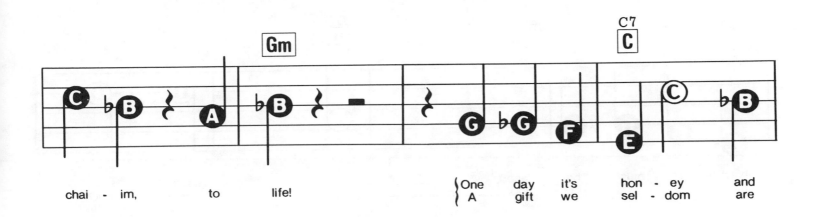

chai - im, to life!

One day it's hon - ey and
A gift we sel - dom are

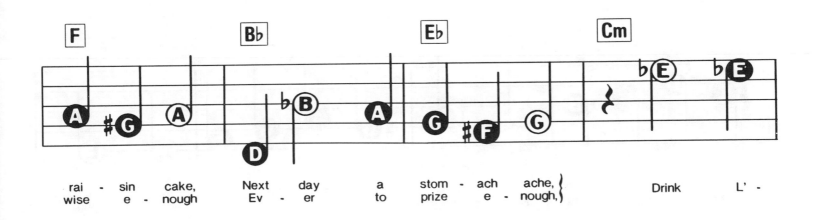

rai - sin cake, Next day a stom - ach ache,
wise e - nough Ev - er to prize e - nough,

Drink L'-

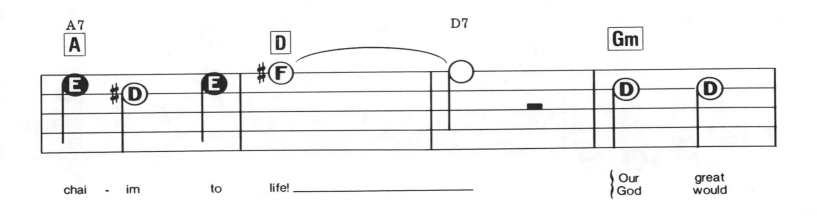

chai - im to life! _____

Our great
God would

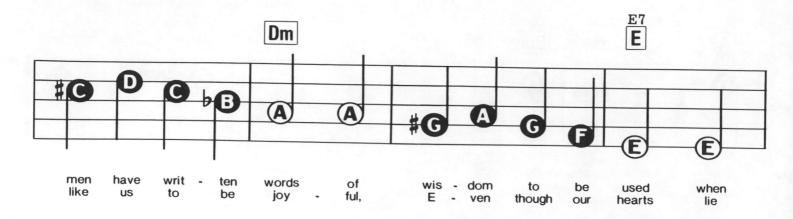

men   have   writ - ten   words   of   wis - dom   to   be   used   when
like   us   to   be   joy - ful,   E - ven   though   our   hearts   lie

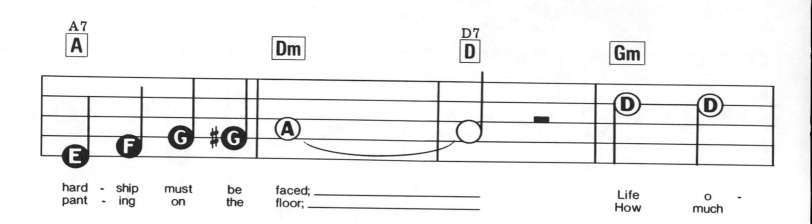

hard - ship   must   be   faced; _____
pant - ing   on   the   floor; _____   Life   o -
                                                                        How   much

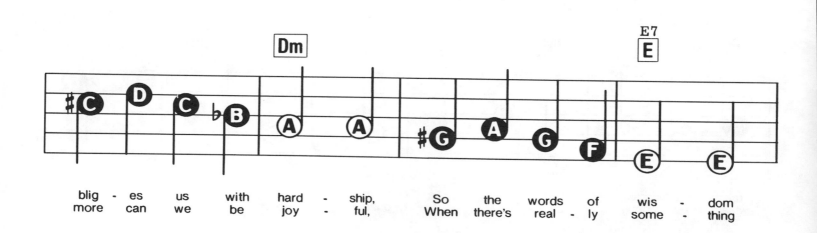

blig - es   us   with   hard - ship,   So   the   words   of   wis - dom
more   can   we   be   joy - ful,   When   there's   real - ly   some - thing

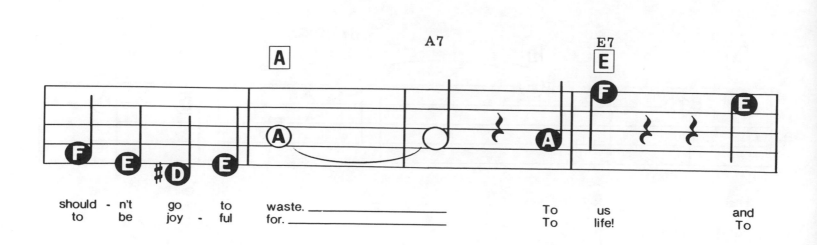

should - n't   go   to   waste. _____
to   be   joy - ful   for. _____   To   us   and
                                                                     To   life!   To

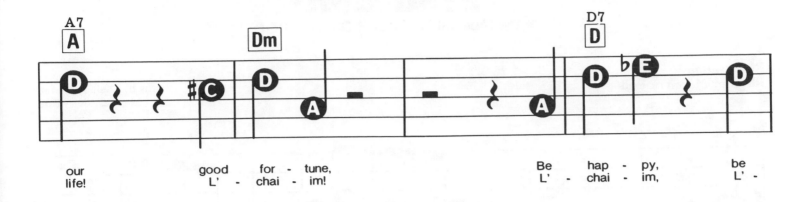

our
life!

good for - tune,
L' - chai - im!

Be hap - py,
L' - chai - im,

be
L' -

health - y,
chai - im,

long to
to

life!
life!

And if our good for - tune
It gives you some - thing to

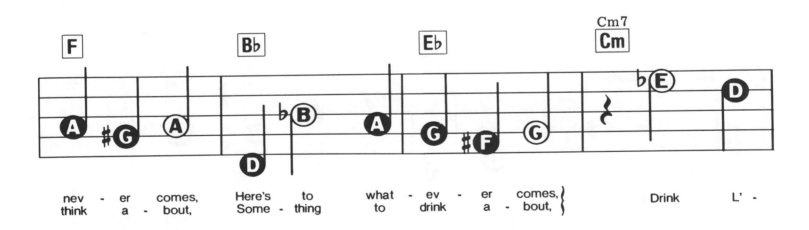

nev - er comes,
think a - bout,

Here's to what - ev - er comes,
Some - thing to drink a - bout,

Drink L' -

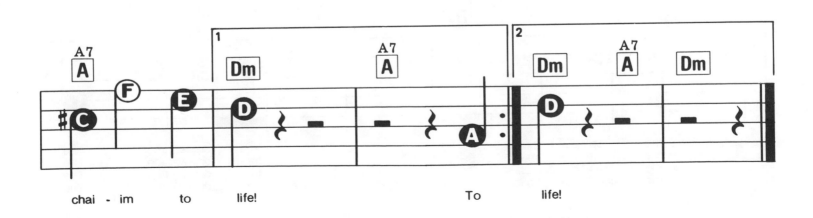

chai - im to life!

To life!

Tradition
(From the Musical "FIDDLER ON THE ROOF")

Words by Sheldon Harnick
Music by Jerry Bock

Registration 1
Rhythm: March or Polka

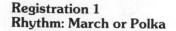

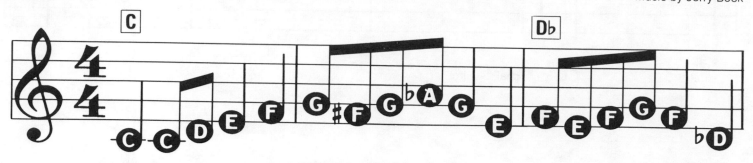

Who day and night must scram-ble for a liv-ing, Feed a wife and chil-dren,

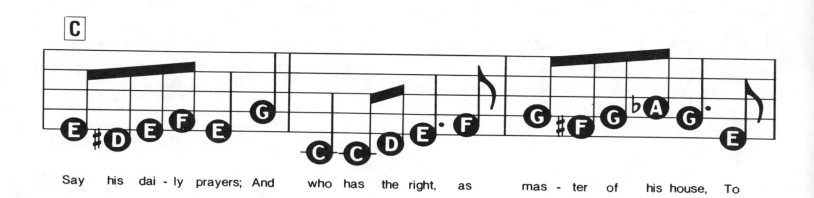

Say his dai-ly prayers; And who has the right, as mas-ter of his house, To

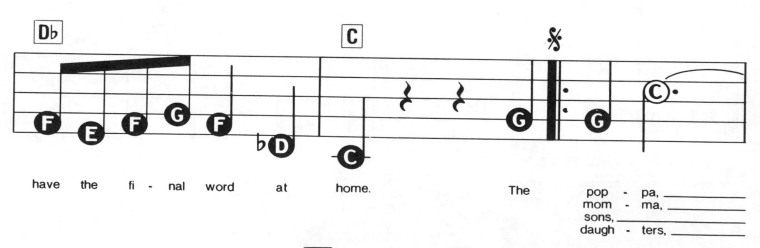

have the fi-nal word at home. The

pop - pa, _____
mom - ma, _____
sons, _____
daugh - ters, _____

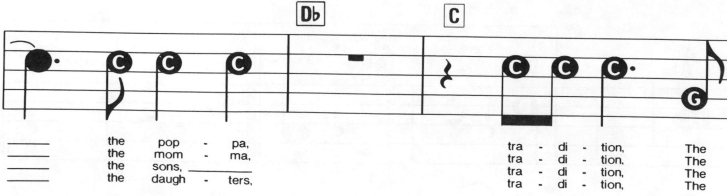

_____	the	pop - pa, _____		tra - di - tion,	The
_____	the	mom - ma, _____		tra - di - tion,	The
_____	the	sons, _____		tra - di - tion,	The
_____	the	daugh - ters,		tra - di - tion,	The

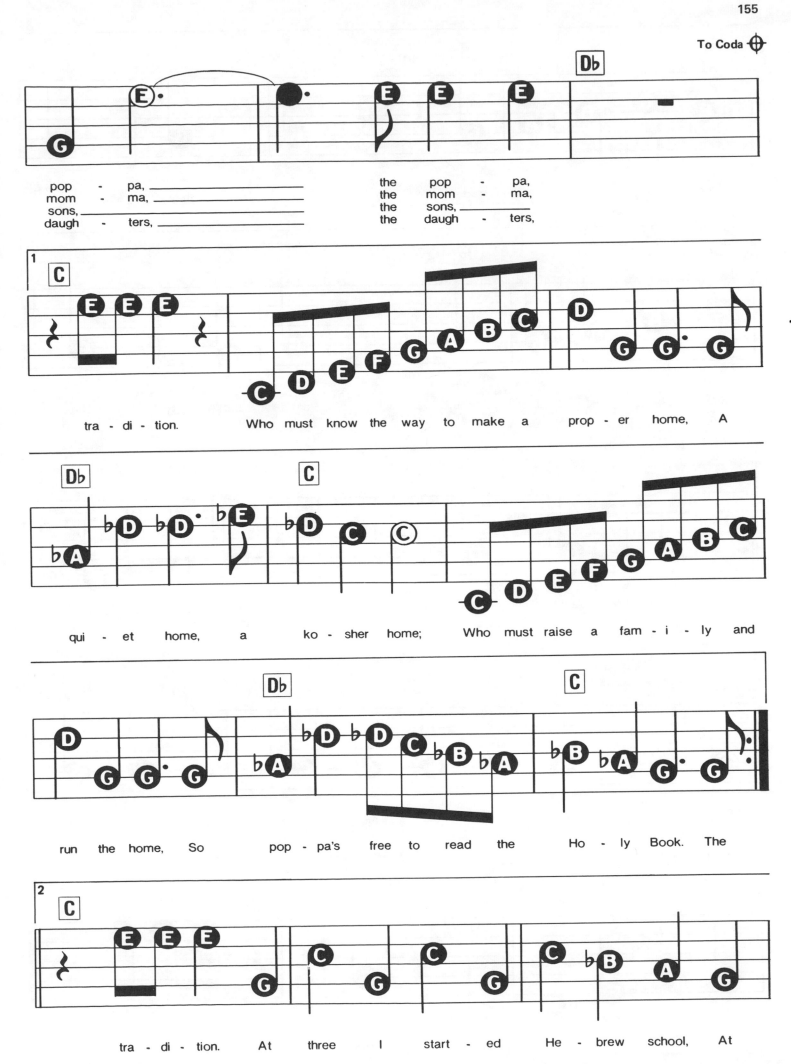

pop - pa, _____ the pop - pa,
mom - ma, _____ the mom - ma,
sons, _____ the sons, _____
daugh - ters, _____ the daugh - ters,

tra - di - tion.   Who must know the way to make a prop - er home, A

qui - et home, a ko - sher home; Who must raise a fam - i - ly and

run the home, So pop - pa's free to read the Ho - ly Book. The

tra - di - tion. At three I start - ed He - brew school, At

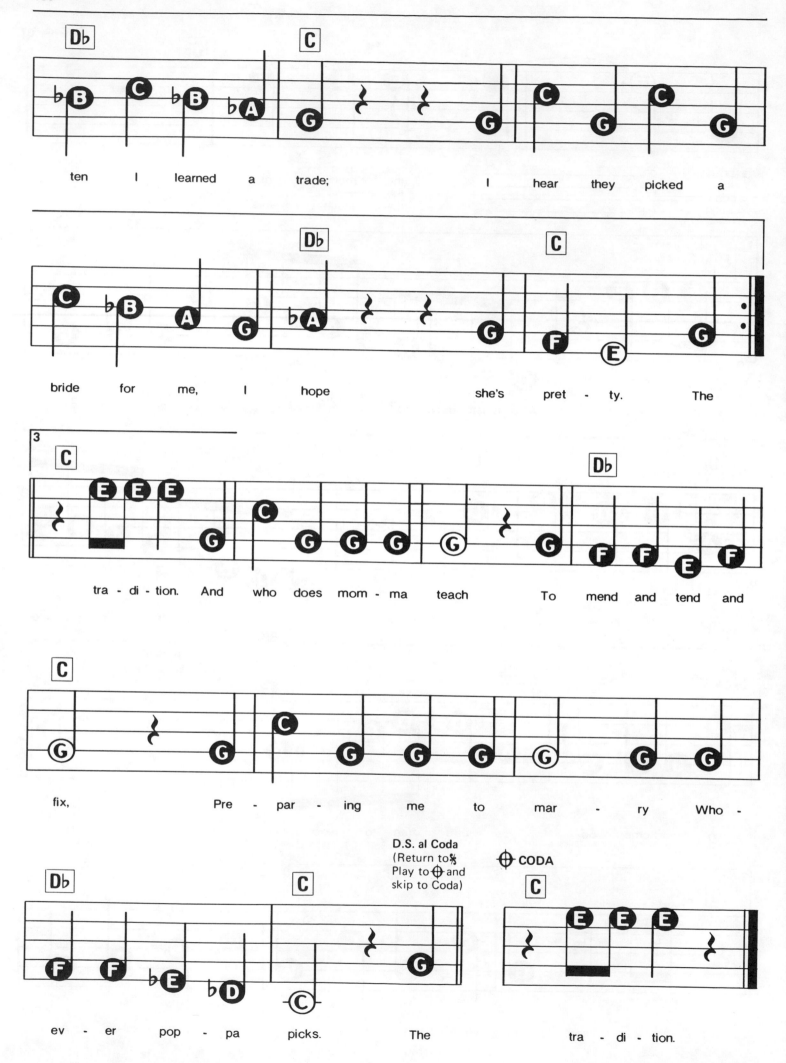

Who Needs You?

Registration 5
Rhythm: Waltz

Music and Lyrics by
Billie Holiday and Jeanne Burns

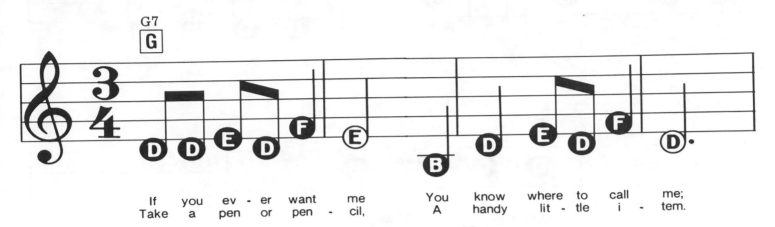

If   you   ev - er   want   me   You   know   where   to   call   me;
Take   a   pen or   pen - cil,   A   handy lit - tle   i -   tem.

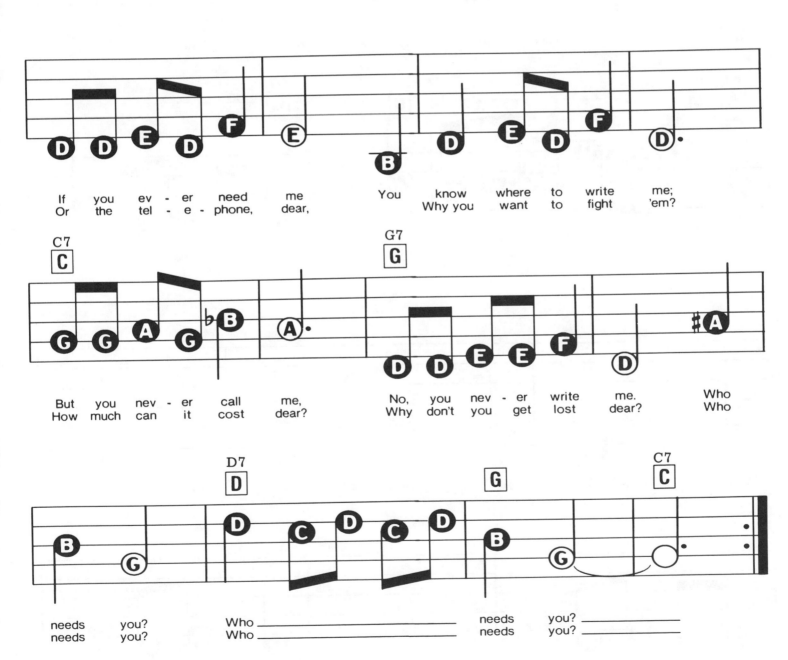

If   you   ev - er   need   me   You   know   where   to   write   me;
Or   the   tel - e - phone,   dear,   Why   you   want   to   fight   'em?

But   you   nev - er call   me,   dear?   No,   you   nev - er write   me.   Who
How   much can   it cost   me,   dear?   Why   don't you   get lost   me, dear? Who

needs   you?   Who _____   needs   you? _____
needs   you?   Who _____   needs   you?

Came on like a big deal. Thought that you could bag

me. Lis - ten Mis - ter Big Wheel,

All you do is drag_____ me. When I real - ly want

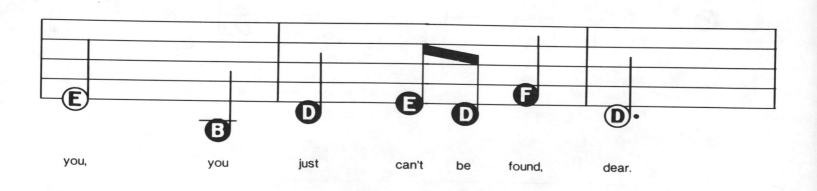

you, you just can't be found, dear.

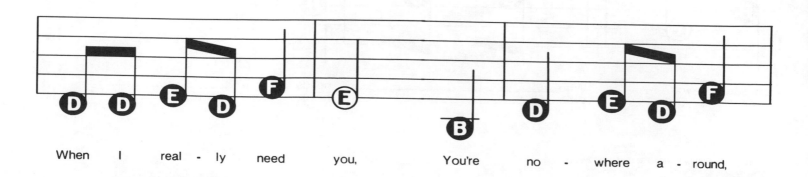

When I real - ly need you, You're no - where a - round,

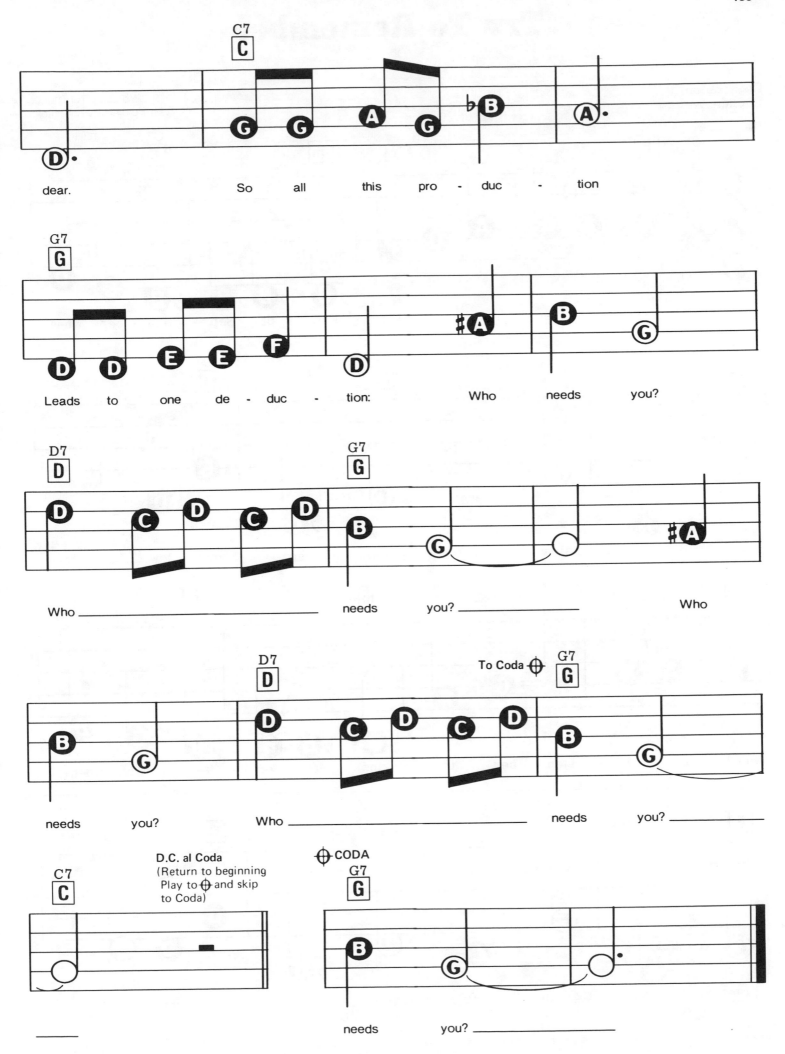

Try To Remember

Registration 10
Rhythm: Waltz

Words by Tom Jones
Music by Harvey Schmidt

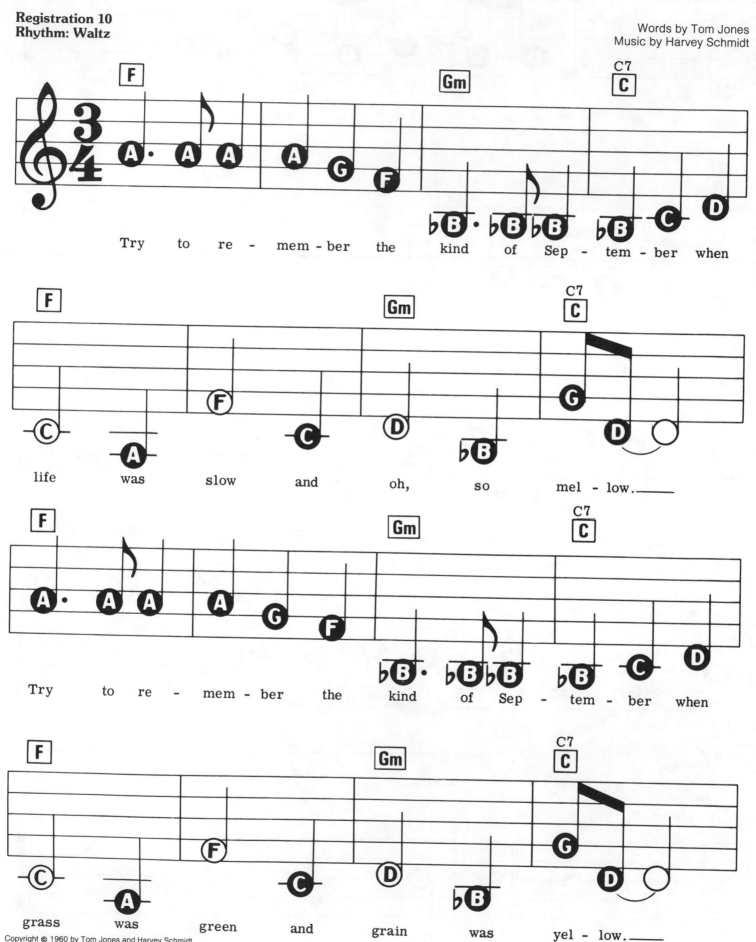

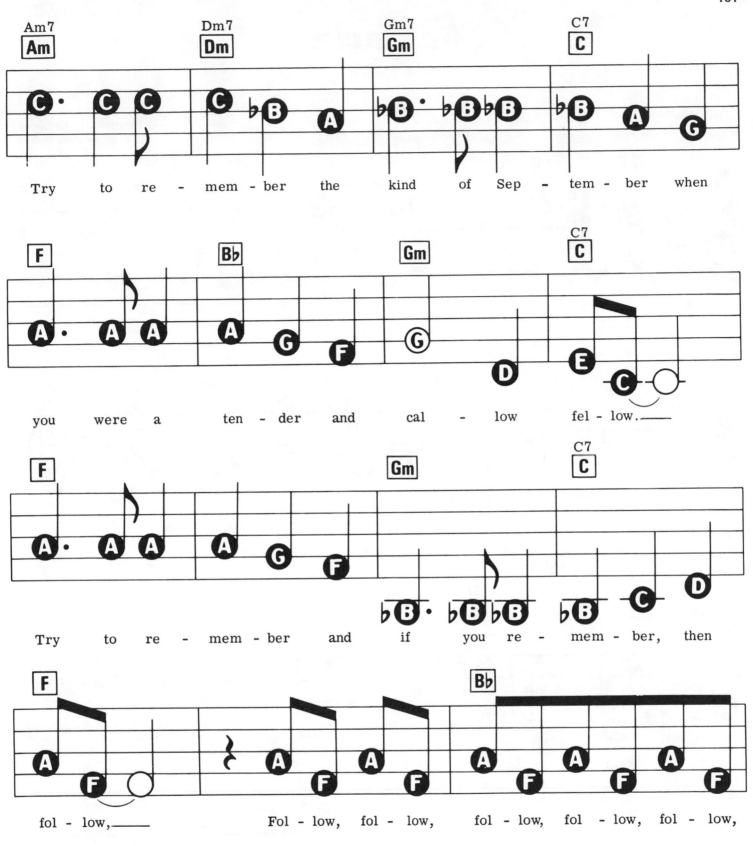

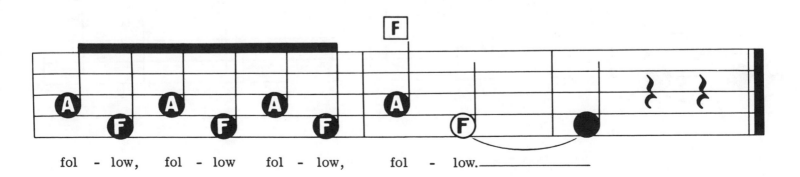

Valencia

Registration 5
Rhythm: 6/8 March

Words by Clifford Grey
Music by Jose Padillo

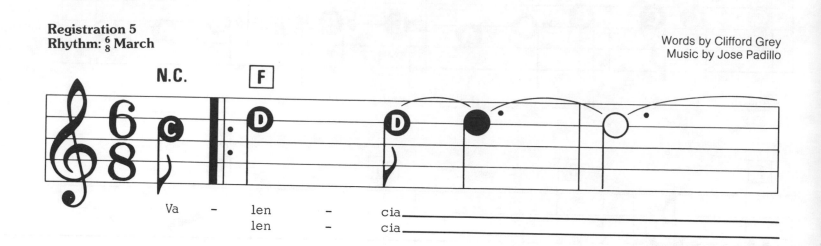

Va - len - cia____
len - cia____

es la tie - rra de las flo - res de la
sin sen - tir co - mo per - fu - ma en tus

luz y del a - mor____
huer - tos el a - zahar____

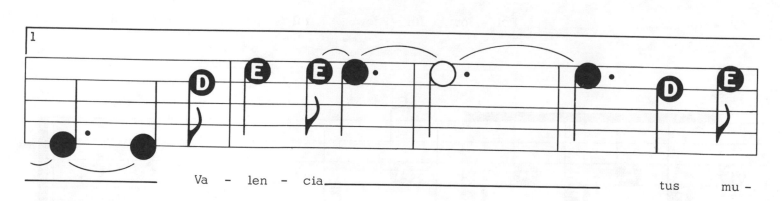

Va - len - cia____ tus mu -

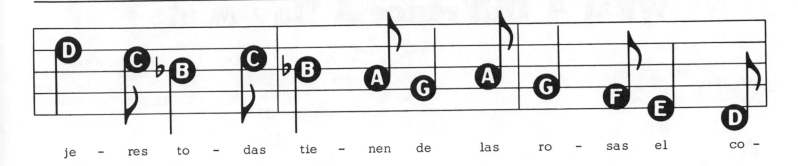

je — res to — das tie — nen de las ro — sas el co —

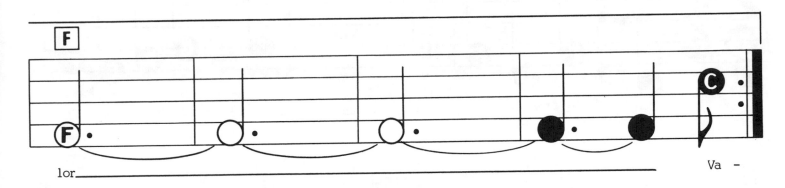

lor_____ Va —

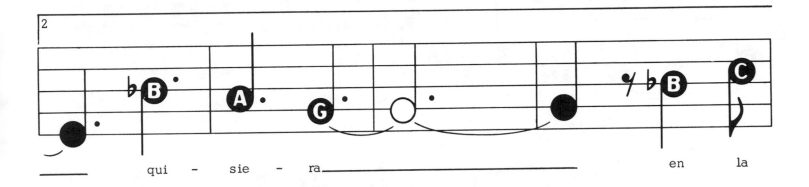

2

_____ qui — sie — ra_____ en la

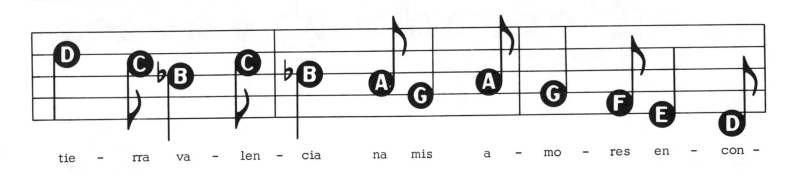

tie — rra va — len — cia na mis a — mo — res en — con —

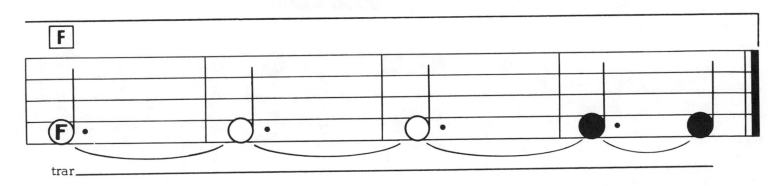

trar_____

What A Diff'rence A Day Made

Registration 8
Rhythm: Latin or Beguine

Lyric by Stanley Adams
Music by Maria Grever

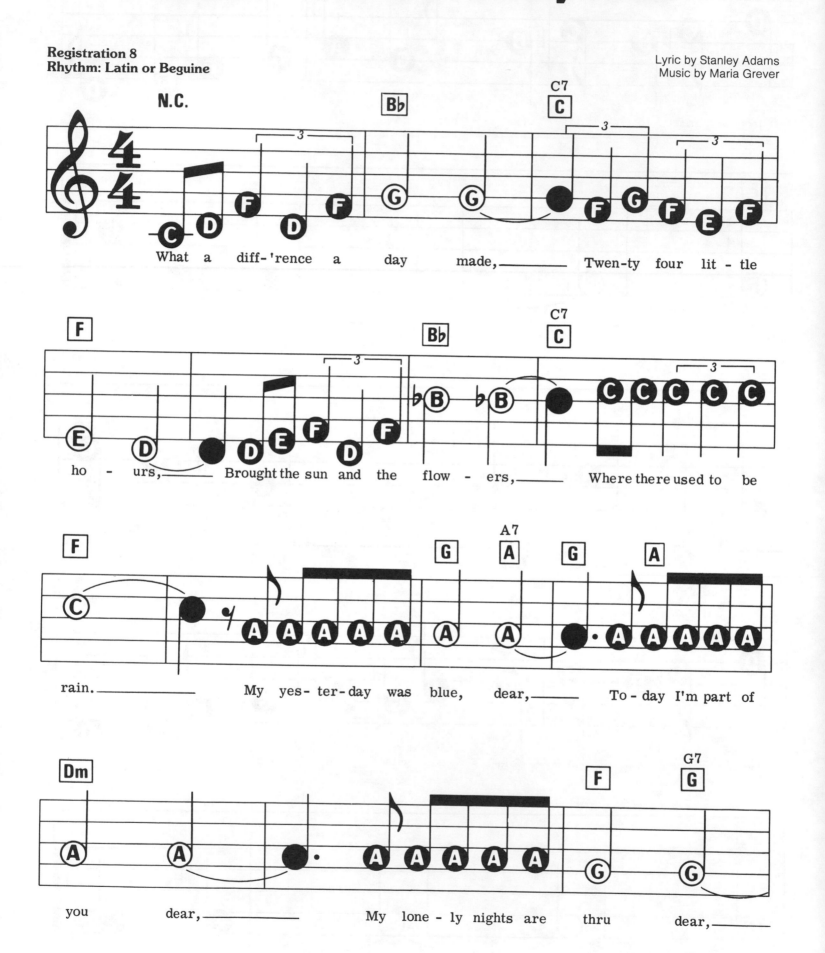

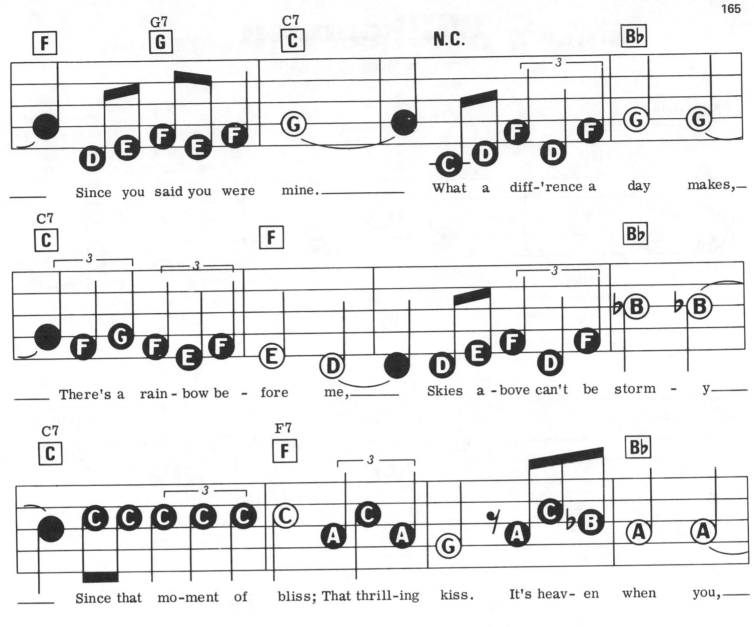

Since you said you were mine.—— What a diff-'rence a day makes,—

There's a rain-bow be-fore me,—— Skies a-bove can't be storm-y——

Since that mo-ment of bliss; That thrill-ing kiss. It's heav-en when you,——

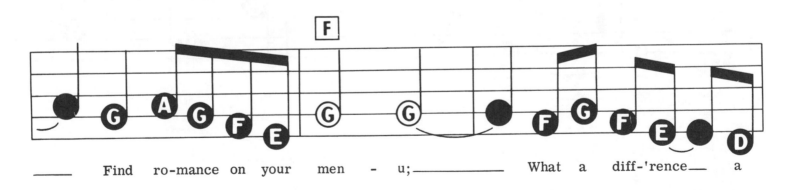

Find ro-mance on your men-u;—— What a diff-'rence—— a

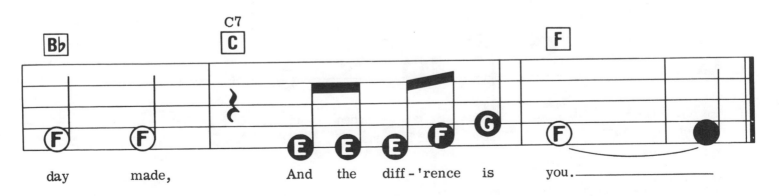

day made, And the diff-'rence is you.——

Willkommen

(From the Musical "CABARET")

Registration 7
Rhythm: Swing or Jazz

Words by Fred Ebb
Music by John Kander

Will - kom - men!   Bien - ve - nue!   Wel - come! _____
Spoken: Meine damen und herren, Messieurs et mes dames, Ladies and

_____   Frem - der,   E - tran - ger,
gentlemen,   *Guten abend,*   *Bon soir,*

Stran - ger. _____   Glück - lich   zu
Good - evening;   *Wie gehts?*

se - hen.   Je suis en - chan - té. _____
comment sa va?   *Do you feel good?*

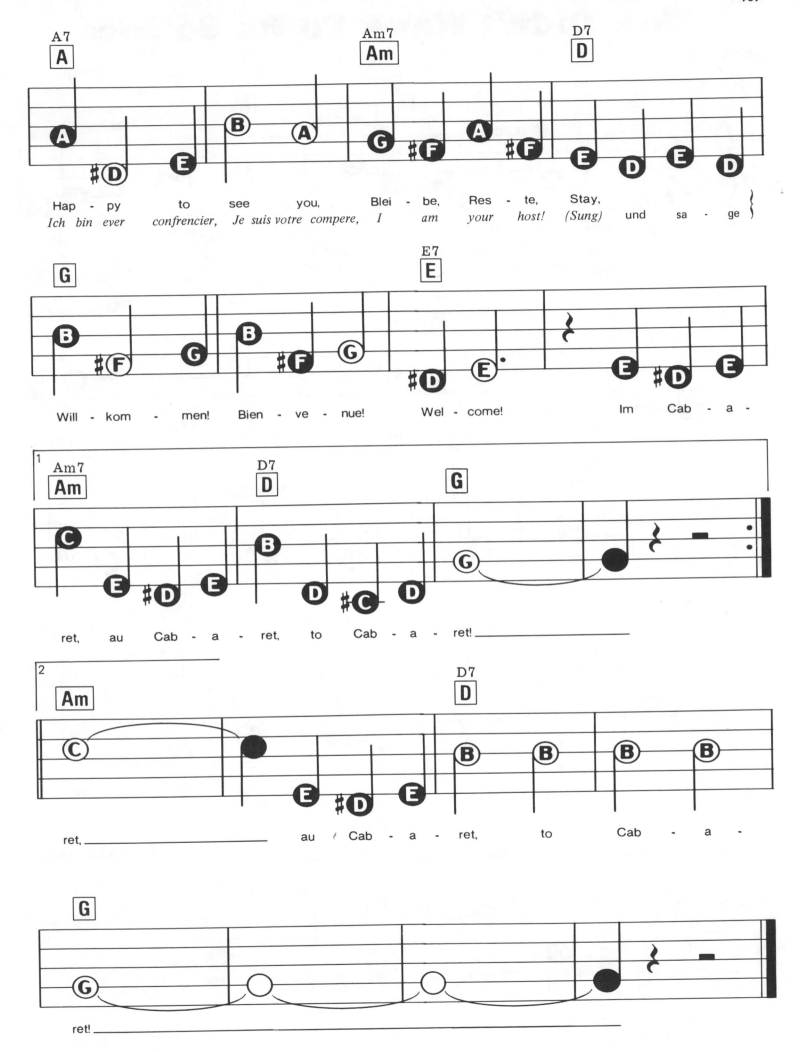

You Didn't Have To Be So Nice

Registration 3
Rhythm: Country

Words and Music by
John Sebastian and Steve Boone

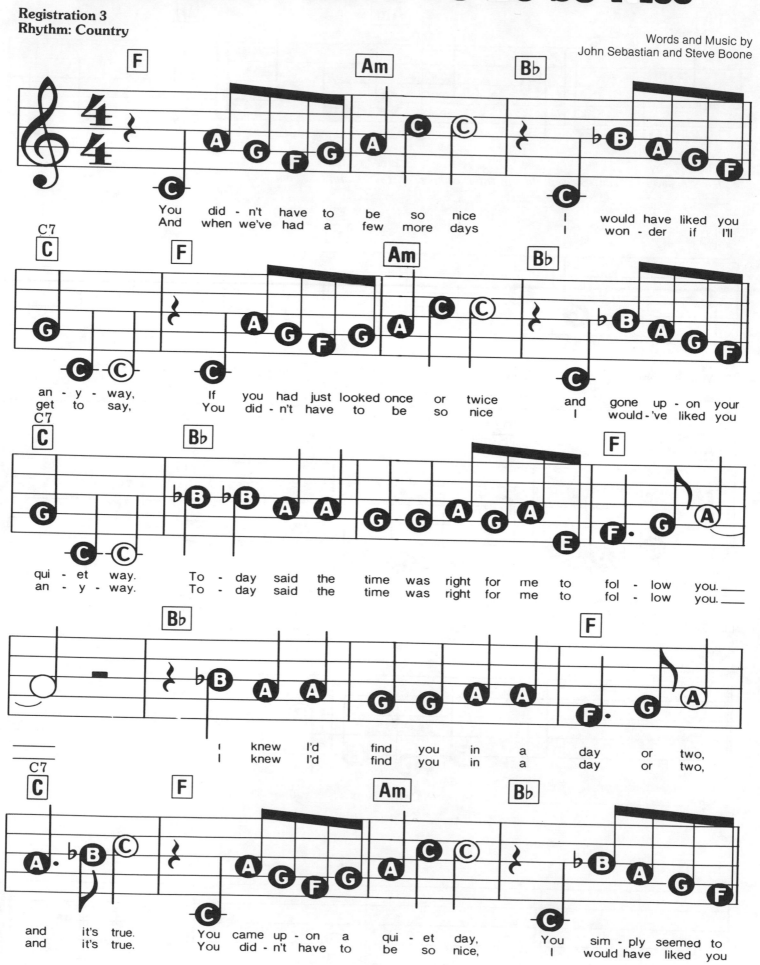

169

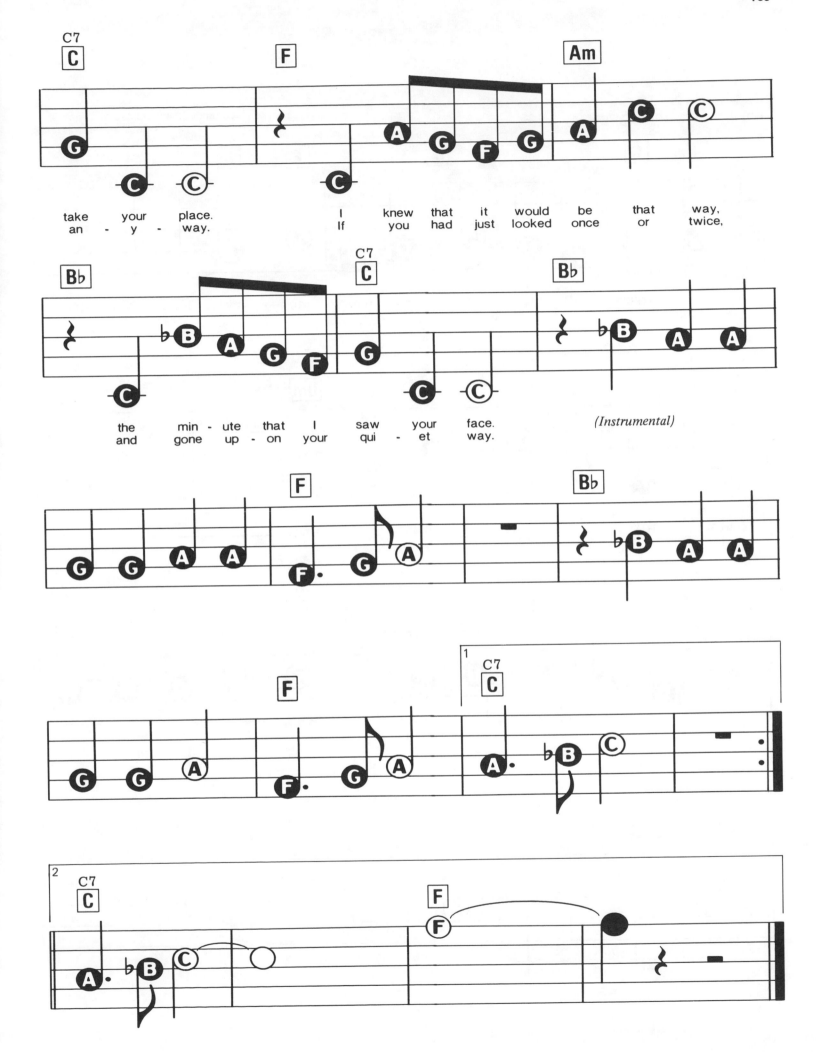

Yours

Registration 2
Rhythm: Fox Trot or Swing

Words by Albert Gamse and Jack Sherr
Music by Gonzalo Roig

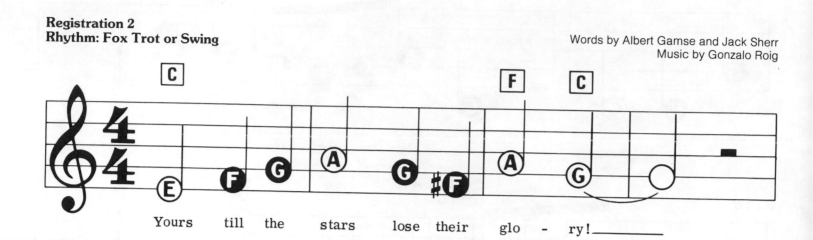

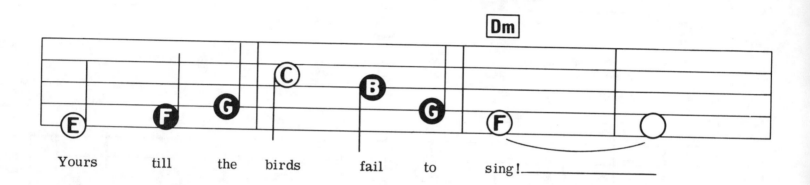

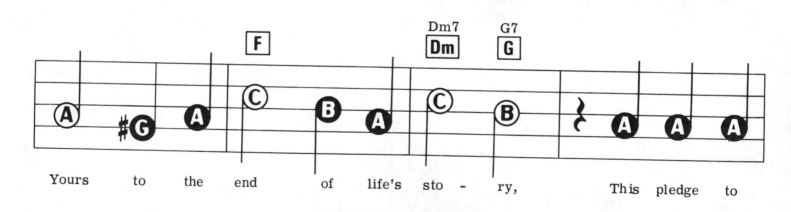

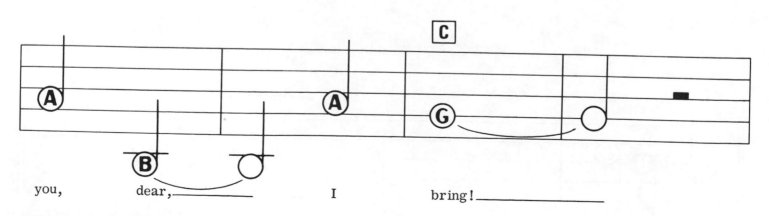

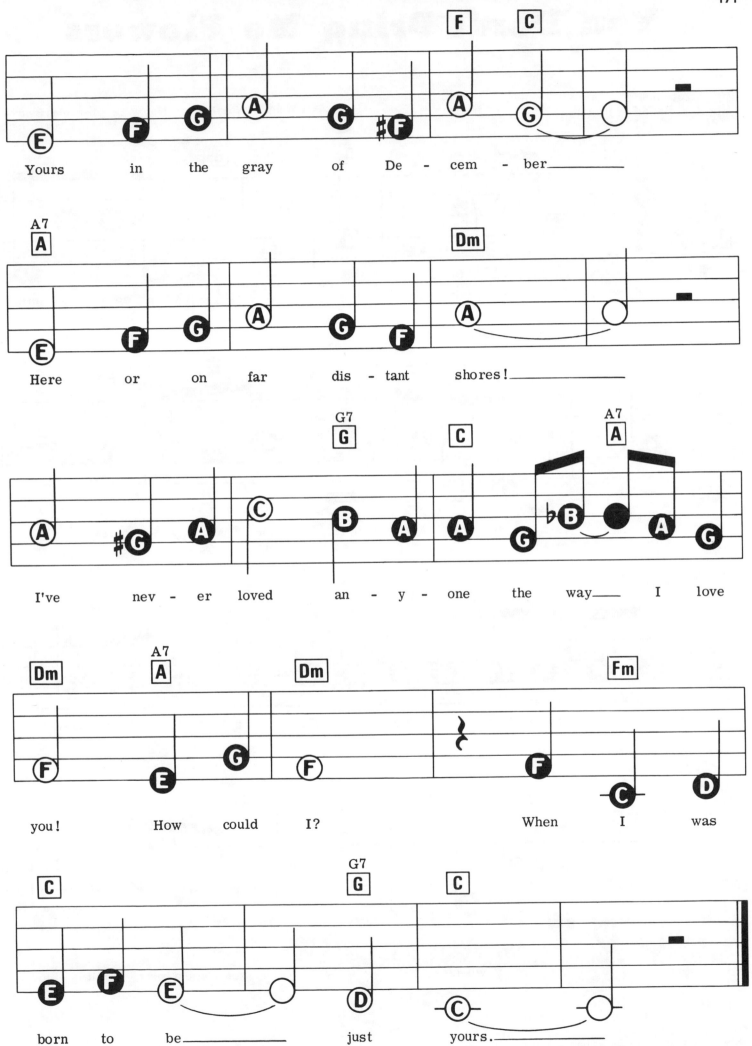

You Don't Bring Me Flowers

Registration 4
Rhythm: Ballad or Fox Trot

Words by Neil Diamond, Marilyn Bergman, Alan Bergman
Music by Neil Diamond

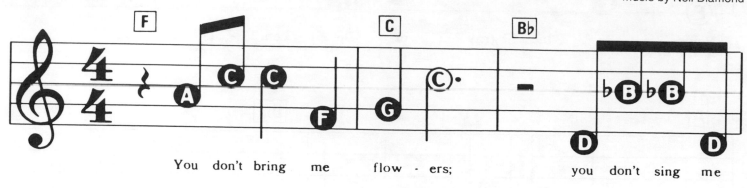

You don't bring me flow - ers; you don't sing me

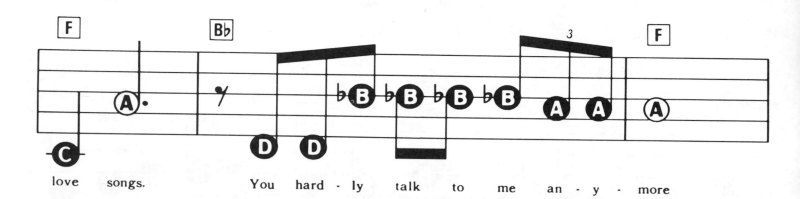

love songs. You hard - ly talk to me an - y - more

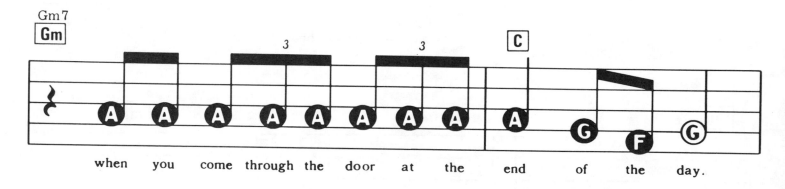

when you come through the door at the end of the day.

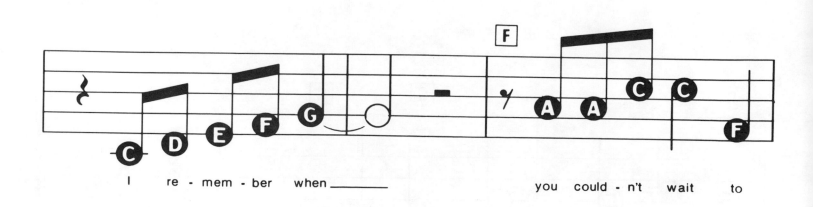

I re - mem - ber when _____ you could - n't wait to

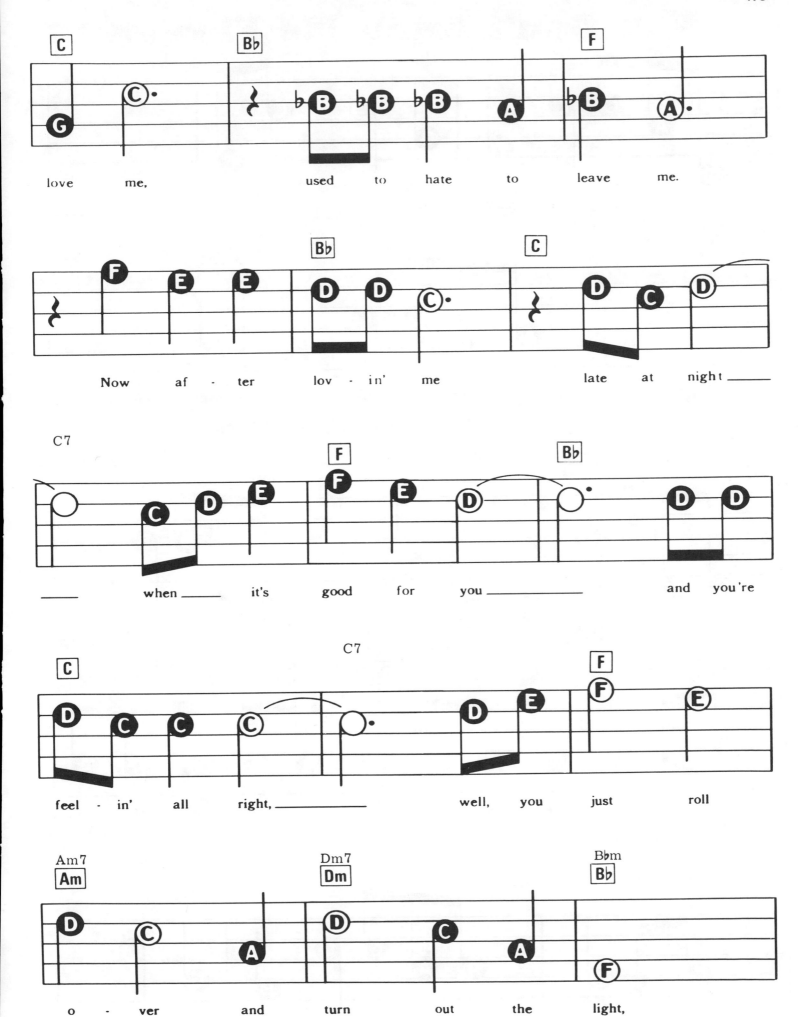

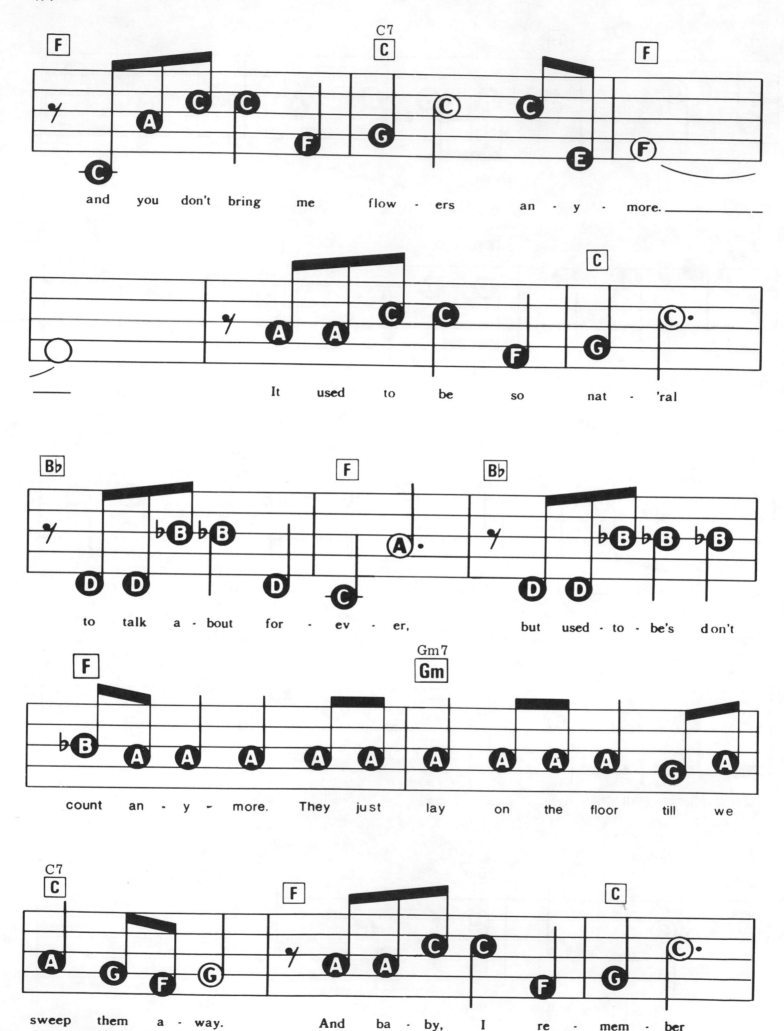

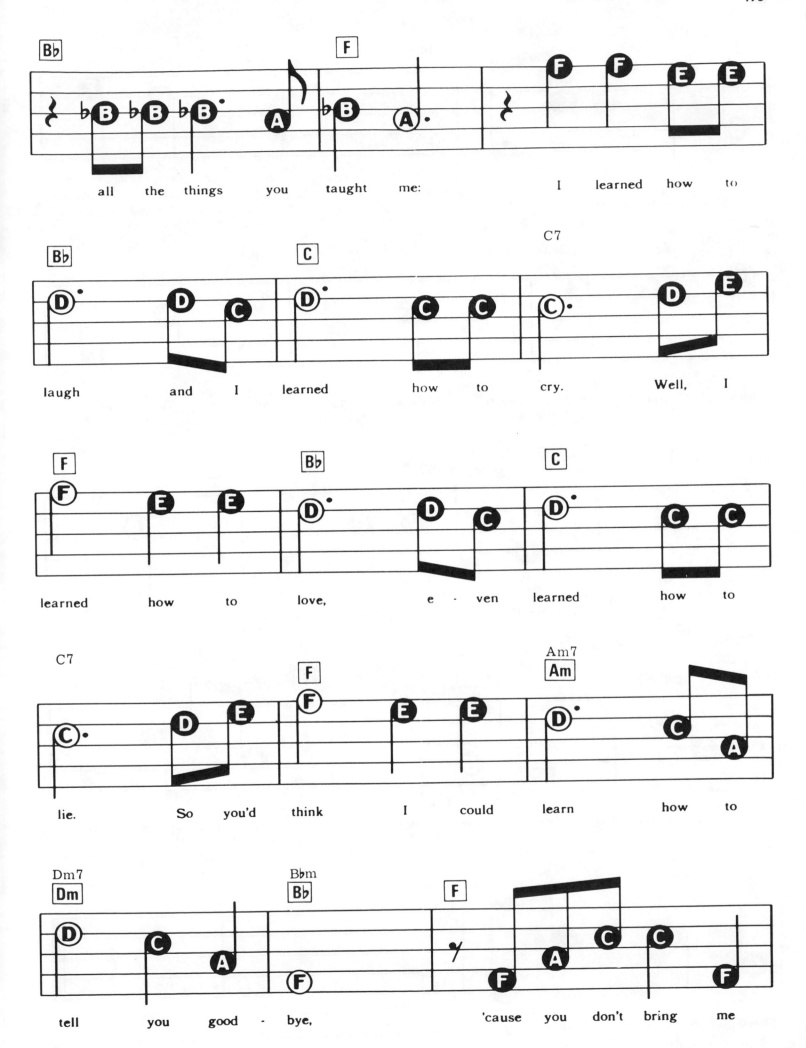